A Gamer's Introduction to Programming in C#

Turn your love of video games into a new love of programming by learning the ins and outs of writing code while also learning how to keep track of high scores, what video game heroes and loot boxes are made of, how the dreaded RNG (random number generator) works and much, much more. This book is the first in an ongoing series designed to take readers from no coding knowledge to writing their own video games and interactive digital experiences using industry standard languages and tools.

But coding books are technical, boring, and scary, aren't they? Not this one. Within these pages, readers will find a fun and approachable adventure that will introduce them to the essential programming fundamentals like variables, computer-based math operations, RNG, logic structures including if-statements and loops, and even some object-oriented programming. Using Visual Studio and C#, readers will write simple but fun console programs and text-based games that will build coding skills and confidence.

Packed with practical examples and plain-language explanations, this book is structured like a video game, complete with levels to progress through, bonus levels for extra practice, cutscenes that offer info-packed coding breaks, and end-of-level code rewards to illustrate how everything fits together. Gain even more experience by exploring the resources and bonus materials at the companion website: https://welcomebraveadventurer.ca. Engaging and concise, this book is appealing to both a general readership as well as course convenors and students of programming.

Put on your cap of +5 courage and level up by joining the coding adventure that awaits you inside!

Aaron Langille (PhD) is a public speaker and radio columnist, game player and designer, writer and editor, and award-winning post-secondary educator. After teaching computer science for almost two decades, he recently leveled up to teaching video game design. In his current role, Aaron sits happily at the intersection of video games, education, visual arts, media, technology, and storytelling.

A Gamer's Introduction to Programming in C#
Welcome Brave Adventurer!

Aaron Langille

CRC Press
Taylor & Francis Group
Boca Raton London New York

CRC Press is an imprint of the
Taylor & Francis Group, an **informa** business

A CHAPMAN & HALL BOOK

Cover Design by Joshua Roberson

First edition published 2025
by CRC Press
2385 NW Executive Center Drive, Suite 320, Boca Raton FL 33431

and by CRC Press
4 Park Square, Milton Park, Abingdon, Oxon, OX14 4RN

CRC Press is an imprint of Taylor & Francis Group, LLC

ISBN: 978-1-032-39123-6 (hbk)
ISBN: 978-1-032-39122-9 (pbk)
ISBN: 978-1-003-34848-1 (ebk)

DOI: 10.1201/9781003348481

Typeset in Palatino
by MPS Limited, Dehradun

This book is dedicated to everyone who learned how to code because of video games.

Illustrations by Joshua Roberson

Contents

Acknowledgements

These books wouldn't be possible without the help and support of a lot of great people. First and foremost, to my amazing life-partner Victoria, thanks for believing in me through the whole process, start to finish. Thank you to my awesome editorial team, especially Randi and Solomon who helped me turn a vague idea into something tangible. Thank you to Josh, the books' illustrator, for levelling up the joy and fun in these pages. Finally, I owe a debt of gratitude to all my past, present, and future programming students who ever-so-patiently let me try out new wild and wonderful ways of teaching people to code.

1

Cutscene 1: Backstory

Press Start to Begin

Welcome brave adventurers, epic heroes, empire builders, jewel organizers, space pirates, zombie hunters, monster collectors, ghost chasers, castle defenders, candy smashers, and everyone who simply likes to jump from one platform to another! There is an adventure contained within this book – an adventure that changes you along the way. As you progress through these pages, your skills and knowledge will level up, preparing you to tackle ever-greater challenges. At times, the path will be easy. At times, the path will test your resolve. But, through patience, perseverance, and practice – a fine trio of video game skills – you will be triumphant in your quest to learn to program using C# (and MonoGame, if you choose to continue your adventure in the next book). But first, like so many great video games, let's set the scene for our adventure with a bit of backstory ...

Why These Books?

I've been teaching intro-to-programming courses for almost two decades. I started out with undergraduate computer science students, but recently I moved to a college game design program. Both groups of students have the same basic goal – to learn to program – but the path we take for each of those groups is often quite different.

The first way is the classical computer science approach of moving games and game design off to the side in order to focus on core programming fundamentals – data types, variables, conditional logic, object-oriented design, graphical user interfaces, and so on. When you feel comfortable with those essential elements, you "graduate" to using full-featured game engines. This approach usually involves writing simple text-based programs where you focus on one or a few coding principles at a time. The

DOI: 10.1201/9781003348481-1

programs aren't very exciting, but they are simple enough to see the direct cause and effect of the code that we write.

The second way, more common for game design students, is to jump into a game engine right from the start and learn to program with a specific language (like GameMaker Studio, Construct3, or Stencyl) and in a specific video game development context. When we do this, we combine learning to program with learning the ins-and-outs of game engine functions. Without a doubt, working in a game engine is exciting – the examples are more interactive and visually awesome (when they work). But the complexity of many modern game engines (like Unity or Unreal Engine) can also be overwhelming, frustrating, and distracting if the primary goal is learning how to program. It's hard to stay focused on source code when we are worried about which way our camera is facing, how the collision physics are reacting, why our animations aren't playing properly, and a whole bunch of other game engine-specific issues. This level of distraction often leads to "surface" learning – learning to program just enough to satisfy our game engine's needs, but not deeply enough for the skills to be used in different contexts (like other programming languages, other development environments, or even other game engines).

Both of these approaches can be effective – I don't want to give the impression that they don't work – but their success depends a lot on your specific goals and also on the materials and resources available to help guide you. This series of books is designed with a different approach in mind, an approach that sits in the space between ignoring games until you are a confident programmer and immediately overwhelming you in a complex game engine. In this first book, we'll start our coding adventure with simple but fun, game-centric text-based examples on the console to build up some essential coding skills and confidence using Visual Studio and C# (C-sharp). In the follow-up book, *A Gamer's Introduction to Programming in MonoGame: Welcome Brave Adventurer*, we'll build on what we've learned here and further level up our C# and Visual Studio skills by using the MonoGame framework!

Along the way, we're going to use games and game ideas to keep our journey motivating and entertaining. In this book, you'll learn how games use fundamental programming elements like variables, math operations, random numbers, decision logic, loops, and simple objects (more on the decision to introduce object-oriented programming in Level 10). In the next book, you'll learn how to use sprites and images, make game objects collide and react to each other, keep score, use keyboards, mice, and game controllers to move characters around, create dynamic scenes using images and sound, and much more. Don't let all the fun fool you – these books are designed to help you develop programming skills that are useful beyond simple games, and everything you'll learn on this adventure will apply to writing software of many different kinds. When you're done, my hope is that you'll feel like a "programmer", even if these books are just the start of your journey.

Now that we know where we're going, let's take a quick look at why this journey uses C#, Visual Studio, and the MonoGame framework.

Visual Studio, the Console, and MonoGame

Every choice of game engine, development environment, programming language, or approach to "learning how to program" has its advantages and disadvantages – and what is being offered here is no different. Our focus is on learning how to program, not making publishable games (yet), and the development environment and programming language has been chosen with that in mind. If your goal is to become a game developer or designer, don't despair! The skills that you'll be introduced to in these books are transferable to all modern game engines – more on that shortly.

In this book, we're going to use Visual Studio (Community Edition), an industry-standard development environment, and C#, an industry-standard programming language. C# is a modern object-oriented programming language that is commonly used to write software, apps, games, and more. It also happens to be the language used in one of the most popular game engines – Unity. Visual Studio – the program we'll use to write and run our programs – is free, has lots of awesome features, and is a good choice for most beginners to start with. It has syntax highlighting that makes our code easier to read and understand and built-in error-checking, compiling, and running for our programs. Visual Studio and C# are also the environment and language supported by MonoGame – a code-first game development framework that you can explore in the next book.

The examples in this first book are all console-based programs. This means they're going to be simple and look a bit plain (Figure 1.1). We'll do this – keep things simple and plain – so that we can really focus on the programming concepts introduced in each of the coming chapters (or levels, as we'll call them).

With console programs, it will be clearer how each line of C# code impacts our program. In a short amount of time and with a bit of practice, you'll have both the skills and the confidence to handle the extra complexity of coding games. That's where the next book and MonoGame come in – the next phase of your programming adventure!

Most game engines are specifically designed to help people create games – that probably makes sense, right? Game engines have tools to deal with all the aspects of video games that make your characters move and interact, help you keep score, tell a compelling game narrative, create animations, art, and sound effects, handle physics and particle effects, render lighting and material surfaces, and so much more. That's a long list of really cool things

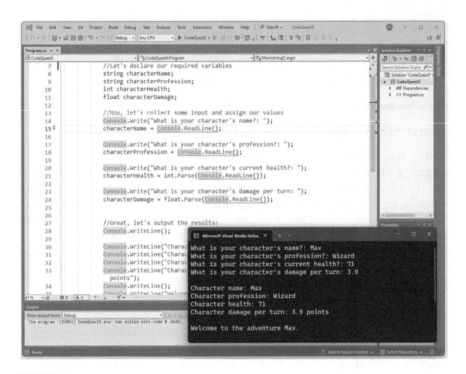

FIGURE 1.1
Even though the black console window isn't as fancy as a video game, it's very helpful for writing programs that focus on coding fundamentals.

to work on and to worry about! These features are important for creating publishable games, but it means that engines are complex tools with complex interfaces full of buttons, toggles, and switches (oh my!) that can be distracting when our goal is learning to program.

Unlike full-featured game engines, MonoGame is a framework (or set of C# libraries) that runs under Visual Studio – which you'll already be familiar with from this first book. MonoGame may not be as convenient as a full-featured game engine, but it does allow us to learn and practice our programming skills while designing simple games and digital experiences (Figure 1.2). Learning to program in MonoGame will help to ease your transition to an engine like Unity if, or when, you're ready to shift your focus from programming to full-on game design.

If you want to know more about MonoGame, scroll through the online showcase (https://www.monogame.net/showcase/) to see what it's capable of – you might find that you've heard of, or even played, some of the amazing games (Stardew Valley, Celeste, Bastion, Axiom Verge) that were made using the language, tools, and environment that you are about to start exploring.

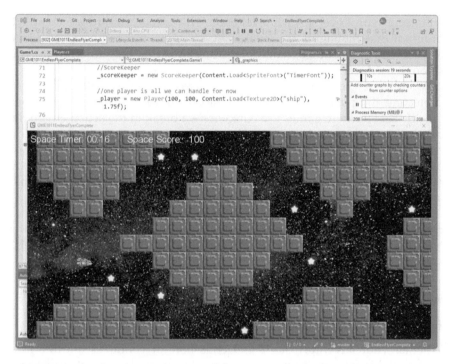

FIGURE 1.2
If you decide to continue your journey into the next book, you'll build more coding knowledge and write extended examples that are more complex but also more visual, interactive, and more game-y!

Books That Are Like Games

Since we're going to be talking a lot about video games in these books, they might as well be set up like video games. Instead of "chapters", you'll find levels – like a game! Each level will introduce you to a specific idea or concept that will be reinforced with multiple code examples that you can try for yourself. Every level builds on the previous one, so you'll be literally "leveling up" as your coding journey progresses. Each level ends with ideas on more things to learn or try.

After each level, you'll find a quest to test your new knowledge and skills. While each code quest is designed to focus on a particular coding concept, as you progress they will get more complex and challenging as they combine ideas and techniques. Like a game that slowly introduces you to each new mechanic, by the end you need to put them all together to complete the final quest(s). Each code quest ends with optional side quest variations on the main quest to help you with more coding practice opportunities.

Starting with Level 4, each level ends with a code reward – a complete program that highlights the level's key concepts and coding ideas. Code rewards are the bonuses, loot, points, or extras that help to motivate you through the level.

When we're crushing candies, being chased by ghosts, crafting items, or protecting the planet, sometimes it's nice to have a break and catch our breath. That's where games use cutscenes – a break in the action where the player gets to learn more about what they're doing without having to do much themselves. You'll find cutscenes in these books as well. They push our story forward, but with fewer code examples and no follow-up code quests. Like video game cutscenes, they can also be skipped – but you'll know more in the end if you don't.

At the end of each book, you'll also find optional bonus levels with extra content for those who want to complete the whole journey. Each bonus level has information that, while cool and useful, didn't make it into the levels.

How to Use These Books (for Instructors and Everyone Else)

Whether your adventure starts and ends here or continues into the next book with MonoGame is up to you (or maybe you and your instructor), and how you use these books depends on your goals and any previous programming experience you might have. Here are a few suggestions on how you can customize the journey for yourself (or for your students):

For Instructors:

- *Full speed, all the material*: The first two books in this series are based on my experience teaching two back-to-back intro-to-programming courses for game design students and computer science students in a game design track. Some advanced material on inheritance, polymorphism, and data structures has been removed, and some optional material has been moved to the Bonus Levels. The contents of both books could be compressed into a single term – particularly if your students have some programming experience or are very keen to dig in.

- *Half speed, all the material (Option 1)*: If you prefer to deliver this material in a more laid-back way, I recommend splitting the two books across two terms. The first way of doing this would be to cover the first book in one term and the second book in another term.

- *Half speed, all the material (Option 2)*: My second recommendation for a two-term delivery is to cover most of the C# fundamentals from this book (up to Level 9), followed by some of the MonoGame content from the second book in a single term. Several of the

MonoGame Levels and Code Quests don't use objects. This means that some MonoGame content can be introduced earlier. In the second term, you might start by finishing Levels 10 and 11 from this book and then completing object-oriented levels from the second book. If there are gaps in either term, you might consider supplementing with topics from the Bonus Levels in both books, introducing the ideas of inheritance and polymorphism, or introducing another game design engine such as Unity to show the similarities and differences with MonoGame.

- *Breaking up the set*: If you are interested in only one of these books for your courses, they can be used separately. Keep in mind that this first book covers only C# with console examples, while the second book, which covers MonoGame, will require some C# coding experience.

For everyone else:

- *Straight line, start to finish*: If you're a beginner or are interested in the whole experience these books have to offer, this is the path for you. With each level (or chapter), you'll build the skills needed to tackle more fun and complex programs.
- *Straight line, second half only*: If you're an experienced programmer in C# or a similar language, you can try jumping straight to the second book and diving right into MonoGame. If you find that you're struggling with certain topics, you can always "retreat" to the first book for some review or extra examples.
- *Basics + MonoGame, then objects + more MonoGame*: If you're a beginner, I highly recommend working your way through Level 9 in this first book, but if you are really anxious to get started in MonoGame, you can safely skip Levels 10 and 11 and jump to the first few levels and Code Quests in the second book. But you will likely need to go back and do Levels 10 and 11 before you can charge through the rest of the second book.
- *Choose your own adventure*: You are, of course, free to use these books in any way that best suits your own needs and goals. Read only the first book. Great. Read only the second book. Awesome. Read both books back-to-back. Fantastic. Read both books by jumping around to the levels that interest you the most. Godspeed brave programmer and game designer!!

All the examples from these books, as well as code rewards, starting projects for code quests, and extra code quests, are available online. See Bonus Level 6 for details.

What Is Not Covered in These Books

Alas, there are limits to what we can cover in these introductory books. Here are some of the things that won't be covered:

- *Every single thing there is to know about C# or MonoGame*: I wish we could cover every detail, every algorithm, and everything that both C# and MonoGame can do. But books have page limits, both students and authors have patience limits, and these are intro-to-programming level books. If you enjoy what you learn here, and want to know more, there'll be suggestions on how to go beyond at the end of each level.

- *Certain C# conventions*: There are certain C# conventions that are supercool, but not as easy to understand. In some cases, I may use syntax or conventions that are meant to be clear and support beginner-level learning. Experienced coders may disagree with this approach, and I encourage everyone to modify examples in a way that suits their own learning style and programming needs.

- *How to specifically program in other languages, development environments, and game engines*: This book focuses on C# and Visual Studio, and the next book in this series will introduce you to the MonoGame framework. Much of what you learn will be applicable in other coding situations, but the specific details are for your future adventures.

- *How to write very specific or very efficient code or algorithms*: These books are meant to be approachable and accessible. In other words, there will be times that I'll write examples or descriptions in a way that (hopefully) maximizes clarity and learning over efficiency and programming "fanciness". As you get more comfortable with the tools and techniques that you're learning, I encourage you to look around for other ways – maybe even better and fancier ways – to get things done in your programs.

What About AI That Writes Code?

At the time these books are being written, there are daily news reports, blog posts, and social media updates on what can be automated using artificial intelligence (AI). A bunch of AI tools are now writing essays, passing standardized tests, and even producing computer code! Should you stop reading these books, give up on learning to code, and outsource your programming needs to AI instead? I'm going to say "no way!" to that idea. Here are three reasons why you should feel confident in starting (or continuing) your programming journey:

1. AI tools are still relatively simple. Of course, what they are able to do will improve over time, but for now and for the foreseeable future, programmers – along with their experience and skills – are still very much in demand.

2. Code-writing AI, like most automation technology, is not perfect. If you ask an AI tool to generate some code for a game project you are working on, how will you know if it's working as effectively and efficiently as you need it to? You can certainly test the code to see if it works, but the only way to be certain that you've received what you actually need, and the only way to modify it if it's not perfect, is by learning to read and write code yourself.

3. AI might end up being part of your coding journey. This might be the most exciting point of all. If we assume, as many people do, that AI tools are here-to-stay, the best solution for many programming projects will be a combo of skilled programmers and AI tools. Even now, many programming environments are integrating AI tools to help programmers (beginners through experts) code more effectively.

In many video games, there are characters who join you for parts of your journey. At specific times, often when they are needed most, they lend their specific skills to help you solve puzzles or progress to the next stage. AI tools are like those supporting characters – there when you need them. You're likely to find AI helping you early on in this journey too. Visual Studio and other development environments routinely include tools that try to anticipate what you're typing and offer suggestions on what lines of code should go next. The more you practice the fundamental programming concepts from this book, the more you'll feel confident in knowing when these tools are making helpful suggestions and when they're not.

Introducing Your Coding Journey Companions

I consider myself (Figure 1.3) very lucky to have grown up playing video games. I have wonderful memories of playing Pong with my friends, skipping recesses at school so I could have some quality time with the classroom Commodore 64, and being irresistibly drawn to every arcade cabinet or pinball machine I came across in the wild. In my time, I've loaded

FIGURE 1.3
This is me, your trusty author and quest-giver – more or less.

games from audio cassettes, several sizes of floppy diskettes, CDs, DVDs, and cartridges, and downloaded them from the Internet. I've owned almost every kind of console that Nintendo has sold, and a few from other companies as well. I've battled countless dragons, robots, zombies, geometric shapes, evil toys, and even possessed foods. I've been the drummer in a virtual rock band, a private investigator solving fictional crimes, and I've even been a frog who just wants to survive crossing a busy street. I've played good games, bad games, scary games, funny games, serious games, games designed to make me smarter, rhythm games, adventure games, story-driven games, casual games, free games, and expensive games – you name it, I've probably played it – or something like it.

Not only did I grow up playing video games, like many of you, I also grew up alongside video games. While I was getting older and (somewhat) more mature, so too were games moving from casual pastime to "serious", multi-billion-dollar industry. As every generation of video game hardware became more powerful and less expensive, the games themselves became more engaging and more readily available to a wider audience. This created a need for more game designers. Unfortunately, when I was finishing high school, there weren't any college or university programs to help me get into a game design career. So, I did the closest thing that was interesting to me – I studied computer science and computer programming. Even though the topics in many of my courses could have been applied to designing and creating video games, it wasn't something that was done at that time and I didn't really have the specific knowledge, opportunities, or tools to combine my new skills with my favorite pastime.

Eventually, I became a computer science professor, and I would find ways to bring video game ideas into my lectures and assignments to help make learning to program more fun for my own students. A few years ago, the department I was working for introduced a video game design minor to our degrees and I was able to teach game-programming classes as well as traditional computer science programming. Game design programs are now common in colleges and universities, in part because the game industry continues to grow and, in part, because many prospective students have parents that, like me, grew up playing video games and recognize their potential for career and personal growth.

Now, I'm at a college where I am the coordinator of a game design program. Unlike the first program I helped to create, this new program is all game design, all the time. How fantastic is that? From my perspective, it's very fantastic, but it also comes with new challenges. My former computer science students would take 2 full years of general programming courses before moving on to the unique challenges of game programming. But my game design students need to learn both programming and game design simultaneously – sometimes with little or no experience in either. There is also a perfectly reasonable expectation that the programming skills they learn are general enough to be applied outside of game design. And that's why this book exists – to bridge the gaps between learning to program, learning to program games, and having some fun while we're at it.

Speaking of having some fun, aside from me as quest-giver, and you as quest-doer, we have another brave coding companion joining us on our journey. The awesomely talented Josh Robertson (Figure 1.4) teaches both game design and animation, and when he's not teaching, he's probably practicing his art, game design, and coding skills by joining a zillion game jams. Josh's drawings can be found throughout these books, and we hope they help to illustrate and bring a bit of fun to concepts like if-statements, loops, code-gremlins, algorithmic thinking, object-oriented programming, and more.

FIGURE 1.4
This is Josh – more or less – a brave companion and the illustrator for our coding journey.

A Brief Pep Talk

I hope you're excited to get started so let's keep this section brief and to the point – you've got this! The trick, if that's the right word, for learning to program is to stick with it. Like any new skill, you'll get better by practicing and by pushing through the parts that feel frustrating or confusing. Also, be patient with yourself. You're going to learn new ways of thinking and problem solving, and that takes time. Don't forget to be excited too, because programming and programming games can be really fun and very rewarding. You're taking your first steps to leveling up your own technical and creative potential.

Now, on to Level 1 where we'll gather up a bit more information and a few resources to prepare us for our programming adventure …

2

Level 1: Prepare for Adventure

Video Games Are Software That Use Hardware

If you read the introduction, you know that I've been around video games for a long time. In my time, I've played games on consoles of every size and shape – all the way from tiny, single-game liquid crystal handhelds to fancy custom-built personal computers (PCs) and specialized laptops. I've played on almost every console from Nintendo, Microsoft, Sony, Sega, Atari, Colecovision, and more. I've used two-button controllers, four-button controllers, zillion-button controllers, ergonomic controllers, and uncomfortable controllers, as well as joysticks, flightsticks, trackballs, almost every brand of mouse and keyboard, and even specially powered gloves (if you know, you know). I've played games on arcade cabinets, special watches, smart (and no-so-smart) phones, and more recently, a bunch of different virtual reality (VR) headsets. I've played games on more kinds of hardware than I can list here, or even remember.

All that cool hardware is just plastic and metal "stuff" and to make it come to life and give it purpose I've installed or played games from cassette tapes, many shapes and sizes of floppy disks and physical cartridges, CDROMs, DVDROMs, BluRay discs, and of course, downloaded and streamed from the Internet.

Even if you haven't been around games as long as I have (or maybe you've been around even longer), no matter what you've played in the past, are playing now, or will play in the future – all video games are software that run on digital hardware. Sure, video games are a special kind of software that is interactive, goal-driven, and (usually) fun, but the way we write games and the hardware that they run on are very similar to any other app or computer program. Afterall, our PCs, laptops, smart phones, and even consoles run non-game applications too.

Before we start writing our own games, apps, or programs, it's helpful to have a working understanding of what software is and what we mean when we say that it runs on hardware. Let's start this part of our adventure by looking at the differences between software and hardware.

DOI: 10.1201/9781003348481-2

Software vs. Hardware

A quick internet search will show you that, quite often, hardware and software are defined together – the two are closely connected, and neither is very useful without the other. Software is the collection of programs, instructions, and data (information) that run on computer hardware, and hardware is the set of physical components needed to run software. Software examples include video games (of course!), social media apps, word processors, internet browsers, operating systems (like Microsoft Windows, MacOS, and Linux), and more. Hardware examples include monitors, central processing units, memory, keyboards, mice, game controllers, and more. One way to keep track of the difference between the two is this – anything you can physically put your hands on is hardware; everything else is software.

As programmers, we write source code – the human-readable instructions that are converted into software that can be run (or executed) on computer hardware. Here's an analogy – if we were writing a recipe book instead of video games, the hardware would be the physical book including the cover and pages, while the software would be the recipes printed inside. But, since we're not actually here to write recipe books, let's take a very brief look at some of the common hardware components that our video game software needs in order to run.

Common Computer Hardware Components

It turns out that video game consoles, handhelds, and even smart phones are all just computers and that the common hardware components exist, in some form or another, in all of our modern game-playing devices. The size, shape, and features might change a bit, but the parts and the way they work are similar from one device to the next. In fact, the hardware is so similar that we can write a game (or other software application) for one type of device, and it can often be easily (sometimes automatically) adapted to another device type. Below are some brief descriptions of the most common hardware components that can be found in almost all modern devices that run your favorite games.

CPU or Central Processing Unit

This is often described as the "brain" of a computer. I'm not a big fan of this comparison because brains think … CPUs don't. What CPUs do is process instructions and carry out mathematical operations, and they do it really,

really quickly. A modern CPU can carry out BILLIONS of calculations every second! What those calculations are and what they mean depend on what we're doing – playing games, surfing the Internet, grading homework, writing this level in our book, etc.

When we are programming, we are writing the instructions that the CPU will eventually carry out. Sometimes the instructions are relatively simple (like when we want to add points to a player's score), and sometimes the instructions are more complicated (like when we're telling our game camera to follow the hero in 3D space). Either way, through the code we write, we are telling the CPU what we want it to do.

RAM or Random Access Memory

RAM is a computer's short-term or working memory. Think of it this way – your friend says you are out of milk and you need to write it on the shopping list. You put that piece of information in your short-term memory, long enough to find a pen or pencil and make it to the shopping list to write it down. Then, you release it from your short-term memory and don't think about it anymore. RAM is kind of like that – your computer uses it to store information (usually called data) that it currently needs but will eventually be replaced with other temporary information or data. Oh, and when you turn your computer off, anything that was in RAM is lost, so we don't use it to store things that are important to keep around long term (those things get stored on the hard drive).

When you load a game on your personal computer (PC), laptop, phone, or console, parts of the game that you need right now – current level, visible enemies, objects nearby, etc. – are loaded into RAM. When they are no longer needed (enemy is defeated, objects are collected, the player moves to a new level), they get removed, and new game elements get loaded in their place.

When we are first learning to program, we don't think or worry too much about RAM. Later on, when we are writing very complex games or programs, we may have to think about having more data than we can store in memory, but by the time you are working on things that complex, you'll most certainly be more familiar with RAM, its limitations, and how to work within them.

Hard Drive Storage

If RAM gets cleared out every time we turn our device off, we need somewhere to store things – game saves and data, apps, photos, music, programs, etc. – long term. That's where hard drives come in. Hard drives are really similar to RAM, especially these days, except that they keep their data intact even when the power is turned off. They are also many times larger in terms of how much information they can store. To understand why, think about how many videos you can watch at one time – without getting into a big discussion about how poorly (or well) people can multitask, the answer is only one. But how many videos do you have stored on your computer at a time? Probably many more than one. The RAM handles the current video you are watching the hard drive holds the rest for watching later. Games work roughly the same way – you can play (part of) one game at a time, so the RAM is active with the current game elements, while the hard drive stores your ridiculously large (or not) game library to be played in the future.

When we program, we use hard drives in two ways. First, we often write programs that request data from the hard drive. For example, we may want to load a user's name, high score, and current progress level from a file that we saved the last time they played. We might also need to load sprites (game images), sound files, and more resources that our game needs to function. Second, our game itself is stored on the hard drive.

Input and Output Devices

Computers work best when there is a way to send information in and receive information out, and for this, they rely on input and output devices. These are the devices where our players or users tell the computer (or phone, or console, or whatever) what to do, and the computer (or phone, or console, or whatever) "replies" with the results.

Input devices send information into whatever digital thing we are using – keyboards, mice (or trackpads), and game controllers are common examples. Think about all the things you are communicating when you use these devices – how to move your player avatar and when to jump, which website you want to visit, where to find the video you want to watch next. But there are other ways of inputting information as well, ways that might not be as obvious. For example, microphones and cameras have become more common. Also, while they are normally output devices touchscreens are also input devices – acting as keyboard, mouse, and game controller on mobile devices.

Speaking of touchscreens, they are great for input using gestures, swipes, and taps, but they are also output devices – showing you the result of your input on the computer/phone/console. Other output devices include (non-touchscreen) monitors, speakers (audio output), and even printers (yes, printers).

GPU or Graphics Processing Unit

In the history of computers, graphics processing units (or GPUs) are considered new-ish hardware components. During the early days of video games (pre-1990s), the job of drawing text and graphics to the screen belonged solely to the CPU. As PC games (and other graphics-heavy programs) evolved and pushed the limits of jaw-dropping 2D and 3D output, CPUs struggled to keep up with all the required calculations. That's when GPUs appeared to share the computational work by taking over the graphics-specific tasks. CPUs still do a lot of work on modern computers, but they work together with GPUs to make sure that our games run smoothly.

Now that we know a bit about the most common computer hardware parts, let's look at the programming languages, tools, and libraries these books use for our coding adventures.

Software Tools for Our Adventure

If we're going to learn to program and write software, we'll need some tools. In this book, we're going to learn the C# programming language, and we're going to use the Visual Studio development environment to write C# code. For those who want to extend their coding adventure, we'll continue with C# and Visual Studio, but we'll also introduce the MonoGame framework in the next book. All three are described below:

- C# is a programming language as well as a set of tools and libraries that we can use to write many types of software, including video games. The C# language determines the specific syntax (words and structure) of our programs. It has a compiler (more on that below) to turn the code we write into software that we can run on a variety of devices. It also has a set of libraries (pre-written software) that we can use to make our coding tasks easier.

- Visual Studio (VS) is the development environment. To be clear, Visual Studio is not our programming language that's C#. VS actually supports many languages (including C#), the same way that your word processor might support writing a letter in many writtent languages. VS is designed to have everything we need to complete our programming projects including an editor, a way to access our language's compiler, and a place to see the results. It also has some fancy features like code auto-completion and syntax highlighting. Again, the goal of these features is to make our coding job easier and more efficient.

- MonoGame is a video game design framework that can be used along with C#. Writing games from scratch without support libraries or a framework can be done, but it's tough and time consuming. Learning how to control each pixel on a monitor, learning how to process sound files, and learning how to interface with a Bluetooth wireless game controller ... these are all interesting puzzles, but aren't things I would recommend when you're new to programming. The MonoGame framework is a collection of pre-written libraries that

have solutions to many of the common game development tasks that
we can use in writing our own games.

All the examples you come across in this book should work with any version
of Microsoft Visual Studio and should work on both Microsoft Windows and
Mac OS. If you are already familiar with Visual Studio, you might be using
Professional or Enterprise versions, but in all screenshots and examples I'll be
using Visual Studio Community Edition – the free version – for Microsoft
Windows. As of the writing of this book, all versions can be found on
Microsoft's Visual Studio web page. You might also find a product called
Visual Studio Code on the same web page – I recommend against installing
this version as it does not integrate as well with MonoGame.

This would be a great place to include some instructions and screenshots on
how to install Visual Studio, but you'll soon notice there aren't any. Modern
software is known for often changing the steps needed for installation, and I
worry that any instructions or screenshots would be out of date between the
time I write this sentence and when the book arrives in your hands or on your
screen. But don't worry – as of right now – installing Visual Studio is a simple
matter of downloading the installer and following the prompts. During
installation you might see some options for installing different modules or
"Workloads". Here are some that you should install if they are made
available to you: .NET desktop development, Universal Windows Platform
development, and Game development with Unity (if you're going to try out
Unity at some point in the future). If all goes well, you'll have it up and
running in no time! In the unlikely event that you run into any installation
issues, there is an active community a web search away!!

In the next book, we're going to move away from console programs and
start developing more visual, interactive, and leveled-up examples using
MonoGame. The good news is this will still happen in Visual Studio. If you
are excited and want to install MonoGame now, you can – it won't interfere
with any of the console examples in this book. If you would rather wait and
see how the first part of your adventure unfolds before installing anything
extra, you can skip to the next section and return here later – none of the
console examples in this book need the MonoGame framework.

For now (at the time of writing this sentence), installing MonoGame in
Visual Studio 2022 means:

- opening Visual Studio
- opening the Extensions → Manage Extensions menu
- searching for MonoGame in the Online: Visual Studio Marketplace
- clicking Download

Visual Studio will require a restart, but assuming all goes well (again),
you'll be able to try out the Bonus Code Quest at the end of this book. If you

do the installation now and if you run into any problems, MonoGame has a very active online community – and a web search of the error you are getting or a post to their support forum is very likely to help you get things fixed up.

How We Program – Write-Compile-Run (and Debug)

Ultimately, how we program is the main quest that we're here for, but before we dive into the specific details of programming using C# and Visual Studio, let's take a look at the general steps that are involved in almost all programming.

My favorite way to summarize the steps involved in programming is write-compile-run! These three separate steps form a cycle that we repeat over and over – whether we're writing a simple program or a AAA blockbuster game, we are always writing, compiling, running, and repeating. We're going to take a look at each of these steps, but don't worry if they seem complicated or confusing at first. We're going to break them down again in Code Quest 1, and you're going to get lots of practice with the examples in these books!

Write

As you might have guessed, in this step, we write source code – human-readable instructions for the computer. To do this, we open Visual Studio (or whatever development environment we are using) and write statements in C# (or whatever language we are using). Statements are to code what sentences are to everyday writing – they are how we express to our program that we want something to happen. Many statements are a single line in length, but they can be longer, as we'll see in later levels. In the example below, I've written three statements in a Visual Studio project called SimpleDemo (Figure 2.1).

Pay attention to the dash-highlighted panel – this is where we write and edit the C# code for our program. Writing code is "easy" – we can type whatever we want in the editor window. But problems (and frustration) pop up in the next step when we try to compile code that isn't written properly.

Compile

The second – and maybe trickiest – step of our three-step programming cycle is compile. The compiler is a tool that is included when you install the C# language and libraries. The compiler takes the code we've written and

FIGURE 2.1
In Visual Studio, we write and edit code in the editor pane (dashed line).

converts it into something that the computer understands and can run (or execute). As people, we process information differently than computers, and it is important for us to be able to write programs in a way that makes sense to us (or will eventually make sense to us when we've practiced programming for a while). We write our programs in C#, which is a high-level or human-understandable programming language, but our digital devices prefer to receive their instructions in a more low-level or machine-understandable language. The compiler takes our C# source code and converts it to machine instructions that our device can then run. Think of this this way – you, an English-speaking person, have written a letter to your friend who only speaks Japanese. You hand your letter to a translator who knows the words and structure (or syntax) of both languages. The translator hands you back a version that you can't read but that you can now deliver to your friend who can read it. Compiling is a bit more technical, but still very similar to this.

The compiler's main job is to convert the high-level code that we've written into machine language, but to do that, it has to check that we've written something that can actually be translated. The compiler asks: Does this code make sense, and can it be converted into something executable? More formally, the compiler checks to see if the syntax of what we have written is acceptable. In programming, syntax is the set of rules that determine how the parts and pieces of a language can be correctly combined. Sounds a bit complicated, but let's look at an example. Here is a silly sentence that I used to write over and over in my high school typing class:

The quick brown fox jumped over the lazy dog.

Here it is written another way:

thequick brown foxJumped overthelaZyd.og

All the pieces are there, but it doesn't really follow the syntax of how we write and read sentences. In particular:

- the spacing is a mess, that makes it hard to figure out where words begin and end
- capitalization is off, so we can't really tell where the sentence starts
- the . is in the wrong place so we can't really tell where the sentence ends

If you handed this syntactically-challenging sentence into your grade-school grammar teacher, they would say that you didn't follow the rules, and you'd probably be asked to review last week's lessons.

Coming back to programming and compiling, the C# code we write also has to follow syntax rules – and failure to follow them will cause the compiler to quit, complain, and throw errors at us – the compiler loves to throw tantrums. Here are some of C#'s syntax rules that the compiler will try to enforce:

- C# is case-sensitive, so capitalization matters! *Hello* is different from *hello*, which is different from *HellO*.
- There's lots of punctuation like . and ; and they mean different things, and both are important. For example, almost all statements in C# end with ; (semicolon) – that's how C# knows that a statement is over. The . separates different parts of the statement (we'll see this more in our upcoming examples).
- Special characters like { } tell us when parts of our program are beginning or ending – kind of like chapters in a story.
- Spacing matters, but not necessarily in the ways you might think. You'll see different examples throughout the levels and quests.
- Some words like *using, class, float,* and *double* are called keywords and have special meaning. Other times, you can create unique words or labels to suit your needs.

That's a lot to worry about when you haven't written your first program yet. I mention some of these rules early to plant the following seed in your mind – the code we write throughout this book needs to follow certain rules. The syntax rules listed above aren't all the rules that C# syntax follows, but they are some of the most immediate and important ones.

In the end, the point is this: you can write whatever you want in the editor window, but Visual Studio and the C# compiler will tell you if you've put in (or missed) something it doesn't like. When we mess up or make mistakes, we call these errors that the compiler finds "syntax errors", and they stop the compiling process. If that happens, we return to the writing step and fix the issue before trying to compile again.

Here is what happens when my example is changed to have two syntax errors (Figure 2.2).

The errors in the program are quite small – I changed the word Console to console, and took away a ; (semicolon). Yup, that's it, from C to c and a lost ; and the whole thing fails (remember, C# is case-sensitive and uses a whole bunch of punctuation types). The syntax highlighting of Visual Studio shows some hints – those squiggly lines highlight syntax warning and errors – and you can also look at the bottom panel (with the dashed box) for more details. If you don't see the errors in the bottom panel, try clicking the red circle with an "x" in it. We'll ignore the specific details for now (there'll be SO MANY opportunities to work through syntax errors as you practice), but that's where you can find them.

Until we fix all the syntax errors in our program (replace the capital c at the start of line 11 and the ; at the end of line 9), we can't successfully

FIGURE 2.2
Visual Studio shows us syntax errors in realtime, as we're coding! Make sure to keep an eye on bottom pane (dashed line) if your program isn't compiling properly.

compile it, and if we can't compile it, we definitely can't run it. Sorry, that's just how it is – I didn't make these particular rules. In the beginning, much of your time spent programming will be trying to satisfy the grumpy and fussy compiler. But don't lose hope, it does get easier with time and practice. When the program successfully compiles, we can proceed to the next, and maybe funnest step – Run!

Run (Finally!)

How do we know if our program does what we want it to? We run it! This can be the most rewarding step, and sometimes the most heartbreaking. It's rewarding when the program does what we want and heartbreaking when it doesn't. But it's a very important step, and we can't skip it.

Once we have satisfied the compiler by writing a program that meets all of C#'s syntax rules, we can ask Visual Studio to compile and run the fruits of our labor. To do this, we click the green "go" button at the top, press the F5 key on our keyboard, or use the Debug → Start Debugging menu option (this is not the same kind of debugging that is described below, don't worry about the labeling in this menu). If our example program compiles successfully, we'll see a window that collects some input from the user and shows a message we crafted (Figure 2.3).

FIGURE 2.3

When your program's syntax is correct, and the compiler is happy, you'll see the results of your program in a console window like the one shown here.

Success! The compiler is happy with our simple program, and the program runs and does exactly what we asked. It won't always be that way, but in this example, we're good-to-go. There will be times that our program will run, but it won't do what we expected. In these cases, we have either logic or runtime errors in our program. Both of these error types are described in later levels.

In a perfect world, we would write source code, compile it into computer or machine code, run it, and enjoy the amazingly perfect results of our programming efforts. In this magical and imaginary world, the steps we follow would always look like this (Figure 2.4).

But this rarely happens, especially as games and programs grow more complex, so there is another unofficial "step" in the write-compile-run process – debugging. Debugging is where we have a problem – or bug – in our code and we need to repeat either the write and compile steps, in the case of syntax errors, or the whole set of steps including write, compile, and run, in the case of logic or runtime errors. In practice, the steps we follow look more like this (Figure 2.5).

This isn't a beginner-only problem, even lifelong programmers need to spend time debugging their source code. Here are a couple of tips to help:

- *Compile and test often*: Instead of sitting down to try and write an entire program all at once, write only one or two (or a few) lines of code before compiling and testing. This way, if there's a syntax error or your code doesn't do what you thought it would do, you'll be able to find the problem more quickly. Thankfully, Visual Studio will keep track of your syntax errors as they appear in your code, which saves you from having to manually compile the code each time, but it's still worth keeping this idea in mind to keep your debugging time at a minimum.

- *Read your code and error messages carefully*: At times, the compiler will feel like your enemy. When you are first learning to program, you're going to make a lot of mistakes – misspelled words, missing semicolons, capitalization errors, missing { or }, etc. The compiler

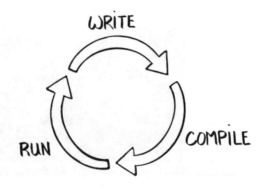

FIGURE 2.4

First, we write the code, then we compile the code, then we run the code. Then, we do it all again. This is the write, compile, run cycle.

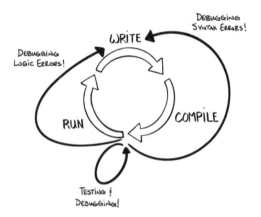

FIGURE 2.5
In reality, the write-compile-run cycle gets a bit messy when we're fixing syntax errors and troubleshooting problems with our program.

will NEVER miss an opportunity to point out your syntax errors – that is its job afterall. When this happens, read the error carefully. Sometimes the error text will tell you exactly how to fix what went wrong. Other times, it won't be so obvious, but with practice, you'll learn how to easily correct many of the common syntax errors.

- *Get help*: When the errors in your program are outside of your experience level, don't hesitate to look them up and ask for help. Many languages, development environments, and frameworks (such as C#, Visual Studio, and MonoGame) have active communities that are ready and willing to help.

- *Keep calm and code on*: Remember, you're new at this. Even video games often seem complex and frustrating when we first start playing them – the mechanics and controls become smoother and more natural as you work your way through them. With practice – yes, even practice making errors and debugging issues – you'll spend less time being stuck and more time enjoying the results of your code.

Side Quests

Want to Know More?

More hardware components: Those with more hardware experience might notice that we skipped a whole bunch of standard computer components. If you want to know more about digital hardware, look up these parts:

- networking devices – allow us to connect to private networks or the Internet

- computer cases and cooling – hold all the pieces together and make sure they don't overheat
- motherboard – connects all the main components like CPU, RAM, hard drive, GPU, and input/output devices and coordinates all the tasks and information

Many Hello, Worlds!: C# is just one of hundreds of programming languages in use today. Look up some different "Hello, World!" examples and compare the different syntaxes to C#. Wikipedia has a great entry for this, but there are other websites and resources as well.

Machine code: All of our examples will be compiled from C# to machine code before they are run in Visual Studio. Look up examples of machine language or machine code to see what it looks like and take a moment to appreciate why we program in high-level languages like C# instead of in lower-level machine code.

C# syntax: I've listed some of the common C# syntax elements, but there are certainly more of them. Wikipedia has a comprehensive entry for C# syntax, but there are others if you take a moment to search for them. Some of the syntax elements that you find will be more important in later levels, but it's worthwhile to be aware of these resources early.

Want to Do More?

Code Quest 1: If you have Visual Studio installed, head to Code Quest 1 and give it a try!

Bonus Code Quest: If you have Visual Studio and MonoGame installed and want to test it out, head to the Bonus Code Quest at the end of the book and give it a try!

3

Code Quest 1: Hello, World!

Before proceeding with this quest:

- review Level 1 contents
- install Visual Studio (covered in Level 1)

Here's the moment you've been waiting for: It's time to create your first Visual Studio project and practice the write-compile-run cycle for yourself! The programs in this first Code Quest are going to be low on complexity, but the steps we follow here are going to be the same for every example that you'll see in this book. Going forward, we're not going to repeat these initial steps with the same level of detail because we'd be repeating the same images and using up valuable page space. It might be worth putting a bookmark on this page so that if you forget one or more of the steps you can easily come back here for a quick reminder.

Ready to embark on your first Code Quest!? Excellent. Let's go!

Main Quest: Hello, World!

For this first Code Quest, we're going to write a classic console program that prints a message to the screen. I say it's a classic program because whenever we (coders or programmers) learn a new programming language, we start with an example known as "Hello, World!". This starter coding example is so common that it has its own Wikipedia page (seriously, check it out). There are four main goals when we write a "Hello, World!" example in a new language:

- To make sure we know how and where to write our code – in our case, this will be the Visual Studio editor window.
- To make sure that we understand the correct code and syntax to output a message to the screen.
- To make sure we know how to compile and run our code.
- To make sure that all the tools we need – development environment, compiler, and so on – are installed and working properly.

DOI: 10.1201/9781003348481-3

There's nothing game-like about this example, but it's still a great place to start our coding adventure. If you've used other development environments and programming languages before, and you want just a high-level overview rather than all the details, the steps we're going to follow for our "Hello, World!" example are as follows:

1. Open Visual Studio and create a new console project called HelloWorld.
2. While it's likely that Visual Studio will create the code automatically for you, make sure that the statement Console.WriteLine ("Hello, World!"); appears between the innermost curly braces { } around line 7 (or so).
3. Run the program using the green "play" button, the F5 key, or the Debug → Start Debugging menu option.

If you're brand-new to Visual Studio or to programming in general, let's take a detailed look at each one of those three steps.

Creating a New Console Project in Visual Studio

The first step for any new program is to create a project in Visual Studio. To do this, open Visual Studio and select Create a new project (Figure 3.1).

Next, we're going to tell Visual Studio that the project is a Console App. This will change when we start writing MonoGame examples in the next book, but for now, scroll or search through the list of templates for Console App (Figure 3.2). If you see more than one Console App option, be sure to select the one that has the C# icon.

Next, we need to tell Visual Studio what we want to call our project. I'm going to call this first project CodeQuest1, and I'm going to save it in my Book Examples folder. I'm going to leave the other options as shown – you can change these if you want, but if your project doesn't work the way you want it to, try creating a new project with settings like mine (Figure 3.3).

This next step is a bit unusual. Newer versions of Visual Studio have an option that says, "Do not use top-level statements". When this option is left blank or unclicked, Visual Studio hides some of the basic program structure and makes the code appear more streamlined. When the option is selected or clicked, the full structure of the program is shown. For all the console examples in this book, I'll be clicking "Do not use top-level statements" so that the full program structure appears – I believe this is the best way to fully understand what is happening in our project code (Figure 3.4).

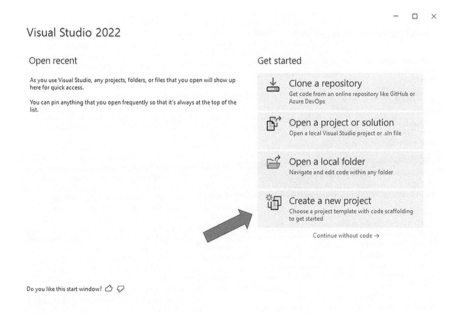

FIGURE 3.1
For most of our new projects, we select the "Create a new project" option in Visual Studio.

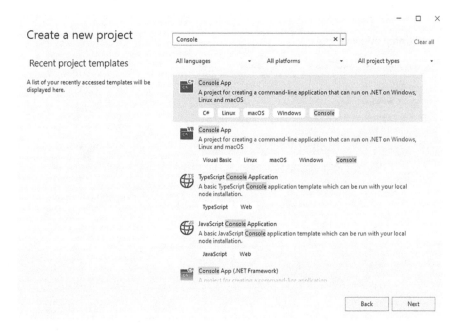

FIGURE 3.2
It's important to select the right type of application when we're starting a new Visual Studio project. In this book, we'll be writing C# console applications.

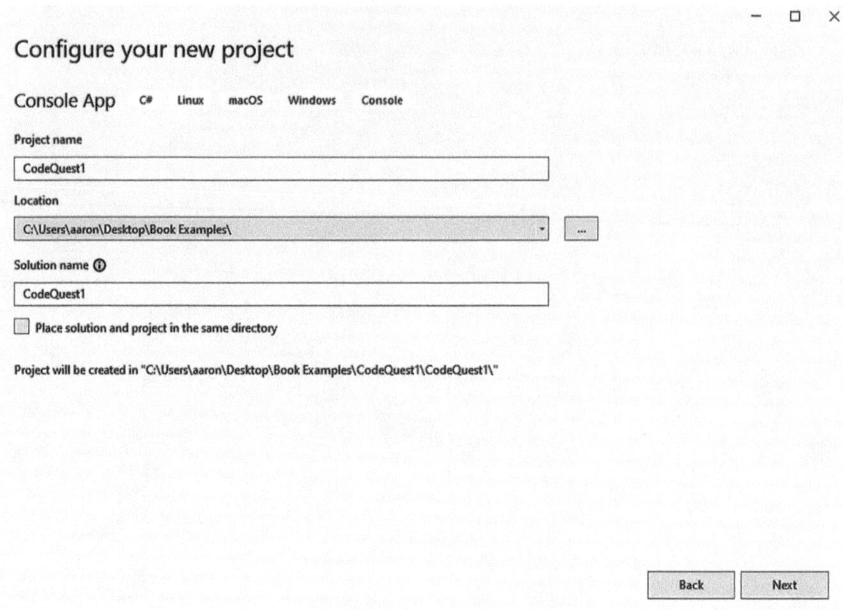

FIGURE 3.3
When you're creating a new Visual Studio project, make sure to give it a descriptive name and save it in a location where you can find it again later.

FIGURE 3.4
Your version of .Net might be newer than mine, but the important thing on this screen is to check that box that says "Do not use top-level statements".

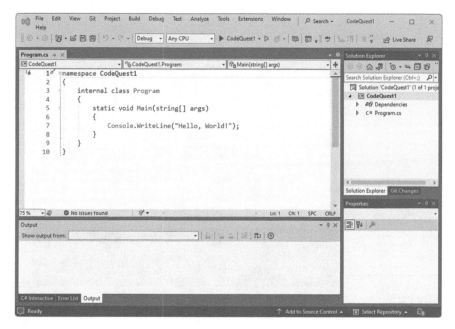

FIGURE 3.5
Here is our first Visual Studio C# console app project. It's even got some code that is ready to compile and run.

With those few steps done, we click the final "Create" button, and we have our first Visual Studio project – and our first C# code too (Figure 3.5)!!

Compiling and Running a Console Project in Visual Studio

Each time we create a new project, Visual Studio fills in some code for us. This code includes the basic structure of all C# programs including a namespace, a class, and a Main() section – we'll talk more about this structure in the next level. Visual Studio also gives us a single C# statement that you can see on line 7. This statement says that our program will display "Hello, World!" to the console when we compile and run the program. In fact, we can do that right now (yes, even though we haven't written any code of our own yet) by pressing the green "play" button at the top of Visual Studio (or by pressing F5, or by using the Debug → Start Debugging menu option). When we do, we see a console screen that looks like this (Figure 3.6).

You've created your first program. Or, you've created your first C# program. Or, you've successfully compiled and run your first C# project since installing Visual Studio. Whatever the case – congratulations! Assuming

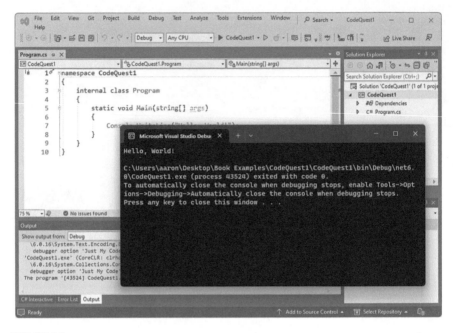

FIGURE 3.6
If all goes well, when you compile and run the code that was given to you when you created your project, you'll see a console window with the classic "Hello, World!" message.

everything went well, you can see a console window that says "Hello, World!" along with a bunch of random-looking text below it. Even though Visual Studio did the write part of write-compile-run for you, you've officially taken your first courageous steps in this programming journey. When you're done admiring your work, feel free to close the console window by clicking the "X" in the top-right corner. You can get it back (to admire your work some more) by running the program again.

At this point, you might be wondering what you saw when you ran your program. A console window is something we don't really see anymore. Operating systems like Microsoft Windows and Mac OS do a good job of hiding old-school features like console windows because they favor visually pleasing and user-friendly graphical windows instead. Console windows are a throwback to a different time in programming and computing but we're going to see them for a while as we work through our first batch of programming examples and concepts. Console programs are much simpler in structure than MonoGame or other graphical user interface programs (fancy windows), and the simpler structure or console programs makes it easier for us to focus on the core programming ideas. After learning and practicing the core programming elements, we'll be able to move into MonoGame (in the next book) and level up our programs! Don't worry, we'll get there soon.

Your Own Hello!

The "Hello, World!" example is a great way to make sure that Visual Studio and C# are installed and working properly, but since all the code was put in place for us, we didn't get to do any code-writing ourselves. Let's quickly fix that.

Using the same CodeQuest1 project, edit the code so that the statement on Line 7 (or thereabouts) says "Hello, <yourname>!" instead of "Hello, World!" For example, after editing, my code would look like this:

```
Console.WriteLine("Hello, Aaron!");
```

Then, re-compile and re-run your program ("play" button, or F5, or Debug → Start Debugging). The output of your program should be different now, here's what mine looks like (Figure 3.7).

This is a very small change, but this time, we completed all three steps ourselves – write-compile-run. Your coding adventure is now truly underway!

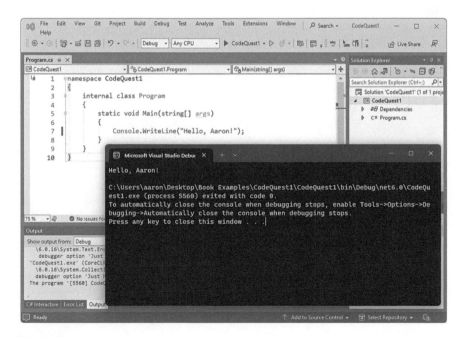

FIGURE 3.7
What's better than seeing "Hello, World!" for the first time? How about seeing "Hello, your own name!" for the first time?

Side Quests

Keep practicing: We haven't learned much about C# yet, but we've learned enough to practice creating new projects and the write-compile-run programming cycle. Try repeating the steps from Code Quest 1 a few times – create more Visual Studio projects and change the "Hello, World!" text to whatever you want! Remember to compile and run your program to make sure that it works properly.

Make mistakes: This might sound weird, but try editing the code in one of your projects to have on-purpose syntax errors! Here are some ideas to try:

- add or remove a curly brace ({ or })
- add or remove a semicolon (;)
- change the case of a letter or word
- add a random word in a random place

Be sure to pay attention to the errors that Visual Studio reports – knowing about different syntax errors and how they happen will help you solve future problems more quickly.

4

Level 2: Adventure Begins

Level 1 Recap:

- Video games and other programs are software that run on physical computer (and smartphone and console) hardware.
- As programmers, we write software or source code in a language like C#. Then, we compile that code into machine code, and run the software to make sure it works. We repeat these steps often.
- C# has a syntax – or set of language rules – that need to be followed.
- Visual Studio is the development environment we're going to use to write our programs.

Video Games Show Us Things

Close your eyes and imagine yourself in the early days of video games, particularly PC games. It's the late 70s or early 80s, and your home computer has a black and white monitor, a really slow CPU (by today's standards), a small amount of RAM, and a keyboard. There's no mouse, not even a trackball. Oh, and GPUs are about 20 years away from being invented and sold. Internet? No way. But, still, these are the early days of PC games, and those games looked something like this:

> I am standing on a beach.
> To the north is a palm tree. There is a parrot in the tree.
> To the east and west, there is more beach.
> To the south is the ocean.
> What shall I do now? *go north*
> You are standing near a palm tree. There is a parrot in the tree.
> What shall I do now? *chop down tree*
> I don't know how to do that.
> What shall I do now? *shake tree*
> The parrot flies down from the tree and lands on your shoulder.

DOI: 10.1201/9781003348481-4

Or, maybe something like this:

Day 6.

The forecast for today is calling for sun and a temperature of 25 degrees C. You currently have $12.25.

The cost of lemonade is 25 cents. How many cups will you make: *20*

The cost of advertising signs is 50 cents. How many will you make: *10*

What price do you want to charge for lemonade (in cents): *75*

Your expenses were $10.00.

You sold 15 cups of lemonade at 75 cents each for a total of $11.50.

At the end of Day 6, you have $13.75.

These two examples are similar to the classic text games *Pirate Adventure* and *Lemonade Stand*, but there were quite a few early PC console video games that worked exactly this way. Even though they don't really "look" like modern video games, they show off two very important points. First, games need to get information to the player – this is output. Output tells our player the state of the game and lets them know if more information is needed. Second, games need to get information from the player – this is input, and it's needed to change the game state (or move the game forward). Even though the types of input and output are different, both of these points are equally true for old-school, text-based console games, or modern, graphically rich games. The console examples we write in this book will be of the old-school, text-based kind. The simple nature of these examples will allow us to focus on our programming fundamentals before we make the leap to MonoGame and fancier graphics in the next book.

We're going to start this level by writing our own code to display simple messages on the console. Then, we'll look at the different types of data we can use in C# and revisit our output statements to see how we can combine text with other data types. We'll end this level by looking at some of the structural pieces that are common in all of our games and programs.

Ready? Let's write some code!!

Displaying to the Console

Displaying to the console is one of the first things we do when we're learning to code because our programs aren't very useful if we can't show off the results to our users or players. Aside from showing you the steps to create a new Visual Studio project, the goal of Code Quest 1 was to introduce you to the statement(s) needed to create console output in your own programs. Here's a reminder of the code for our Code Quest 1 example:

```
namespace CodeQuest1
{
    internal class Program
    {
        static void Main(string[] args)
        {
            Console.WriteLine("Hello, World!");
        }
    }
}
```

Despite all the structure – that we'll learn more about at the end of this level – the only line doing any real work here is:

```
Console.WriteLine("Hello, World!");
```

Maybe you already guessed the purpose of this statement from the "WriteLine" part – write, or output a line of text. In general, we can think of it this way:

```
Console.WriteLine(something to output to the console);
```

We did this in Code Quest 1, but for some extra practice, create a new console project and replace the "Hello, World!" with anything else. I'll replace it with my full name like this:

```
Console.WriteLine("Hello, Aaron Langille!");
```

Assuming I don't make any syntax errors – like erasing a quotation mark or round bracket or forgetting the semicolon – when I run the program, it will display my name. Try it for yourself with your name, your pet's name, your favorite game character's name, your favorite game title, or wherever inspires you! Even though this exercise might seem simple, it's a great way to practice the write-compile-run steps that are part of all programming projects.

Now, let's try adding a brand-new line of code instead of changing one that was already there! You can do this in the same project you were using above or create a new one – your choice. Try adding a new line of code below the existing "Hello, World!" (or Hello, whatever) line, like this (don't forget the semicolons to tell C# where your new statement ends):

```
Console.WriteLine("Hello, World!");
Console.WriteLine("I like playing video games!");
```

Since our output is getting a bit more complex, I'll show what these two lines will display:

```
Hello, World!
I like playing video games!
```

Maybe this output comes as no surprise, but let's make sure we know what's happening – when we call Console.WriteLine() we print what's inside the round brackets (or parentheses, more formally) followed by a new line character. We don't "see" the new line character, but it's there after World! and after games! and because it's there, we have two separate lines of output. Here's another example:

```
Console.WriteLine("Let's");
Console.WriteLine("play");
Console.WriteLine("a game.");
```

which, outputs the following:

```
Let's
play
a game.
```

Three Console.WriteLine() statements, three separate lines of output! If, for whatever reason, you don't want three separate statements, there's another C# output statement that does not print a newline character at the end of the output line. Can you see what's different in the code below?

```
Console.Write("Let's");
Console.Write("play");
Console.Write("a game.");
```

It can be hard to see at first because it's very close to what we did before, but these statements say Console.Write(), not Console.WriteLine(). If we compile and run a program with this code, we would have the following output:

```
Let'splaya game.
```

That output is a bit hard to read, and we can fix it up a bit by adding some spaces after Let's and play like this:

```
Console.Write("Let's ");
Console.Write("play ");
Console.Write("a game.");
```

Console.Write() and Console.WriteLine() print exactly what is inside the quotation marks, so adding spaces gives us the more readable output of:

```
Let's play a game.
```

Both Console.WriteLine() and Console.Write() print information to the console and we're going to use one or both in almost all of our example programs – it's how we get information from our games to the player or ourselves while we're testing our code. So far, all the examples in this section output words – letters, spaces, and punctuation inside quotation marks. This kind of output is important, but games are made up of much more. Try writing a program with the following statements:

```
Console.WriteLine(10);
Console.WriteLine(3.14159);
Console.WriteLine(-0.5f);
Console.WriteLine(true);
Console.WriteLine('Y');
Console.WriteLine("games");
```

The output for these statements might seem obvious – after all, C# simply outputs what you ask it to. But something rather special is happening. Each one of these statements is outputting a different built-in data type that we can (and will) make use of in our games and other programs. What are built-in data types? Let's answer that question, and then we'll take another look at the statements above.

Built-In Data Types

Before we look at the details of built-in types, I want you to imagine you are building a model out of some generic brand of small interlocking plastic bricks. Your completed model might be a futuristic spaceship, a medieval castle, a race car, or something else fun and magical, but, when you first take it out of the box, it's just a bunch of individual pieces – pieces that you need to assemble yourself (that's the fun part). Each of the individual pieces has its place and each type of piece serves a purpose. While they don't look like much when they are spread across the table, floor, or in the carpet, in the end they come together to create something that is more complex and cooler than any of the individual pieces (Figure 4.1).

Writing games is a lot like building toy models – we use a handful of simple "pieces" to create complex game code. The pieces that a programming language gives us are often called built-in data types, but you might see them called fundamental or even atomic data types. Mostly,

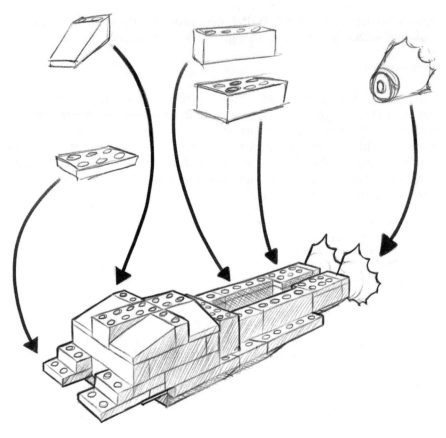

FIGURE 4.1
Built-in types are like toy model bricks – alone, they aren't much. But, they can be combined to create awesome and complex things.

these built-in, fundamental, or atomic data types are numbers and text (as we'll see below), and each type has a particular use in our programs.

With that in mind, let's look at a few of C#'s built-in data types – some of which we'll use often and some we'll use only in very special cases. I recommend paying close attention to the frequently used ones, but a quick read of the special case data types should be enough.

Frequently Used C# Built-in Data Types (and Some Special Case Ones)

There are four built-in data types that we use in almost every game and program we write. Think of these as the most common model pieces in our coding toolkit.

- *int:* int is short for integer and is used for whole numbers ranging from roughly negative 2 billion to positive 2 billion. When we want to work with numbers that have no decimal and are between ± 2 billion, int is the right choice. An integer is stored in 32 bits, or 4 bytes of memory.

- *float*: float is short for floating point number, which is a programming term for decimal number. Floats can store large negative decimal numbers and large positive decimal numbers between $\pm 1.5 \times 10^{-45}$ to $\pm 3.4 \times 10^{38}$. Float is our go-to for storing decimal numbers. Like ints, floats are stored in 32 bits or 4 bytes of memory.

- *bool*: bool is short for boolean, and bools are quite different from ints and floats. A bool stores a value that means true or false. We use bools (or booleans) when we write code that needs to make a decision. We call these decisions conditional logic, and we'll get to them in Level 7. Booleans are a bit unusual in that they are stored in 16 bits (2 bytes) of memory, even though they only store true or false (which technically could be done in 1 bit – see Bonus Level 1).

- *string*: string is the type we use to store text. Strings are actually made up of characters (or chars, see below), so the amount of memory they use depends on the length of the string.

The four data types described above are the ones we use most of the time. However, there are a few that can be used in special cases.

- *char*: char is short for character, and we use this type to store single letters, numbers, punctuation, and a bunch of other printable and non-printable stuff. Even though char can store single numbers, we use it for printing or input and not for math – int and float are better when we want to calculate something. A char is stored in 16 bits, or 2 bytes of memory. We could have put char in "frequently used", but in this book and when programming games in general, it's much more common that we'll use strings instead.

- *byte, long,* and *short*: These are all whole number (no decimal) data types. You choose which one to use based on your needs. If you need to save on memory and only need to store numbers that fall within a small range, using byte or short is the right choice. If you need a really big range of numbers, you can use long, but it will cost you more memory. The int data type strikes a balance between memory usage and the range of numbers you can store, and that's why they are our default whole number data type.

- *double* and *decimal*: These are the other two floating point data types. Double uses twice the memory that a float needs (hence the name double) but is more precise (more decimal places), while decimal is four times the memory size of a float and provides even more precision (even more decimal places)! Float is usually enough precision for most of our decimal work, and at half the size of a double (one-quarter the size of a decimal), is a good trade-off between precision and memory requirements. There is one more reason that we'll use floats here instead of doubles – game engines like Unity use floats as their default decimal data types.

You might be wondering why there are so many data types in C# (and in many other languages). The technical answer has a lot to do with the compiler, languages that came before C#, and how computers store data in memory. A simpler explanation is that many data types give us programmers more options to handle data in different ways. If we want to store small integers and save memory (see Bonus Level 1 for more on bits and bytes of memory), we can do that. If we want to be ultra-precise and memory isn't an issue, we can do that too. Don't forget, there are only four built-in data types that we'll use consistently in our programs – int for whole numbers, float for decimal numbers, bool for logic (Level 7), and strings for text. Here are the key takeaways from our first look at built-in data types:

- C# has many built-in data types.
- Each data type has a specific range of values.
- Data types have different memory requirements (see Bonus Level 1 for more information).
- int, float, bool, and string will handle most of our data needs, and other data types are available if we run into any special cases.

Data Literals

For most people starting out in coding, literals are an unusual concept. Literals are the data whose values we can see in our code, and they are important for two reasons – it's important to be able to identify the different parts of our programs, and we use literals in almost every game or program we write. Let's try to illustrate this idea with a non-code example:

> *Store the result of 171.2 multiplied by 12. Divide that result by -0.19 and subtract 10.*

I don't actually want you to do the math, but I do want to point out some things that are happening in this "sentence". First, we have some information that we know for sure, like the highlighted numbers:

*Store the result of **171.2** multiplied by **12**. Divide that result by **-0.19** and subtract **10**.*

We also know the operations we want to perform – multiply, divide, and subtract – but that's less important right now. There are also unknown elements in this example – "the result" and the final combined value from all the operations are things we don't know (for now) and depend on both the literals (data we can see) and the operations between them. The parts we don't know or can't see in our code will be stored in containers called variables (Level 3). But, for now, let's focus on the literals.

If we were to write this example using C# code, it might look something like this:

```
float tempResult = (171.2f * 12);
float finalResult = (tempResult / -0.19f) - 10;
```

In this code, we have 4 literals – 171.2f, 12, −0.19f, and 10. Everything else in the code is an operator (*, /, -, =, and ()) a variable (float tempResult, float finalResult), or a syntax element (;) – all things we will explore in the next couple of levels. Here are some more example literals for each of our four commonly used built-in data types (and a special appearance by double):

- int: 12, 10, 0, 1024, −369, 1000000, and −212458736712. int literals have no decimal point, no commas, are positive or negative, and are between −2147483648 and 2147483647.

- float: 12f, 10.168f, 0.0f, −3.69f, and −212458736712.9f. float literals have f (or F) at the end, often have a decimal place, have no commas, are positive or negative, and are between $\pm 1.5 \times 10^{-45}$ to $\pm 3.4 \times 10^{38}$.

- bool: true, false. bool literals can be only true or false – nothing else. Bool literals have no double quotation marks around them.

- string: "apples", "I like video games and have played 10 different games this month", "10", "Y", "true". string literals have double quotation marks around them. Even though some of these might look like other data types, the double quotations mean they are strings. Watch for this when you are first starting to code.

- double: 12.0, 10.168, 0.0, −3.69, −212458736712.9. I know what you're thinking – why am I showing you double literals when I said that we would be using floats in our programs? It's important to recognize double literals because they are the default decimal literal in C#. What this means is that if I write a decimal number in my code and I don't put f or F to label it a float literal, C# will treat it like a double literal – and this will cause us problems when we try to do certain operations or calculations. As a reminder, we're using floats in our programs because game engines, like Unity, use floats instead of doubles to save memory.

With our new understanding of literals, let's revisit some code we've seen before:

```
Console.WriteLine(10);
Console.WriteLine(3.14159);
Console.WriteLine(-0.5f);
Console.WriteLine(true);
Console.WriteLine('Y');
Console.WriteLine("games");
```

When we last saw these statements, I said that something special was happening – each one is outputting a different type of literal. Can you tell which type of literal is being output for each statement? Here's the answer key for our little quiz:

```
Console.WriteLine(10);       – int, whole number, no decimal
Console.WriteLine(3.14159); – double, decimal number, no f
Console.WriteLine(-0.5f);    – float, decimal number with f
Console.WriteLine(true);     – bool, true with no quotation marks
Console.WriteLine('Y');      – char, single character with single
                                     quotations
Console.WriteLine("games"); – string, anything in double quotation marks
```

Yes, maybe I was a bit sneaky by including double and char, but did you get them all otherwise? If you didn't, don't worry you're going to see many more example literals throughout this book (and beyond).

We're going to take a closer look at the syntax and structure of our console programs, but before we do, let's practice coding some output statements that use literals and a new operator called concatenation.

Revisiting Output – Now with Concatenation!

It won't take very long for us to want to output text and other data types together. Maybe we'll want to say:

- High Score: 333333360
- Enemy wave #6 starting, now!

- Game over. You lasted 1.7 minutes.
- Hero has 51 health, 19 stamina, and 3 mana points. Next move?

We could write statements like this:

```
Console.WriteLine("High Score: 333333360");
Console.WriteLine("Enemy wave #6 starting, now!");
Console.WriteLine("Game over. You lasted 1.7 minutes.");
Console.WriteLine("Hero has 51 health, 19 stamina, and 3 mana points. Next
move?");
```

This would display what we want to the screen ... sort of. When we output using statements like the ones above, we are outputting unchangeable text. Every time we run the program, the output will be the same. But, when we are writing games, we want to be able to write the text "High Score:" followed by the actual high score that the player earned. When another wave of enemies is about to enter the battle, we want to know what wave number it is, not simply say "wave #6" every time. The same goes for however many minutes the player lasted and our hero's stats. In short, we need a way to separate the text that we print each time, from the data, information, or values that change.

Unfortunately, we can't simply put multiple things to output in the same output statement like this:

```
Console.WriteLine("High Score: " 333333360);
```

Try coding that statement and reviewing the syntax error that Visual Studio shows you. We could break our output up like this:

```
Console.Write("High Score: ");
Console.WriteLine(333333360);
```

This will give us the output we want, but I'd rather do it in one line of code instead of two. Some of the examples above would take 3, 4, or even 7 statements if we were to do it this way. A more efficient way to do this would be to use a special operator like this:

```
Console.WriteLine("High Score: " + 333333360);
Console.WriteLine("Enemy wave #" + 6 + " starting, now!");
Console.WriteLine("Game over. You lasted " + 1.7f + " minutes.");
Console.WriteLine("Hero has " + 51 + " health, " + 19 + " stamina, and " + 3 +
" mana points. Next move?");
```

Each of the statements above is a combination of strings and other types – ints and floats in these cases – and the concatenation operator, +, allows us to join strings and other data types into a single string, most often for creating dynamic or changing output. These statements aren't really flexible because we're still using literals for our score, wave number, survival time, and hero stats. But, once we understand how variables work (Level 3), using concatenation to build complex strings from multiple data types will allow us to write code like this:

```
int highScore = 333333360;
Console.WriteLine("High Score: " + highScore);

int waveNumber = 6;
Console.WriteLine("Enemy wave #" + waveNumber + " starting, now!");

float survivalTime = 1.7f;
Console.WriteLine("Game over. You lasted " + survivalTime + " minutes.");

int heroHealth = 51;
int heroStamina = 19;
int heroMana = 3;
Console.WriteLine("Hero has " + heroHealth + " health, " + heroStamina
   + " stamina, and " + heroMana + " mana points. Next move?");
```

Try coding the above examples before moving on – even the example that uses variables, everything you need is there. Try changing the text and the numbers; make the examples your own!

Before we move on to our next section, it's worth repeating that the concatenation operator is used to join strings with other strings and other data types. If you try to use + without a string somewhere in the expression, you'll be doing regular math addition. Consider the following:

```
Console.WriteLine("2" + "8");
Console.WriteLine(2 + 8);
Console.WriteLine("2" + 8);
```

Of these three statements, two are doing concatenation, and one is doing regular number addition. Can you tell which two lines will output "28" and which one will output 10? If you're unsure, go ahead and code the example to see the output that these statements display. Just in case you're still unsure what is happening – lines 1 and 3 have string literals in them (look for the " ") so they output the string "28" (that's concatenation). Line 2, on the other hand, has two int literals, and no strings, so C# does addition, not concatenation, and the output is 10.

Now that we're more familiar with console output, built-in data types and literals, and building flexible output with concatenation, let's finish this level by revisiting our familiar "Hello, World!" (Code Quest 1) example to discuss some of the structural pieces that make up all our programs.

Revisiting "Hello, World!" – Basic Console Program Structure

Below is the code that Visual Studio gives to us each time we create a new console project:

```
namespace CodeQuest1
{
    internal class Program
    {
        static void Main(string[] args)
        {
            Console.WriteLine("Hello, World!");
        }
    }
}
```

From Code Quest 1, we know this program simply prints "Hello, World!" to the console window. We can see Console.WriteLine("Hello, World!"); and that's the one statement that does something really cool and visible in this program. But, what are all the other lines doing? Why is there so much structure for such a simple program? And, what are all those curly braces { } for? It's important to remember that all programming languages have a syntax that needs to be followed. Even simple programs need to be set up in a specific way. As you practice and write more programs, these "structural" pieces will fade into the background. In fact, the most important thing to know for most of our console programs is that the code we write will go between the curly braces that start on line 6 and end on line 8. With that in mind, let's take a very quick look at each of the parts in this simple program, so that you feel a bit more comfortable with this code.

namespace CodeQuest1

Namespaces are a way of saying "what's in here belongs to this project" – in this case the project CodeQuest1. It's most useful in larger projects where you might have more than one program or class (big projects often have many parts that work together) and namespaces help keep all the parts organized. The word namespace is a C# keyword – meaning it's built into the language. In this example, the specific namespace is CodeQuest1, and unlike the keyword namespace, this is something that can be chosen by you – the programmer. Visual Studio uses the project name (we chose the name CodeQuest1 for the project in the previous chapter) as the default namespace.

internal class Program

Let's work backward with this one. Program is the name of our … program and it is where we write our code. If you look in the Solution Explorer in Visual Studio, you'll also see that the code we write in Program is stored in a file called Program.cs. The name of our class, Program, must match the name of our file – Program.cs. But, don't worry, Visual Studio takes care of all of this for us. You can change the word Program in the code, and you can change the name of the file Program.cs, but I wouldn't recommend it. In Level 10, we'll write classes that are named and stored in something other than Program and Program.cs.

"class" is another C# keyword that means we are doing object-oriented programming (OOP) and that we are working in a class named Program. We'll learn more about this in Level 10, but for now it's worth keeping in mind that almost everything in C# is in a class, so you'll see this in every program we write.

The keyword "internal" is a protection label that prevents the code we write here from being accessed directly by another program. That might sound confusing, but it's a good thing. Sometimes programmers lose track of all the code's details, especially in complex projects, and they try to access parts of other programs in a way that might cause the program to crash or do something else undesirable. The internal word protects against this.

static void Main(string[] args)

Despite all those unusual words and symbols, Main is simply the "entry or starting point" for our program. In later chapters, our examples will get more complex with more classes and files, but Main will always be where our program begins. For now, all the code we're going to write goes inside Main's curly braces { }.

"static" is a C# keyword that Main needs in order to run the program properly. Like internal, it has protective meaning.

"void" is another keyword and means this section of our program – called a method – will not "return" any values. We'll learn more about methods in Level 10.

() are parentheses and they show where any arguments – data passed into Main – will appear.

string[] args are the specific arguments for Main – they are a way for use to pass information into the program (if we need to) when it runs. We won't be using command line arguments in our programs, but this line will always be there.

Curly Braces { }

Curly braces organize our code into "blocks" or sections. For example, the curly braces on lines 2 and 10 create a block of code that says the whole program is part of namespace CodeQuest1. The pair on lines 4 and 9 are a block for the class Program, and the final pair on lines 6 and 8 are for Main – these are the curly braces we are most interested in for now. Here are a few things to keep in mind when it comes to curly braces:

- Every opening brace { must have a corresponding closing brace }.
- Sets of curly braces can exist inside of others – in our example, the Main curly braces are inside of the class curly braces which are inside of the namespace curly braces.
- A lot of syntax errors happen because we lose track of where our curly braces are and what they are doing in our code.
- Curly braces define the scope, or sections of code, where our variables can be accessed (see Bonus level 6 for more).

That's a lot of technical detail – C# keywords, parentheses, square brackets, curly braces, and more! Are all of those pieces required? Yes. Are all of those pieces important? Also, yes, but most of those structural pieces are put in place for you by Visual Studio when you first create your project. We covered them quickly here because they appear in all of our programs (console and MonoGame) and for some people, knowing what they are and what they do will be helpful, but we don't need to worry about them, most of the time. Think of all those structural pieces like the parts of a car – when we drive, the engine, doors, tires, electronics, and seats are all very important, but when everything is working properly, all we really think about are the gas and brake pedals, mirrors, and the steering wheel.

Revisiting Top-Level Statements

Before we move on to writing some code of our own, let's revisit an important point from Level 1. In the instructions for Code Quest 1, I mentioned clicking the checkbox that says "Do not use top-level state-ments" on the last step of creating your projects in Visual Studio. If you leave that checkbox empty, the code in your Program file will look like this:

```
// See https://aka.ms/new-console-template for more information
Console.WriteLine("Hello, World!");
```

Where are all the C# keywords, parentheses, square brackets, and curly braces? In short, they are hidden in a way that's designed to make it easier to jump right in and do some programming. We won't be using this feature for our examples – instead, we're going to immerse ourselves in all the wonderful structure C# has to offer. If you accidentally forget and create a project with this feature enabled, you have a few options:

- Keep going! The code you write will look a bit different from my examples, but most of it should work, at least for the first few chapters.
- Delete the project and create it again with the checkbox enabled.
- Use the "Convert to 'Program.Main' style program" option that shows up if you move your mouse to the line numbers to the left of your code in Visual Studio. This will give you back most of the structure, but not the namespace line.

Now that we know a bit more about how console programs are structured, and what to do if we accidentally create a project with top-level statements, let's push forward to Level 3 and learn how to store data in variables, collect user input, and write comments to help us keep track of what our games and programs are doing.

Side Quests

Want to Know More?

Show me all the built-ins: Even though we've looked at the most common built-in data types in this Level, there are more. Some of them are pretty handy, some of them are for very specific cases and needs. Find a list or description of all C# data types and their corresponding literals.

A different way to output: There are actually two common ways to create output strings in C#. I've shown you concatenation here because, in my humble opinion (imho), it is the most straightforward and intuitive. Here's a concatenation example that we've seen in this Level:

```
Console.WriteLine("Hero has " + 51 + " health, " + 19 + " stamina, and " + 3
                    + " mana points. Next move?");
```

Another way to do this uses a syntax called composite formatting like this:

```
Console.WriteLine("Hero has {0} health, {1} stamina, and {2} mana points
left. Next move?", 51, 19, 3);
```

These two statements produce the same output. In the concatenation version, we build the output string using + with the data (or variables in the next level) exactly where they'll show up. It's like the cars of a train, and the data goes exactly where it will appear. In the composite formatting, we put placeholders like {0}, {1}, and {2} directly in the string portion of our output and follow that with the list of data (separated by commas) after the string. Neither of these two formats is "better" than the other and all of the output examples in this book can be reworked to use composite formatting.

Look up some more examples of composite formatting to see if you might want to use that in your code instead of concatenation.

Another different way to output: There is a third way to build output strings, it's called interpolation formatting and while it makes more sense to use it with variables (Level 3), it looks like this:

```
Console.WriteLine($"Hero has {51} health, {19} stamina, and {3} mana points
left. Next move?");
```

Find more examples of interpolation formatting, maybe that'll be the one you like best.

Bits, bytes, and binary: To understand more about how built-in data types are stored in memory and how computers differentiate between different data types, look up definitions, and explanations of bits, bytes, and binary data. Bonus Level 1 is another good resource for this.

Want to Do More?

What's your data story: Write a program similar to the examples in this level. Make the output something that is either about you, or something that is interesting to you. Try to write at least five output statements and use a combination of Console.Write() and Console. WriteLine() statements.

Complex concatenation: Practice writing output statements that use concatenation. Make your output statements complex or interesting enough to include more than one built-in data type. Use concatenation to separate your data types, but make sure that your output is readable by yourself or your users.

5

Code Quest 2: Great Game Quotes

Before proceeding with this quest:

- review Level 2
- complete Code Quest 1
- create a new Visual Studio Console project. If you need a refresher, detailed instructions can be found at the beginning of Code Quest 1.

Games are full of great quotes. Sometimes they are part of meaningful dialog, and other times they come from important moments in the story. They can even come as sarcastic, thoughtful, or potent one-liners. Wherever they come from, quotes help us remember and relive great game moments. In this Code Quest, you'll practice using Console.Write() and Console.WriteLine() to output some popular, and perhaps familiar, game quotes to the console.

Main Quest – Great Game Quotes

Using only Console.WriteLine() statements and string literals, write a console program that outputs the following quotes:

- It's dangerous to go alone! Take this.
- The cake is a lie!
- Stay awhile, and listen.
- Thank you Mario! But our Princess is in another castle!

Here is my output – see how closely you can duplicate it! (Figure 5.1).

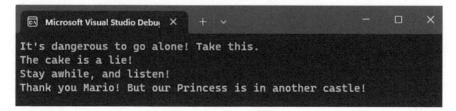

FIGURE 5.1
Can you write a program that duplicates my console output?

DOI: 10.1201/9781003348481-5

Side Quests

A small change: Starting with the code from the Main Quest, change it so that the output looks like this instead (Figure 5.2).

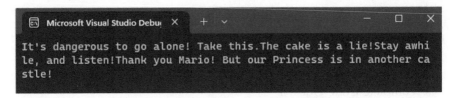

🔲 Microsoft Visual Studio Debug   ✕   +   ∨   —   ☐   ✕

```
It's dangerous to go alone! Take this.The cake is a lie!Stay awhi
le, and listen!Thank you Mario! But our Princess is in another ca
stle!
```

FIGURE 5.2
Here is some new output for you to duplicate.

Hint: It's a small change to each of the output statements.

Let's get literal: I've made some "creative" changes to a few of the game quotes:

```
The PI 3.14159 Is A Lie!
Stay awhile, and listen true!
Thank you Mar10! But our Princess is in another castle!
```

Redo the Main Quest, but this time, use concatenation and some different literals in your output. To help with this side quest, my non-string literals have been bolded.

Make it your own: Most of the game quotes in this Code Quest come from games that I've played or am familiar with. Redo the Main Quest or any of the Side Quests using your own favorite game quotes.

6

Level 3: A Variable Inventory of Items

Level 2 recap:

- We can display output to the console using Console.WriteLine() and Console.Write().
- Built-in data types like int, float, bool, and string help us to work with different kinds of numbers, text, and data in our code.
- Literals are data values – specific numbers, text, and more – that we see in our code.
- We can build cool output strings that combine different data types with the concatenation operator +.

Video Games Use Dynamic Data and Information

Think about the last video game you played. It doesn't matter what kind of game it was or what kind of hardware you were playing it on. What matters is what was happening in the game. Were there enemies swarming you? Were you grinding through new areas looking for equipment upgrades and more experience points? Were you moving colorful shapes around the screen to make triples or full-lines so that your score would go up? Whatever was happening in your specific game, I'll bet that things were changing often: Enemy positions changed as they moved toward you, items were added and removed from inventory, XP counters went up, colorful shapes disappeared and new ones appeared to fill the gaps, the old high score was replaced by your awesome run, and so on.

Video games are dynamic programs – this means they are constantly changing. This also means that when we write them, we need a way to store data (information that our game needs) so that it can change as the game goes on. Literals won't work because we need to edit and recompile the code to change those. So, what do we use for our game's dynamic data needs?

Variables.

As their name suggests, variables are variable or changeable. A complex game might have hundreds, or even thousands of variables, each storing some kind of information about the current state of the level or area. Every

DOI: 10.1201/9781003348481-6

time something changes in the game, some variables change value. Variables are also one half of what we need to make games interactive. The other half is user input, and that's the topic of Level 4.

If things aren't clear from this quick introduction, worry-not-brave coding adventurers – Level 3 is here to help us make sense of how our games use variables!

A word of caution before we charge forward – variables are a truly fundamental programming concept – almost everything we do going forward depends on a solid understanding of variables. I recommend "bookmarking" this level and coming back to it if, later on, you find yourself needing a refresher on variables and how to use them.

Now, without further delay ... 3, 2, 1. CHARGE!!!

The What and Why of Variables?

In Level 2, we learned about different data types and literals. We know that C# has built-in data types like int, float, bool, string, and more. We also know how to use them in our code: 16, −4.9f, false, "Ready Player 1?" and so on. But we can only do so much with literals alone. Let's revisit these Level 2 example output statements:

```
Console.WriteLine("High Score: " + 333333360);
Console.WriteLine("Enemy wave #" + 6 + " starting, now!");
Console.WriteLine("Game over. You lasted " + 1.7f + " minutes.");
Console.WriteLine("Hero has " + 51 + " health, " + 19 + " stamina, and " + 3 +
" mana points left. Next move?");
```

In each of these lines, we are outputting text literals and number literals to the console. That's cool, but the way this code is written, it produces the same output each time it's run. If you're skeptical, try coding these lines in a new project and running the program at least five times. It will produce the same output every single time you run it. These statements are hard-coded to use literals – hard-coded means there is no input from the user and the data is part of the code itself with no way to change it apart from editing and re-compiling it. When we play games or run other programs, we don't edit and re-compile the code to change values. Instead, programmers – like us – use a powerful combo of variables and user input (Level 4) to make the game (or program) work with a range of possible values.

Technically speaking, variables are named locations in RAM memory that store data or values, but I like to think of them like labeled storage boxes (Figure 6.1).

FIGURE 6.1
Variables are like labeled storage boxes in memory. They have a name (that's the label), and they can only store a specific type of thing.

The fact that our labeled storage boxes exist in RAM memory is something we don't really have to worry about – C# will take care of that. What is more important for us are the following facts about variables. They each:

- can store data values that we need for our game to work properly
- have a name that makes it easier for us to identify and access them
- can have their value changed – this is where the word variable comes from
- can be accessed to see what is being stored
- can only store a specific data type

Let's wrap these variable facts into an analogy that involves you flying to Mars (stay with me on this).

In your Mars spacecraft, you have several fuel storage tanks. Each one has a name, such as FuelTank1, which makes it easier for you to know which fuel tank you're currently working with or investigating. The fuel tank can store something specific – fuel. The amount of fuel in FuelTank1 goes down as you travel to Mars. But if there are any Mars-fuel refueling stations along the way, the amount of fuel in FuelTank1 might go up. In other words, the fuel in FuelTank1 changes – it's variable. At any point, we can check the amount of fuel in FuelTank1. Oh, and in case this wasn't clear, the only thing FuelTank1 can properly and safely store is … fuel.

Here's another example that is closer to what we'll do with variables in our game code.

To practice your programming skills, you are creating your own version of PacMan (classic!). You have a variable named playerScore that keeps track of the player's current score. You store 0 (zero) as the starting value in the playerScore variable. As the player moves around the screen and eats dots and vulnerable ghosts, the player's score goes up (so the value in playerScore changes). The player's up-to-date score is visible on the game screen at all times. The playerScore variable is a whole number (because we don't need a decimal in our score).

Now that we have some idea of what variables are and what they can be used for, we need to learn three variable-related programming tasks – creating a variable, storing a value in a variable, and checking what value is currently in the variable. We call these three tasks declaring, assigning, and accessing.

Declaring Variables

To create a variable, we must declare it – and to do that we need to tell C# what type the variable will be (what kind of value it will store) and give it a name (a programmer-defined label that will we use to access the variable). In general, a declaration statement looks like this:

```
type variableName;
```

Here are four separate example declaration statements that use each of our main built-in data types:

```
int playerScore;
float scoreModifier;
string playerName;
bool playerHasHighScore;
```

Try putting the four declarations in a project of your own. Remember to put them inside of Main's curly braces. You can compile and run this code, but it won't output anything. As long as it compiles and runs without errors, you've succeeded with this mini-practice quest.

Each of these four lines is creating a variable to store some data for our (hypothetical) game, and each has both a type and a name that match what we plan to store:

- int, or whole number, for our player's score
- float, or decimal number, for a score multiplier
- string, or text, for our player's name
- bool, or true/false, to know if our player currently has the high score

One of the reasons we need to specify the type of our variable is so that C# knows how much memory to set aside. The actual amount of memory space being used by each variable doesn't matter too much – modern devices have lots of RAM – but look back to Level 2 if you want a reminder of how much memory our built-in data types need. The other thing that is happening in our four lines of code is that our variables are being given names. The name we give to a variable (sometimes called a variable identifier) is up to the programmer and can be *almost* anything. But there are some rules and conventions to variable naming that we'll discuss shortly. Also, like most statements in C#, variable declarations end with a semicolon.

When you get more comfortable with declaring variables, you might want to save a bit of space in your code by declaring multiple variables – of the same type – on the same line, like this:

```
int playerScore, playerHealth, gameHighScore;
float scoreModifier;
string playerFirstName, playerLastName;
bool playerHasHighScore, gameOver;
```

Here is the same code, with each of the declarations on a separate line:

```
int playerScore;
int playerHealth;
int gameHighScore;

float scoreModifier;

string playerFirstName;
string playerLastName;

bool playerHasHighScore;
bool gameOver;
```

Both of these examples do the same work – declaring multiple variables. Which of them you use is a matter of personal preference. Personally, I like the compactness of declaring multiple variables on a single line, but it really is up to you.

Finally, and very importantly, a variable declaration only creates the variable, it doesn't store a value. Think of a declaration as creating an appropriately sized, but empty, box. To store something in our variables, or appropriately sized boxes, we need to learn about assignment statements.

Assigning and Accessing Variables

So, you've declared a variable, and now you want to store something in it – maybe a number, maybe some text, maybe a true or a false value. Let's take a look at one of the most common statements in almost every programming language – the assignment statement. In general, an assignment statement looks like this:

```
variableName = someValue;
```

One of these pieces we've looked at before – the variable name. We set this during the variable declaration. The = is new, and it's known as the assignment operator. The assignment operator basically says, "take the value on the right and store it in the variable (memory storage box) named on the left" (Figure 6.2).

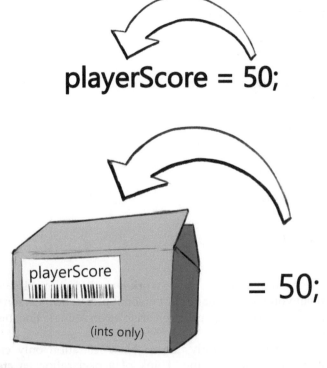

FIGURE 6.2
When we assign variables, we store a value in our labeled memory "box".

Here are some example assignments to go with the declarations we coded above. The declarations are repeated above the assignments to save you from flipping back to look them up:

```
int playerScore;
float scoreModifier;
string playerName;
bool playerHasHighScore;

playerScore = 50;
scoreModifier = 2.5f;
playerName = "Aaron";
playerHasHighScore = false;
```

There are a few things going on in these eight lines of code:

- A variable must be declared before it can be assigned – the same way that a box must exist before you can put something in it. In this example, all four variables are declared before any of the assignments happen, but you don't have to do it that way. Experiment in your own code with declaration and assignment placement.
- Assignment statements, like declarations, always end with a semicolon.
- While the type of the variable matters, we don't repeat it in the assignment. The variable type is set during declaration only. Notice that the assignment statements don't (and cannot) repeat the int, float, string, and bool that we used in the declaration.
- Each assignment statement has a variable name on the left and an appropriately typed literal on the right of the assignment operator (=). The variable name always appears on the left, and the value to be assigned (or stored) always appears on the right. It's not always going to be a literal, but it must always be a type that is compatible with the variable.

This last point is REALLY important and worth repeating – the right side of an assignment statement must be of an appropriate type for the left side variable (or box). Think of it this way – you can't store a refrigerator in a shoe box. In all of the examples below, I will be very careful to make sure that the right-hand side is compatible with the left-hand variable. There are some ways to bend these rules a bit, but we won't look at them until Level 6 (or Bonus Level 2).

Here is another example with a single variable that stores the health of our player character. We start by declaring it:

```
int playerHealth;
```

Then, we assign a value of an appropriate type. Since our variable is type int, we'll use an int literal:

```
int playerHealth;
playerHealth= 100;
```

Easy-peasy, right? Now, with a third statement, I can double check that it worked properly by accessing (or reading) the value that was stored in the playerHealth variable:

```
int playerHealth;
playerHealth= 100;
Console.WriteLine(playerHealth);
```

The final line of this example will print 100 – the value stored inside the variable. Whenever C# comes across a variable name – and assuming the variable has been properly declared and assigned a value – C# will replace the variable name with the value stored inside. In other words, the final statement in this example says: "output to the console the value stored inside variable playerHealth, whatever it might be". Since the value stored in playerHealth is 100, the output statement is equivalent to:

```
Console.WriteLine(100);
```

Try coding this example for yourself. It might seem trivial, but with this small amount of code you're practicing three of the most common things we do in programming – declaring variables, assigning values to variables, and accessing the values stored inside variables. These steps are so important that we're going to do some more examples. Let's try working with a float:

```
float distanceToTarget;
distanceToTarget = 10.9f;
Console.WriteLine("Distance to target: " + distanceToTarget);
```

Here we have declared a float, assigned it a value of 10.9f, and used an output statement with concatenation to output some text and the value of the distanceToTarget variable. When assigning float literals to variables, we need to remember the f that comes after the 10.9. If we forget the f, C# will treat our literal like a double and double values are incompatible with float variables. Try out these three lines of code – but try the second line with and without the f and pay close attention to the error that Visual Studio shows you.

How about a string example?

```
string inventoryItem;
inventoryItem = "purple gem";
Console.WriteLine("In my inventory: " + inventoryItem);
```

In each of the above examples, we've assigned a literal to our variables. While these examples are good to show how assignment works in the simplest cases, we can and will get fancier. Here's a pretty common game scenario. Our player earns a score through normal activities in the game. But they might also earn an extra bonus by clearing out all the enemies or finishing the game with a speedy time. Here's how we might show off this idea in code:

```
int playerScore;
int bonusEarned;
int finalScore;

playerScore = 100;
bonusEarned = 15;
finalScore = playerScore + bonusEarned;

Console.WriteLine("Final score: " + finalScore);
```

Try coding this example before reading on for the explanation.

The variables we need are declared in the first three statements. In the next three statements, we assign values to our variables. In the last statement, we access the finalScore variable to show the player the result. So, what's new about this example? In the statement "finalScore = playerScore + bonusEarned;" we assign a value to finalScore – but instead of using literals, we use the values that we previously assigned to playerScore and bonusEarned. If we were to describe this statement in words, it would be something like this:

- access the values stored in playerScore and access the value stored in bonusEarned
- add these two values together
- store the added values in finalScore

There are two new ideas for us in this one line of code. First, we can, and very often do, use variables on the right-hand side of an assignment – the values don't need to be literals. Remember, when C# sees a variable name in your code, as long as it has been previously declared and assigned a value, that value will be substituted for the variable name. That means that our new statement is essentially:

```
finalScore = 100 + 15;
```

Second, until this example, + for us meant concatenation (combining values with strings, Level 2), but when only number types are used, it means addition (regular math). Since both playerScore and bonusEarned are number types, we simply add them together here. We'll learn more about C#'s math operators in Level 4.

It's very normal to be questioning the point of variables – instead of using literals, like we did in the previous level. It seems as though we're simply using literals stored in boxes. But we wouldn't go to all this trouble to introduce the idea of variables if they weren't really, really useful. To level up our variables, we need to understand two important ideas – the value in a variable can change, and the value in a variable is sometimes unknown to us. Read on to unlock these two key variable concepts.

Reassigning Variables

If literals are values or data that we can literally see in our code, what are variables? We know they are named storage containers in memory – but why not call them memory boxes or data containers? As I've mentioned before, they are called variables because they are variable (or changeable). Once you've declared a variable, you can change its value any time you want or need to! This is a good thing in programming because it means we can use a single variable to store a player's score, and it will be updated as they move through a level. Changing the value in an existing variable is called reassigning. With this new information, we start to see games (and other programs) as a collection of constantly reassigning (changing, updating) variables. Keep this idea in mind as we journey onward.

The good news is that we don't need to learn anything new to reassign a variable. Take a look at the following code:

```
int numberOfEnemies;
numberOfEnemies = 10;
Console.WriteLine("There are " + numberOfEnemies + " enemies");
numberOfEnemies = 100;
Console.WriteLine("Oops, there are now " + numberOfEnemies + " enemies");
```

There really isn't a practical reason that we would declare a variable, assign it a value, and then immediately change it (the bold statement), but this code does show us that it's possible – variables can be changed by simply writing a new assignment statement. This code will compile, and when it runs, it will output that there are 10 enemies, then it will output that there are now 100 enemies, all using only one variable – numberOfEnemies.

It doesn't matter what type your variables are, you can reassign them whenever you want, as long as you remember to use the right type of values:

```
string playerName;
float playerID;

playerName = "Aaron";
playerID = 1976.0211f;

Console.WriteLine("My name:" + playerName + ", and my ID:" + playerID);

playerName = "GamerAaron";
playerID = 2023.0101f;

Console.WriteLine("My new name: " + playerName + ", and my new ID: " +
playerID);
```

We'll see more practical reasons to reassign variables as we learn more programming concepts and as our examples become more complex. For now, let's take a look at some of the common (and most frustrating) variable assignment and reassignment errors.

Common Assignment and Reassignment Errors

Here are a few of the errors that beginners (and pros!) often make when assigning and reassigning variables.

Accessing a variable that doesn't exist yet: Trying to access a variable that doesn't exist is a surprisingly common error.

```
int playerScore;
playerScore = 100;
Console.WriteLine("Player score is: " + finalScore);
```

In this example, we've successfully declared and assigned playerScore. But, in our output statement, we are trying to access a variable named finalScore – which hasn't been declared (or assigned). C#'s way of telling us this is a problem is to error "The name 'finalScore' does not exist in the current context". It would be great if it simply said "you forgot to create the variable finalScore", but it doesn't. The easiest way to fix this example is to replace finalScore with playerScore in the output statement:

```
int playerScore;
playerScore = 100;
Console.WriteLine("Player score is: " + playerScore);
```

If finalScore is something we meant to include, we could always declare it and assign it.

Accessing a variable before assigning it: When we first declare a variable, it has no "default" value stored in it.

```
int playerScore;
Console.WriteLine("Player score is: " + playerScore);
```

If we try to access a variable before we assign it a value, we get the error "Use of unassigned local variable 'variableName,'" or in this case "Use of unassigned local variable 'playerScore.'" To fix this error, find the variable and make sure it has a value before trying to access it.

```
int playerScore;playerScore = 100;
Console.WriteLine("Player score is: " + playerScore);
```

Assigning, or reassigning an incompatible value: Whether we're assigning or reassigning a value, it must be compatible with the variable we want to store it in.

```
int playerScore;
playerScore = "Aaron";

string playerName;
playerName = 100;
```

Both of these assignments cause the same error – "Cannot implicitly convert type X to Y". I've used X and Y here because this error will always put the variable type (int, float, string, bool, etc.) in X and the value type (int, float, string, bool, etc.) in Y – this way you know what types are causing the conflict. The fix this error, make sure that the values you want to assign are appropriate for the variables you're storing them in:

```
int playerScore;
playerScore = 100;

string playerName;
playerName = "Aaron";
```

Redeclaring a variable: A variable declaration specifies the type, but an assignment, or reassignment, does NOT. It is an error to do something like this:

```
int numberOfEnemies;
numberOfEnemies = 10;
Console.WriteLine("There are " + numberOfEnemies + " enemies.");
int numberOfEnemies = 100;
Console.WriteLine("Oops, there are now " + numberOfEnemies + " enemies.");
```

This one is pretty subtle – see if you can find the issue in the code above before reading on.

The error is in the statement that reassigns numberOfEnemies to 100. It's very common for beginners to accidentally "redeclare" a variable when they actually just want to reassign it. By putting the type in front of an assignment statement, you are trying to recreate the variable, and this causes the error "A local variable named 'variable' is already defined in this scope" (scope is discussed more in Bonus Level 6). In other words, C# thinks you want another variable with the same name in your program – which you can't do. Once you have declared a variable by giving it a type and a name, it will be there for you to assign and reassign. The fix for this error is to remove the type from your assignment, or reassignment statements:

```
int numberOfEnemies;
numberOfEnemies = 10;
Console.WriteLine("There are " + numberOfEnemies + " enemies.");
numberOfEnemies = 100;
Console.WriteLine("Oops, there are now " + numberOfEnemies + " enemies.");
```

Remember, it's perfectly normal to make mistakes when you're programming – beginners and pros and everyone else in between. The most important thing is to pay close attention to the errors that Visual Studio shows you so that you can learn how to avoid, or at least correct, them when they happen.

Initialization = Declaration + Assignment

I'll repeat something I've said already in this level – when we're programming, we declare and assign variables all the time. If that's not clear yet, it will be as our examples become more complex and interactive. Take a look at the declaration and assignment below:

```
string playerName;
playerName = "Aaron";
```

There are two considerations – one minor, one major – with these lines of code. First, we have to repeat the variable name playerName in both lines of code. Not a big deal, but if I can skip that and make my code more compact,

I'm happy to do so. Second, and more importantly, after the first line, we have an empty variable. If, for whatever reason, we forget to assign it a value and then try to access it, the program will fail to compile (see *Accessing a variable before assigning it*). There is a way to address both issues at once – an initialization statement:

```
string playerName = "Aaron";
```

An initialization is simply a declaration and assignment mashup! In this statement, we are saying "create a string variable called somePlayer and immediately put the text Aaron in it". This cuts down on the code a bit (one line instead of two) and makes sure there is an accessible value in the variable (even if we're going to reassign it a different value later on). Let's revisit our example from earlier:

```
int playerScore;
float scoreModifier;
string playerName;
bool playerHasHighScore;

playerScore = 50;
scoreModifier = 2.5f;
playerName = "Aaron";
playerHasHighScore = false;
```

but using initializations this time:

```
int playerScore = 50;
float scoreModifier = 2.5f;
string playerName = "Aaron";
bool playerHasHighScore = false;
```

This has the same effect, but takes up half the code space and all of our variables are guaranteed to have values if we try to access them immediately after the initializations. Try coding this second example and then try accessing the variables using output statements immediately after the initializations.

I strongly recommend using initialization statements over separate declarations and assignments, whenever you can. Why then, did we wait so long to introduce them? Two reasons – first, at this point, we know what declaration and assignment mean so combining them into a single statement should make more sense, and second, there will be times where it is actually more appropriate to declare a variable and assign it at a later time. Initialization statements are often the best idea, but not always. Knowing that declarations and assignments can be separate is still very important.

We have one more variable topic to cover before we get to the promise of this level's introduction – interactive programs. It's a short topic, so let's get to it.

Naming Your Variables

It might seem a bit silly to be talking about what we name our variables. But, as with so many things in programming, there are some C# naming rules that we must follow, and some conventions (good practices) that we really should follow.

Rules

- Variable names must start with a letter or an underscore. This one can be a bit frustrating when you want to start a variable name with a number, like 5thEnemy or 2DBackground, but it's just not allowed in C#. Instead, use enemy5 or background2D.

- After the first letter or underscore, I recommend sticking mostly to letters, numbers, or underscores unless you have a really good reason to use something else. Some unusual characters can be used, but others will cause syntax errors.

- You cannot use a space in a variable name. A space actually splits your variable name into two variable names and will confuse the compiler. For example, playerScore is one variable, while player Score will be treated like two variables.

Aside from the rules that we must follow, naming conventions are guidelines, best practices, or the "way things are normally done". They don't cause compiler errors, and they aren't meant to stifle your variable-naming creativity or make things harder for you as a coder. They are meant to make variable names more consistent between programs, projects, and other programmers (often we work with teammates on large projects) so that the code we write is easier to understand. Consider adopting these C# naming conventions.

Conventions

- Variable names should be descriptive. It's easy to get lazy and start using single letters as variable names – like x, y, and z. If you store the player score in x, the number of enemies in y, and the player health in z, how long is it going to be before those variable names cause you or your coding teammates confusion. Instead, use descriptive names like score, enemies, or health – or better yet, playerScore, numberOfEnemies, and playerHealth. It's a bit more to type, but trust me on this one – when you (or your teammates) read your code, it'll be very clear what the variables are being used for.

- Use "camel case" when your variable names have more than one word. Writing multi-word variable names like this – playerfirst-name – is ok, but the words tend to blend together. To make the specific words in the name clearer, use camel case, which means giving each word after the first word a capital letter like – playerFirstName. You can capitalize the first letter, but by C# convention, variable names start with a lowercase first letter.

By now, I hope you're feeling good about variables. We know how to declare, assign, and access them. We know how to make our code a bit more compact and avoid some errors using initializations. We also know how to properly name our variables and why it matters. With all this knowledge, we have reached a truly awesome milestone in our adventure. In Level 4, we're going to write code that is interactive – and variables are going to lead the way.

Side Quests

Want to Know More?

The typeless var variable: This is another variable type known as var. It's a bit tricky because it's not a type like int, float, string, or bool. Instead, var lets the C# compiler guess at the type the variable should be based on what you're trying to store in it:

```
var someText = "Hello there!";
var playerScore = 125;
var scoreMultiplier = 2.5f;
```

It seems like this would be the easiest way to declare all our variables, but there are some very good reasons why we don't do this. There are also some solid reasons when it's okay to use var instead of our other built-in types. Do a bit of research to understand when you might and might not want to try using var.

But I want to store a fridge in a shoe box: The data we store in our variables must be of a compatible type with the variable itself. Most of the time, we store ints in int variables, floats in float variables, strings in string variables, and so on. But, occasionally we need to squeeze some data of one kind into a variable of another kind. We'll talk about this a bit in Level 6, but *if you're really curious*, look up casting and type conversions in C#. We won't do it often in this book, but it's an interesting topic and worth knowing about.

Want to Do More?

Make mistakes: Programmers make mistakes all the time when we declare, initialize, and assign variables. Make some mistakes of your own so that, with practice, you'll be able to identify and fix them quickly. Try assigning some variables before you declare them, accessing some declared variables without assigning them, and mixing up your assignment variable (left-hand side) and value (right-hand side) types – see which ones are compatible and which ones are not!

Code more, change much: Code the examples in this level for yourself. Change the numbers and text so that they are a better reflection of your gaming and programming interests.

7

Code Quest 3: Character Builder (Part 1)

Before proceeding with this quest:

- review Level 3
- complete Code Quest 2 (optional)
- create a new Visual Studio Console project. If you need a refresher, detailed instructions can be found at the beginning of Code Quest 1.

Many role-playing video games, and also many tabletop role-playing games, start by having the player "build" a character using a character sheet. We're going to write a program that does something similar – but we'll keep it simple by not having too many character traits. In this code quest, we're going to practice declaring, assigning, and accessing variables that could be used in a character game character sheet. In Code Quest 4, we'll continue this program by adding some user input to make our character sheet program interactive!!

Main Quest – Character Builder (Part 1)

The code in this quest should accomplish the following tasks:

1. Start by declaring at least four different variables of different types to store your character's traits. My version (output below) has two string variables, one int variable, and a float variable to store my character's name, profession, health points, and damage per turn.
2. Give each of your four variables a value using assignment statements and appropriate literals.
3. Output some character sheet-style text and the values stored in your variables to the console. Use concatenation to combine your text and variable values.
4. Be sure to compile and run your code frequently and solve any coding issues as they come up.

Here is the output from my version of this quest (Figure 7.1).

DOI: 10.1201/9781003348481-7

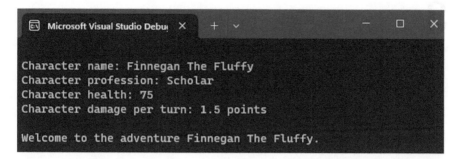

FIGURE 7.1
Try duplicating my output before getting more creative with your own version of this program. Don't forget the variables and literals in your code!

Side Quests

Less code, same output: Complete this quest using initialization statements instead of separate declarations and assignment statements.

Go big or go home: My example has only four variables and five lines of output. Add more variables and more output statements to make your character sheet more interesting and detailed.

Make it your own: Do you find my output uninteresting or uninspiring? Do you prefer pirate games? Do you prefer space games? Do you prefer space-pirate games? Change the text and the variables to make this quest more fun for you!!

8

Level 4: Some Friendly Input

Level 3 Recap:

- Variables are named memory locations where we can store, update, and retrieve information.
- The variable type is specified when it is declared or initialized.
- The value that is assigned to the variable must be compatible with the variable type.
- Variables can be reassigned or updated, as often as we need.

Video Games Use Input

Have you ever wondered what it is that makes video games different from other media like books, music, or movies? Is it the compelling characters and immersive storyline? No, books have that. Is it the soundtrack that resonates with your deepest emotions? Probably not, I have a few playlists that do that. Well, then surely it's the mind-blowing imagery and visual effects? Hm. The latest blockbuster movie also has these things. So, what is it that makes video games unique?

It turns out that, unlike books, music, and movies, video games are interactive. Maybe this seems obvious now that we "say it out loud", but player interaction is the main ingredient that makes games special – games are the only medium where we, as players, can truly impact how the experience "plays" out (pun intended). Here are some examples:

- Each time you play through an action role-playing game, you pick a different character type with different abilities. This changes how the gameplay and storyline unfold.
- The first time you play a mobile platformer, you earn a score of one star after finishing a level. The next time, by knowing what to expect and by making different decisions, you get a score of three stars (way to go)!
- There is a clay pot on the ground. You break it with your sword. Ten gold coins fall out. You put them in your backpack. Later on,

DOI: 10.1201/9781003348481-8

you spend 10 gold on a wooden flute. There is now no gold in your backpack, but there is a wooden flute.

- You find a shortcut in a racetrack, one that your friends don't know about, and finish the race 1.38 seconds faster than anyone else.

- You plant 3 turnip seeds, 13 onion seeds, and 4 cherry tree seeds in your farming game. The next day, when you log in, you will have mature plants and trees to harvest delicious digital fruits and vegetables.

Even though each of these examples seems different, there are a pair of programming ideas that make them all work interactively. The first is a way to "store" data or information. As we know from Level 3, games are made up of all kinds of values that are constantly changing – player and enemy positions, current score, pick-up items, dialog prompts, and much more. This data is stored in variables. The second important concept we need for interactivity is a way to get information from the player – what character type they want to be, how do they want to move across the platforms, do they choose to break the clay pot to collect the gold to buy the wooden flute, do they take the shortcut or the long way around, and finally, which seeds do they plant and then harvest the next day. We call this player-generated information input, and our games need it to move the action forward.

A big part of the joy of video games is our ability to affect the outcome. To make this joy happen, we, as programmers, need variables (check! thanks to Level 3) and user input. Level 4 is going to start out simple, with console-based keyboard input, but if you decide to continue your journey, in the next book we'll look at other input types like mouse input and game controllers. We're also going to start by focusing on the steps involved in collecting input, instead of what we can actually do once we've collected it – that will come over the next few levels.

Getting Console Input from Our Player

What we are about to do is the opposite of outputting values to the console – something we've done many times so far using:

```
Console.WriteLine();
```

Now, we want to read values from the console. Lucky for us, the C# statement we're going to use for input is very similar to the one we use for output:

```
Console.ReadLine();
```

It's very similar in structure (just change the word Write to Read), but Console.ReadLine() has a very different job – it collects input from the keyboard that you can, and really should, store in a variable. This means that a complete input statement looks more like this:

```
string playerInput = Console.ReadLine();
```

This initialization statement (Level 3) says – read input from the keyboard and store it in a new string variable called playerInput. If you prefer a separate declaration and assignment, you could use this code instead (but I'll most often use the more compact form above):

```
string playerInput;
playerInput = Console.ReadLine();
```

Why is our variable a string? Everything that Console.ReadLine() collects from the keyboard is given to our code or program as a string – this is an important fact that we'll come back to in a bit when we want to collect numbers. Before you try programming the previous input statement for yourself, let's add an output statement to go with it. This way, we'll know if the code is actually working.

```
string playerInput = Console.ReadLine();
Console.WriteLine("Your input was: " + playerInput);
```

These two statements are really powerful. In the first, we collect a string from the player and store it in the variable playerInput. In the second statement, we access and output the contents of playerInput. We don't know what the player is going to input, but we output it no matter what it is. With these two simple statements, we have our first truly interactive (but still simple) program. Try coding this example for yourself and running it a few times with different inputs – single words, sentences, gibberish with unusual characters from the keyboard, etc. But be aware – when you run it, the program will look like it's just "stopped". This is because Console.ReadLine() pauses the program and waits for the input. Once the player hits enter (that's the signal that the input is complete), the program will continue, and the contents of our variable will be shown on the console.

Steps to Collect User Input

Technically, the only thing we need to do to collect user input is write a Console.ReadLine() statement. But, as you might have noticed from coding and trying the previous example, having our game (or program) simply stop and wait is a bit awkward. We can make user input clearer and more friendly by breaking it into three steps:

1. Prompt the player by telling them what kind of input you are looking for. I recommend using Console.Write(); for your prompt, instead of Console.WriteLine(); – using Write means the user input will be on the same line as the prompt. Try them both (Write and WriteLine) to see the difference.
2. Collect the input using a Console.ReadLine() statement.
3. Store the input in an appropriately named and typed variable.

Steps 2 and 3 are typically done in the same statement (variable initialization or assignment), but it's worth remembering that two things are actually happening. Here is a simple program that collects input using the steps listed above and then outputs the input that was collected:

```
Console.Write("Welcome, brave adventurer! What is your first name: ");
string playerFirstName = Console.ReadLine();
Console.WriteLine("Fantastic! We are glad you joined us " + playerFirstName
+ ".");
```

Can you see all three steps in this example? The player was prompted (first statement), input was collected and stored in a variable (second statement), and as a bonus, the stored input was output to the console (third statement). Try writing this example for yourself and be sure to run it a few times. When I run it, it looks something like this (my input is **bold**):

```
Welcome, brave adventurer! What is your first name: Aaron
Fantastic! We are glad you joined us Aaron.
```

Or, running it a second time with different input:

```
Welcome, brave adventurer! What is your first name: GLaDOS
Fantastic! We are glad you joined us GLaDOS.
```

If you want to collect input more than once, simply repeat the three steps multiple times:

```
Console.Write("Welcome, brave adventurer! What is your first name: ");
string playerFirstName = Console.ReadLine();
Console.Write("And what is your profession: ");
string playerProfession = Console.ReadLine();
Console.Write("Fantastic! We are glad you joined us " + playerFirstName + " the "
+ playerProfession + ".");
```

Here, we've collected input twice in order to get the player's name and profession. As always, try coding this example for yourself and running it a few times to get a feel for what the code is actually doing. Here is some sample output to compare with (again, my input is bolded to make it stand out):

```
Welcome, brave adventurer! What is your first name: Aaron
And what is your profession: Professor
Fantastic! We are glad you joined us Aaron the Professor.
```

And this one:

```
Welcome, brave adventurer! What is your first name: GLaDOS
And what is your profession: Evil Robotic Overseer
Fantastic! We are glad you joined us GLaDOS the Evil Robotic Overseer.
```

Input is an important part of our console games and programs going forward. If you're uncertain of the steps, spend a bit more time with the content and examples in this section. The next section adds a small amount of complexity to our input collection, but the steps are still very similar.

Inputting Numbers and Other Fun Things

We are not limited to text or string input, though there is an extra step we need to do when we want to collect other types from the user. We know, from the examples in the previous section, that Console.ReadLine() only reads in strings from the keyboard. That's a bit inconvenient when we want to collect other kinds of data, but it turns out that every built-in data type in C# has a handy "parse" method that allows us to convert from strings to other data types. Let's look at a simple(ish) example. Say I have a string that looks like this:

```
string textNumber = "12345";
```

If I want to convert that string to an integer, I can call the int.Parse() method like this:

```
string textNumber = "12345";
int intNumber = int.Parse(textNumber);
```

Until we cover objects and methods (Level 10) in more detail, think of int.Parse () as a helpful C# tool, like Console.WriteLine() and Console.ReadLine(), that allows us to convert from one kind of thing to another. In this case, int.Parse() lets us convert the string "12345" to an int 12345. We put the thing we want to convert, in this case textNumber, into the round brackets ( ), and we store the result in the variable intNumber. If all goes well, intNumber will have the number 12345 that we can then do math (Level 4) and other integer-y operations on. We can do the same type of operation with floats and even booleans using:

```
string textFloat = "12345.67";
string textBool = "true";
float convertedFloat = float.Parse(textFloat);
bool convertedBool = bool.Parse(textBool);
```

There are Parse methods for all of the built-in data types (except for string, which is converted using concatenation or a special ToString() method).

We can convert strings to number (and bool) types – but what does this have to do with input? Since Console.ReadLine() only reads strings from our console keyboard, if we want to read in other types, we need to "parse" them. Suppose we want to ask our player how old they are, and we want to treat their age as a number, not text. We need to make a slight change in our prompt-collect-store steps:

```
Console.Write("Greetings brave adventurer! What is your age: ");
int playerAge = int.Parse(Console.ReadLine());
Console.Write("Wonderful. " + playerAge + " is a fine age indeed.");
```

Everything in this example works as it did before. We prompt the player, we store and collect the input, and we output the result. But, this time, since the input is a number, we need to change our variable to type int (assuming we are interested in whole-number ages), and we have to parse the input in order to convert the string that Console.ReadLine() collects. An expanded version of this code would look like this:

```
Console.Write("Greetings brave adventurer! What is your age: ");
string playerAgeText;
playerAgeText = Console.ReadLine();

int playerAge;
playerAge = int.Parse(playerAgeText);

Console.Write("Wonderful. " + playerAge + " is a fine age indeed.");
```

To the player, the code in these two examples would run the same way. The only difference between the two is that the second example more clearly shows everything that is happening, step-by-step. Here is one last example with a few differences, so pay close attention:

```
Console.Write("Hello player! What is your first name: ");
string playerName = Console.ReadLine();
Console.Write("And, what is your age: ");
```

```
int playerAge = int.Parse(Console.ReadLine());
Console.Write("How many hours of video games do you play per week: ");
float playerGameTime = float.Parse(Console.ReadLine());
Console.WriteLine();
Console.WriteLine("Player stats:");
Console.WriteLine("Player name: " + playerName);
Console.WriteLine("Player age: " + playerAge);
Console.WriteLine("Player Game Time (per week): " + playerGameTime);
```

Here are some important things to look for in this code:

- How many times is the player being prompted?
- How many inputs is the player providing?
- What types of inputs is the player providing?
- Bonus question: What does a standalone Console.WriteLine();
  statement do?

To be clear, there is nothing new in this code – you've seen it all in previous examples. But, sometimes, as our programs get more complex, we can get overwhelmed – the whole program seems somehow greater than the sum of its statements. How can you work through this program? Start by coding and running it for yourself. Before this level ends, I'll show you another way to help fight the growing complexity of our programs – using comments.

Parsing Can Be Tricky

Parsing is a sensitive operation. If I want to parse an integer from a string, the string needs to contain only numbers – like "123456", "101", or "7". If the string contains the word "apples", whether there are numbers in the string or not, parsing isn't going to be successful. In fact, parsing is always doomed to fail if the input string doesn't jive with the type of data being parsed.

Here are some tips for entering console input that can be parsed to our common built-in data types:

- *From string to int*: The string should contain only numbers, no decimal, and no spaces or commas. The string you are converting also needs to be within the allowed range for ints (Level 2).
- *From string to float*: The string should contain only numbers, at most one decimal point, and no spaces or commas. The string you are converting also needs to be within the allowed range for floats (Level 2).
- *From string to bool*: We don't do this very often, but if you're curious, the string must be the word "true" or "false" only.

Dealing with failed parsing is possible, but we won't look at it now – we need a few more programming pieces to be able to tackle this elegantly (see Bonus Level 3). For now, assume that your player (or, more often you) will enter good and parse-able strings on the keyboard, and if not, just go ahead and let the program crash!

Don't Know, Don't Care – The True Power of Variables + Input

Have I mentioned that variables are powerful – like, really powerful? Variables, along with input, make our games and programs interactive, dynamic, and fun. Sure, they can be annoying when you forget to declare them or when you try to put a value into a variable that isn't compatible – but, once you get the common hiccups figured out, things get better.

When we combine input and variables, we unlock the "don't know, don't care" factor. Are you making a puzzled face and scratching your head? I've seen that look many times. Let's unpuzzle this unusual idea. Statements like this are both common and important:

```
int playerScore = 100;
string playerName = "Aaron";
float playerGameTime = 10.5f;
```

In each of these statements, we can clearly see the values in the code – because 100, "Aaron", and 10.5f are all literals. This code is easy to understand but not very flexible because the program always runs the same way. But what happens when we write code that looks like this:

```
Console.Write("Greetings player. Enter your first name: ");
string playerName = Console.ReadLine();
Console.WriteLine("Welcome: " + playerName);
```

We know, from the previous examples, that playerName will store whatever the user enters. Maybe they'll enter "Aaron" (I know I would). Maybe it will be "Patty" or "Osman" or "Natasha" or "Duante" or "Shen" or ..."applesauce" or "3 cups of soup please". Remember, I asked the user to enter their first name, and then I left them alone to complete the task. Will they actually enter their name? Don't know. More importantly, as long as it's text, I really don't care. I'm not trying to be mean or insensitive, but the program will work whether they input "Aaron", "Patty", "Osman", "Natasha", "Duante", "Shen", "applesauce", or even "3 cups of soup please". The point here is to recognize that what is stored in our variables, often, doesn't matter, and the program will do its job regardless.

There are a few considerations that do matter. The value we are trying to store has to be the right type, or the program will crash. The value might also need to be within a certain range or the code we write won't work properly. Part of what we're going to learn going forward is how to make sure the input we get is appropriate for our code, but for now, simply recognizing the "don't know, don't care" nature of variables is helpful.

Here is another example with a sneak peek at some code that we'll cover in Level 6:

```
Random numberGenerator = new Random();
int randomValue1 = numberGenerator.Next(1, 7);
int randomValue2 = numberGenerator.Next(1, 7);
int result = randomValue1 + randomValue2;
Console.WriteLine(result);
```

As a mini practice quest, code these statements for yourself. What is the output of this program? Given the title of this section, you might want to jump right to "don't know, don't care", but the answer is a bit more interesting than that. The output will be a random number between 2 and 12 because two of the variables each have stored random numbers between 1 and 6, and the third variable stores the sum (addition) of the other two. Essentially, this is a program that simulates two six-sided dice that are added together! What are the specific numbers that will be stored in the three variables (pssst, now is the time … .) – don't know, don't care! As long as they are integers and can be added and output to the console, the program will run perfectly!!!

Again, it sounds like we're being flippant about our coding – we don't know what it's doing and we don't really care – but actually what we're doing is realizing that a lot of coding is working with players, users, and data where we can't really anticipate the exact values. So, we code in such a way that the program will work even if we will never actually know the specifics of what it will compute and output when it is run. Variables are the key to this power – and games are made up of variables that are constantly changing based on user input (and sometimes a bit of good old-fashioned random number generation).

Comments (They Matter)

We're finishing this level on a topic that is always a hard sell. In all my (many, many) years of teaching people to program, not one person has come up to me and said "commenting is my favorite part of coding". Not one! There are a couple of reasons for this, and I'll tell you about them at the end of this section. For now, as we move forward in our adventure together, our code is getting (and will continue to get) more complex – both in terms of what it can do and in terms of the amount we need to write to get things done. Here's an example from earlier in this level:

```
Console.Write("Hello player! What is your first name: ");
string playerName = Console.ReadLine();
Console.Write("And, what is your age: ");
int playerAge = int.Parse(Console.ReadLine());
Console.Write("How many hours of video games do you play per week: ");
float playerGameTime = float.Parse(Console.ReadLine());
Console.WriteLine();
Console.WriteLine("Player stats:");
Console.WriteLine("Player name: " + playerName);
Console.WriteLine("Player age: " + playerAge);
Console.WriteLine("Player Game Time (per week): " + playerGameTime);
```

We went through this code before, but seeing it again now, how comfortable do you feel about describing what it does? It's ok to say "I feel great and understand it all", and it's equally ok to say "I don't feel great and there are things that I'm not quite sure of, yet". As it turns out, we have ways of making code easier to read, and understand. One way is to use descriptive variable names, which we've discussed in Level 3, and you can see in the example above. Another way is to add comments to our code. Take a look at the updated example below:

```
/*
This program is very interactive. It collects three pieces of data
from the user, using input, and then displays that data to the console.
This program was written by: Aaron Langille.
*/

//Prompt the player for their name
Console.Write("Hello player! What is your first name: ");
//Collect and store the player name (as a string)
string playerName = Console.ReadLine();

//Prompt the player for their age
Console.Write("And, what is your age: ");
//Collect and store the player age (as an int)
int playerAge = int.Parse(Console.ReadLine());

//Prompt the player for their game playing time
Console.Write("How many hours of video games do you play per week: ");
//Collect and store the player game time (as a float)
float playerGameTime = float.Parse(Console.ReadLine());

//Output a blank line (to make the output nicer)
Console.WriteLine();
```

```
//Output all of variable that were input by the player
Console.WriteLine("Player stats:");
Console.WriteLine("Player name: " + playerName); //output name
Console.WriteLine("Player age: " + playerAge); //output age
Console.WriteLine("Player Game Time (per week): " + playerGameTime);
//output game time
```

The second version of this program is well-commented or well-documented. These descriptive text elements help us and our colleagues (when we work in teams). It's easiest to understand why we would write comments when we're working in a team – so that everyone understands how and why the code does what it does. This is especially true when the project is large, there is lots of code, and many people are working on it. We always want to communicate as much as possible about our code to help people quickly make use of what we've written and to avoid any misunderstandings.

I would argue, and here comes the tough sell, that writing comments is equally important when we are working alone. We might start coding something and then stop working on it for a while – when we come back, it's nice to have reminders of what we were thinking. Similarly, as our projects get bigger, comments can help us keep track of how the different pieces work and how they all fit together. It's hard to appreciate the value of comments when our examples are only a few lines long, but trust me, whether you're working alone or in a team, comments can make a big difference.

With that in mind, there are two main types of comments in C# – line comments and block comments.

- *Line comments*: These start with // and extend only to the end of the line they are created on. In the example above you can see that some comments are the only things on the line – that is, the whole line is just a comment. In other cases, the line comments are at the end of the statement (after the ;). When the compiler reads a line, it reads up to the // and determines that it, and everything after, is part of a comment. Line comments are great for short notes that relate to specific lines of code.

- *Block comments*: These start with /* and end with */. They have as many lines as you choose to place between the start and end symbols. You can see in the example above that my program has four comment lines (Visual Studio will put the leading *'s in the block comment for you). Block comments save us from having to use // over and over again – they are more convenient when we have lots to say. In the example above, there is only a block comment at the top, but block comments can appear anywhere in the code, as long as the proper start and finish symbols are in place.

When you're first starting out, it might not be clear how and when to write comments in your code. Some people write very short comments infrequently, while some write long, wordy comments often. Commenting style is a somewhat personal matter (unless your team, employer, or instructor gives you specific instructions), but here are some general tips for writing good comments:

- put a comment anywhere that you think your code needs some explanation
- use line comments for quick notes
- use block comments for longer, wordier explanations
- comment while you code, don't leave it until the end
- don't under-comment – make sure future-you, or your teammates can understand what you're doing in your code
- don't over-comment – too many comments can make it harder to read the actual code of your program, not every statement needs a comment, and not every program needs your "life's story"

Okay – you made it this far, so you must want to know why no one ever considers commenting their favorite part of coding. Here are the main reasons:

- *Comments don't have any impact on the program*: Comments don't make your program run faster. They don't make your program use memory more efficiently, they don't make your output easier to understand, and they don't make your player character jump any higher or move any more smoothly. In fact, the compiler ignores comments entirely – they don't even make it into the compiled version of your game or program. All they do is make your code easier to read when you or your colleagues need to make changes or understand what is happening.
- *It's boring*: Writing code is exciting. Writing comments about that code is boring, and since it's boring, people tend to put it off until the end – like eating your broccoli last (sorry people who like broccoli, but I think you get what I mean). People often write all of their code, then go back to do all the commenting after-the-fact. Or, even worse, they don't write comments at all. This may seem tempting, but trust me – it's a bad idea. When you return to your code a few days, a few weeks, a few months, or a few years later and have no idea what is happening, you'll be grumpy that your comments are either lacklustre or non-existent.

In a way, I hope the one takeaway from this section is that commenting your code is like eating broccoli (or something else you don't really enjoy) –

not the most fun part, but definitely important and healthy. Do yourself a big favor, write comments while you code and keep your comments up to date. Future-you, and your coding teammates, will thank you!!

Side Quests

Want to Know More?

More data types, more parsing: In this level, we looked at how to collect and parse the common built-in types, but C# has more data types that we can use. Look up parsing examples for some of the less-common (but still cool) data types.

Stop the crashing: In this level, there's no real solution to prevent your programs from crashing if they try to parse bad input from the player or user. You can also look up C#'s try/catch blocks to learn how to exit the program gracefully if the user enters a bad value, or you can read Bonus Level 3 to see examples of the TryParse method. These are interesting topics, but they're going to be less important if or when you move into MonoGame.

Professional commenting: There is a third type of C# comment called Documentation Comments. They're a bit more complicated than our line and block comments and are most often used for professional projects with large programming teams. Find some examples of how to use documentation comments in your code.

Want to Do More?

Crash the input examples: Code the examples from the parsing section ("Reading in Numbers and Other Fun Things") and try entering some ridiculous input for any of the parsed values. How many different ways can you crash your program!? Don't worry, this still counts as programming practice.

Code Reward – The Player Introduction

Congratulations brave adventurer! You made it through four levels and have been introduced to enough programming concepts that we can put together our first complete, interactive program. Starting here at the end of Level 4, and at the end of all levels going forward, I'll provide a full program that highlights the most recent topics we've covered. The programs will be simple at first, but will get more complex and interesting as we level up our skills together.

Our first code reward is a player introduction program, and it shows off several programming concepts, including data types, variables, output, and input. It's similar to some of the examples from this level, but it's a good exercise to try for extra practice.

Imagine you've been contacted by a game tournament organizer. They want a simple program that collects information about a player participating in the tournament. Lucky for us, they want to collect information that we can use to practice our input skills!

Here are the steps to create this program:

- Write a quick introduction output line (this is always a fun thing to do).
- Prompt the player to input their name.
- Collect and store the player name in an appropriate variable – I suggest a string.
- Prompt the player to input their age.
- Collect and store the player age in an appropriate variable – I suggest an int.
- Prompt the player to input their star ranking from the previous tournament. This is a made-up stat for this example – assume a player ranking is a decimal number between 0 and 10 (or something like that).
- Collect and store the player star ranking in an appropriate variable – I suggest a float.
- Finally, ask the player if they think the original arcade version of Donkey Kong is the greatest game of all time. This is a bit of a stretch, but we're practicing collecting and parsing different data types, and this is a silly but reasonable way to ask a true or false question.
- Collect and store the player's Donkey Kong opinion in an appropriate variable – I suggest a bool.
- Write some output statements that summarize our player's tournament information. Be creative here!
- Write some comments that describe your program. Try to include both some block comments and line comments.

Try this code reward for yourself. If you get stuck, take a look at my sample solution for a hint. Even though it looks like a lot of code, pay attention to how much of it is comments, and how many different inputs we are collecting and outputting.

```
/*
This is a program that uses variables, output, and input. The program acts
like a simple player info collection and output tool that could be used at a
(very small and very simple) game tournament.

This program is the Code Reward for Level 4.

Author: Aaron Langille
*/


//here are the variables we'll use
string playerName;
int playerAge;
float playerRanking;
bool donkeyKongIsTheBest;

//This is a helpful welcome message followed by a blank line.
Console.WriteLine("Welcome to the Player Intro-matic version 1.0.");
Console.WriteLine();

/*
When we collect input, particularly numbers, the program can crash if the user
enters input that can't be properly parsed. Assume the user enters meaningful
and parse-able input. Bonus Level 3 has more information.
*/

//Prompt the user to enter their name.
Console.Write("Enter your name: ");

//Assign the player name
playerName = Console.ReadLine();

//Prompt the user to enter their age.
Console.Write("Enter your age: ");

//Assign the player age
playerAge = int.Parse(Console.ReadLine());

//Prompt the user to enter their previous tournament ranking.
Console.Write("Enter your previous ranking: ");

//Assign the player rank
playerRanking = float.Parse(Console.ReadLine());

//Prompt the user to enter their answer.
Console.Write("Donkey Kong is the best game ever (true/false): ");

//Ask the big question …
donkeyKongIsTheBest = bool.Parse(Console.ReadLine());
```

```
//Here's our output!!!
Console.WriteLine(); //start with a blank line
Console.WriteLine("Here is the info for this player: ");
Console.WriteLine("Player name: " + playerName);
Console.WriteLine("Player age: " + playerAge);
Console.WriteLine("Player's previous ranking: " + playerRanking);
Console.WriteLine("Is Donkey Kong the best game ever?: "
+ donkeyKongIsTheBest);
```

9

Code Quest 4: Character Builder (Part 2)

Before proceeding with this quest:

- review Level 4
- complete Code Quest 3 (recommended)
- review or try Code Reward 4 (recommended)
- create a new Visual Studio Console project. If you need a refresher, detailed instructions can be found at the beginning of Code Quest 1.

In Code Quest 4, we created a simple character builder program with a few variables and output statements. But, that program wasn't interactive – to change our character's traits we need to edit and recompile the code. This is good practice (editing and recompiling) when we're learning to program, but the character sheet would be much more fun and useful if we could more easily change the character traits without editing and recompiling all the time. In this Code Quest, we're going to make our character sheet interactive by adding user input. If you're a beginner coder, I strongly recommend completing Code Quest 3 before starting this one – the idea here is to build off of that code.

My completed example will be very similar to my version of Code Quest 3. If your version of Code Quest 3 was different (more exciting or detailed), feel free to adapt the Main Quest instructions to match what you did previously.

Main Quest – Character Builder (Part 2)

The code in this quest should accomplish the following tasks:

1. Start by declaring at least four different variables (just like Code Quest 3). There should be different types in your variables. My example (output below) has two strings, one int, and a float.
2. Prompt the user to input a value by telling them what kind of information the program is looking for.

DOI: 10.1201/9781003348481-9

3. Use Console.ReadLine() to assign a user-input value to your variable. Remember, non-string inputs (like ints, floats, and almost anything else) need to be parsed before they can be stored properly. Trust that your player (or you) will enter input that can and will be properly parsed.

4. Repeat Steps 2 and 3 for each of your declared variables.

5. Once all your input has been collected and variables have been assigned, output some character sheet-style text and the values stored in your variables (by accessing them) to the console.

6. Add a few descriptive comments in your code – preferably while you're writing your program.

7. Be sure to compile and run your code frequently and solve any coding issues as they come up. Hint: You don't need to have all the code written before testing the program. Try coding and testing one variable declaration + prompt + input/assignment + output at a time.

Here is the output from my version of this quest (Figure 9.1).

Remember, the user or player is entering the information this time. This means if we run the program again, with different input, we'll get different output (Figure 9.2).

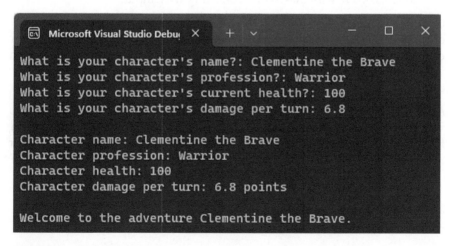

FIGURE 9.1

This is the output from my version of this program, but it also has my input. Be sure to note which text in this screenshot is prompts for the user, which is input from the user (me, in this case), and which text is the final output.

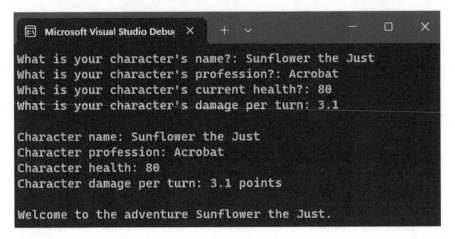

FIGURE 9.2
This is just another execution of the same program, but with different input. Notice how the final output changes.

Side Quests

Less code, same output: Complete this quest using initialization statements instead of separate declarations and assignment statements. Remember, you can initialize your variables while collecting user input.

Go big or go home: My example has only four variables and five lines of output. Add more variables and more output statements to make your character sheet more interesting and detailed. Be careful here – each variable you add will add a prompt, input, and output statement. Your code will grow quickly as you add character traits.

Make it your own: Do you find my output uninteresting or uninspiring? Do you prefer fishing games? Do you prefer farming games? Do you prefer fish-farming games? Change the text and the variables to make this quest more fun for you!!

10

Cutscene 2: Recipes for Success

Video Games Are Made of Algorithms

Your hero is crouched behind a lovely pixelated shrub. They watch quietly as a huge, troll-like guard patrols the enemy campsite. The guard starts their patrol in the northwest corner and moves to the northeastern border of the camp. Then, they march to the southeastern-most point, then to the southwestern limit, and finally back to the northwest corner. This seems to happen over and over again. Your hero watches this movement pattern and hatches a plan to sneak into the closest enemy tent when the guard's back is turned.

Inside the tent, your hero smashes two clay pots and three wooden crates. Oddly, the guard, just outside the tent, doesn't seem to hear anything. Your hero runs around the tent interior and collects the spilled contents of the clay pots and wooden crates – a bunch of gold pieces, a medium axe (how did that even get into a clay pot?), and three perfect rubies. Cool.

Checking their inventory, your hero notices they are now carrying three rubies, nine blackberries, a goblin tooth, and a potato shaped like a small foot. With these items, your hero can finally craft a portal to transport them back home. Your hero arranges all of the items, places them on the crafting altar, and confirms they want to proceed. Moments later and bathed in pale yellow light, they are magically transported away.

What do all these video game features – enemy patrolling, smashing pots and crates, and crafting – have in common? If you said they are all created using computer code – that's absolutely correct! But there's more to it. These features (and almost all game features, events, and actions) are coded using algorithms, or code recipes.

In this short cutscene, we'll look at what the term algorithm means, the common properties of algorithms, and how knowing a bit about algorithms can help us solve coding issues in our own programs and games.

If your hero didn't get transported away and is still in the tent smashing pots and crates, have them finish up and meet us in the next section where we'll see how our games are made of code recipes.

DOI: 10.1201/9781003348481-10

Algorithms Are Recipes for Code

To understand how algorithms are recipes for code, it helps to be familiar with recipes in general. Maybe you already know some deliciously complex recipes – I like making sourdough bread that takes two days from start to finish. That's a bit more complex than we need here, so, let's consider a simple favorite recipe from my house – the ever-popular cake in a cup (Figure 10.1). The ones we make at home have all the ingredients pre-measured in a paper envelope, but I'm going to pretend to be fancy and list them.

Ingredients:

- flour
- salt
- sugar
- baking powder
- cocoa
- water (or milk if you prefer)

FIGURE 10.1
Algorithms are like recipes in our code. They have ingredients, like variables and literals, and they have steps we need to follow in order to make something awesome for our program in the end.

Next, we need to combine and prepare our ingredients.
Steps:

- Combine all the dry ingredients in a microwave-safe mug of your choice. I recommend using a mug with a video game character or theme, but this is optional.
- Add water (or milk) to your mug of dry ingredients. Mix thoroughly.
- Microwave your mug of cake batter for 90 seconds on high.
- Remove your mug cake from the microwave – be careful, the mug might be hot.
- Let it cool a bit, then eat and enjoy.

Whether or not you're a frequent baker or meal-maker, this simple recipe is meant to illustrate a particular way of thinking or problem solving – one where we start with our basic ingredients, then we combine and prepare them in a particular order to end up with something awesome. This is the same approach that we take when writing games and other software, except we call our recipe algorithms, and instead of eating our results, we enjoy them on our computers and other digital devices. Here are a couple of examples to help make this idea clearer.

Collecting Player Name (from the Player)

Ingredients:

- empty string variable
- string literal prompt that asks the player for their name

Steps:

- Declare a string variable to store the player name.
- Display the prompt string to tell the player to enter their name.
- Collect player input and store it in the name variable.

Updating the High Score in a Video Game

Ingredients:

- the player's final score (integer variable with player's final score)
- the game's current high score (integer variable with game's high score)

Steps:

- Compare the player's final score value to the game's current high score value.
- If the player's score is greater than the game's current high score, update the game's high score to be the player's final score.
- If the player's final score is less than or equal to the game's current high score, don't do anything.

In these examples, our ingredients are variables (or literals in some cases), and the steps we follow result in something that our game needs to function properly – collect some input or update a high score value. As algorithms go, these ones aren't very complex. The input example is one we've already seen in code (Level 4), and the high score example is coming up soon (Level 7). We're going to see many more examples of algorithmic problem solving in the coming levels, and there are even more in the next book. As we proceed on our adventure together, the algorithms will become more complex with more code, but their basic properties will always be the same. Let's take a closer look at what those properties are.

The Properties of Algorithms

All computer algorithms have some common features or properties. Specifically, algorithms:

- *Have a finite number of steps or instructions*: this means they can't go on forever. An algorithm that has never-ending instructions can never finish.
- *Are unambiguous in their steps or instructions*: this means the instructions have to be clear. There can't be any room for misinterpreting what needs to be done.
- *Solve a specific task*: this means the algorithm has a purpose.
- *Have data to work on*: even though most definitions of algorithms don't specifically mention data (or ingredients), I think it's pretty safe to assume that most of them need some variables, literals, input, or data to work on, so we'll add that to our list as well.

To understand why these properties are so important for our algorithms, think about our cake recipe again for a moment. What would happen if our recipe had an infinite number of instructions? We'd never get to eat our sweet treat. What if one of the instructions was unclear and just said "bake" instead of being more specific? Some of us would be eating raw cakes, and some of us would be eating burnt ones. What if some of the steps were missing or out of order? I don't even want to imagine what would happen to our delicious desserts in this case. And, finally, what if we didn't even know what we were making? Anarchy!

Now take a moment to think about what would happen in our code if our algorithms had a never-ending number of steps, had instructions that were unclear, confusing, missing, or out of order, or – perhaps worst of all – didn't even accomplish the task that we wanted to accomplish. Just like the recipes, we'd definitely have some issues in our code if our algorithms weren't set up properly.

See if you can find all of these properties in the examples and Code Rewards that are coming up. This is good practice for algorithmic thinking and problem solving and will help you work through algorithmic solutions for your own code quests and future game projects.

Algorithmic Problem Solving

For some people, the logic of algorithms feels perfectly natural. For other people, it's a new and unusual approach to problem solving. Wherever you find yourself, here are some helpful tips:

- *Remember the properties of algorithms*: remember the task you are trying to get done in your code has to eventually come to an end (finite steps), be clear (unambiguous) in its solution, and solve the actual task that you set out to solve.

- *Break each problem down into ingredients and steps*: start by breaking down your task into the ingredients (data) or steps (instructions) that you're going to need.

- *Write the ingredients and steps down before starting to code*: pencil and paper are a programmer's most powerful tools (seriously!). If you can write down the ingredients and steps for your task's recipe using words, you'll be in better shape for translating them into code. If you can't write your algorithm down – you're unsure of what data you need, or what instructions you need to follow – then writing it in code (which you're still learning) is going to be an even tougher job. In this case, you might need to spend some more time thinking the problem through or breaking the task into a set of smaller tasks.

- *Break big tasks down into smaller tasks*: baking a cake is a big task that is actually made up of smaller tasks like measuring ingredients, using the microwave (or oven if like something fancier than a mug cake), stirring, and so on. Algorithms are similar. Big tasks like writing a guessing game, building an RPG character sheet, or having game objects interact are actually made up of a bunch of smaller coding tasks. We can get anxious and frustrated when we focus on how big the overall task is instead of focusing on the smaller tasks that we know how to do. Start with the smaller tasks, and often the overall big task will quickly start to take shape.

- *Be patient and practice*: thinking in algorithms and code can take time but is a skill that is very much worth developing. While you're learning, be patient with yourself, ask for help when you need it, and make sure you practice.

Side Quests

Want to Know More?

Algorithms are everywhere: If you want to know more about algorithms or algorithmic approaches to problem solving, try an internet search on either of those topics. You might be surprised at how many articles, blog posts, and even books are dedicated to logic recipes. In fact, many of them aren't even about coding but instead are about everyday life tasks that can be solved with a finite number of clearly defined steps or instructions.

Want to Do More?

Back to the beginning: At the start of this level, I described three game-related tasks including an enemy patrol route, destroying pots and crates to find treasure, and crafting a portal. With a pencil and paper, see if you can write down the ingredients and steps that each of these tasks would need. Don't think about C# code because we haven't covered everything we need to solve these in code yet. Instead, just use words to tease out a possible solution.

Back to the beginning (Part 2, more detail): It is really common to miss some steps (or even ingredients, variables, or data) the first time we try to write out an algorithm. This is okay for a first pass, but a final solution is usually more detailed than our first attempt. Take one or more of your word-y algorithms (enemy patrol route, treasure pots and creates, or portal crafting) and try to think of any steps that can be broken down into smaller steps. Try to be as detail-focused as possible.

Back to the beginning (Part 2 again, less detail): It is really common to add extra steps to an algorithm by mistake, trying to be too detailed, or even misunderstanding the task we're trying to complete. Review your word-y algorithms one more time, but this time look for any steps that can be removed without actually affecting how the algorithm will complete its task.

11

Level 5: Divide and Conquer

Level 4 Recap:

- User input can make our games and programs more interactive and fun.
- For console input, it's important to prompt the user so they know what kind of input we are expecting.
- All console input is collected with Console.ReadLine(), but numbers and other data types that aren't strings need to be parsed before they can be properly stored.
- "Don't know, don't care" is one way to express the power of variables to store values that we, the programmer, never see.
- Comments are an important part of programming – without them, our code is harder to read and understand.

Video Games Use Math

All the way back in Level 1, we talked about how computers are great at only one thing – math. They run billions of mathematical calculations per second. Luckily, we don't need to worry about the details of those calculations, but as programmers, we do need to tell the computer what math to compute from time to time. We describe how fast our character runs or how high they jump. We say whether the next wave of enemies will go up by one or will be doubled in size. How many health points does the hero lose when they run into a wall of spikes? Want to add some more gold to the inventory? Interested in exchanging some of that gold for health potions? All of these design decisions need math and our games are made of variables that are being updated by math operators and math functions. Math brings our games to life, and Level 5 is here to help us understand how.

When it comes to programming, math is a lot like comments – it's usually no one's favorite topic. I know many people who have avoided game design and programming because they're worried about having to learn a lot of math. The good news is this is not a math book. Modern programming languages (and game design engines) do a lot of heavy lifting for us – we

DOI: 10.1201/9781003348481-11

don't need to worry about the calculus of collisions, the trigonometry of 3D space, or the algebra of movement. We'll introduce some of the simpler built-in math operators and functions here, and for those who continue their journey in the next book, we'll look at some more game-specific math operations when we work with MonoGame.

Common Built-in Math Operators

Working with the four main built-in math operators, the ones you're most familiar with from grade school, is mostly intuitive. These operators are:

- + addition
- − subtraction (and negation, see below)
- * multiplication (this is an asterisk, not an x)
- / division

There are some other important ones like ++ and −− (increment and decrement), % (modulus), and the compound assignment operators, but they need a bit more explanation and will be covered later (or in Bonus Level 2 for modulus). For now, let's focus on the familiar operators and keep things simple by working with number literals.

Each of the first four built-in math operators works roughly the same way. They are known as binary operators because they each take two values (or operands) to do their work. Take a look at these example statements:

```
Console.WriteLine(6.0f + 4.0f);
Console.WriteLine(6.0f - 4.0f);
Console.WriteLine(6.0f * 4.0f);
Console.WriteLine(6.0f / 4.0f);
```

If you code these for yourself, you should get output that looks like this:

```
10
2
24
1.5
```

There probably aren't any surprises with that output – addition, subtraction, multiplication, and division all happened as expected. However, I used floats in that example for a specific reason – so everything would work as planned. If we change all the literals to integers:

```
Console.WriteLine(6 + 4);
Console.WriteLine(6 - 4);
Console.WriteLine(6 * 4);
Console.WriteLine(6 / 4);
```

The output is this now:

```
10
2
24
1
```

Mostly, this is fine, but the last line of output is 1. If you take a second to divide 6 by 4 on a calculator (or in your head if you prefer), you'll see that the answer is actually 1.5, like the float example shows. Why can't C# divide 6 by 4 properly? There is a reason for this – it's called integer division and you can read more about it and the other unusual math things C# does in Bonus Level 2. Aside from the one small hiccup when we divide two integers, everything else in this level should work as we expect, mathematically speaking.

When we did math with float literals everything worked great. When we used integers everything worked out except for division. But, what happens when we mix types like this?

```
Console.WriteLine(6.0f + 4);
Console.WriteLine(6 - 4.0f);
Console.WriteLine(6.0f * 4);
Console.WriteLine(6 / 4.0f);
```

We get output like this.

```
10
2
24
1.5
```

Even though it's hard to tell from the output, two things are happening – first, we have proof that we can do math operations with different, or mixed, value-types, and second, when we do mix types, the result is automatically converted to the "bigger", or most appropriate, of the two types. In this example, when you calculate something using both an int and a float, the result is of type float – behold the decimal in the last line of output. This automatic conversion is important to keep in mind.

Before we start working with math and variables, I encourage you to write some more simple expressions of your own to make sure you have a good idea of how they work. Try some expressions with:

- really big values and really small values
- positive and negative numbers
- floats, ints, and a mixture of both

If anything unexpected happens, make a note of it – we'll probably cover it in this level or the next.

Doing math with literals shows us how the basic operations work, but we quickly run out of fun things to do with them and need to turn to the power of variables. Let's think game-y and pretend we are calculating some scores that have score modifiers – addition for bonus, subtraction for penalty, multiplication for a positive score multiplier, and division as a penalty multiplier (it's a stretch, but try to go with it). With that in mind, consider these four statements:

```
float score1 = 100.0f + 25.0f;
float score2 = 100.0f - 25.0f;
float score3 = 100.0f * 25.0f;
float score4 = 100.0f / 25.0f;
```

If you code these, you should find that there are no issues getting them to compile. If you write output statements to show what is stored in the result variables (go ahead, I'll wait here for you), you'll see output like this:

```
125
75
2500
4
```

But if we're going to use variables, let's do it properly:

```
float baseScore = 100.0f;

float modifier = 25.0f;

float finalScore1 = baseScore + modifier;
float finalScore2 = baseScore - modifier;
float finalScore3 = baseScore * modifier;
float finalScore4 = baseScore / modifier;
```

Remember, any time C# sees a variable name in a statement, if the variable has been properly declared and assigned, C# will access the variable and substitute the value in place of the name. In other words, in the statements above, C# substitutes 100.0 for baseScore and 25.0 for modifier. Just like the previous literal example, if you write the output statements to display the value of the finalScore variables, you should see that everything works, and the output is the same:

```
125
75
2500
4
```

We do need to be a bit careful when we mix variable types in assignment statements. The following statements won't compile – can you guess why (hint: instead of guessing, code this example and read the error that Visual Studio shows you)?

```
int baseScore = 100;

float modifier = 25.0f;

int finalScore1 = baseScore + modifier;
int finalScore2 = baseScore - modifier;
int finalScore3 = baseScore * modifier;
int finalScore4 = baseScore / modifier;
```

There isn't a really good reason for us to mix our baseScore and modifier variable types, but it does help to make a point. Remember from our literal example, if we write math expressions that have different types, the result is automatically converted to the bigger or more appropriate type. This means that for each of our four math statements, the right-hand side is converted to type float. That's cool, but we can't store a float result in an integer variable – integer variables can't store decimals. So, we have to change our code to this:

```
int baseScore = 100;

float modifier = 25.0f;

float finalScore1 = baseScore + modifier;
float finalScore2 = baseScore - modifier;
float finalScore3 = baseScore * modifier;
float finalScore4 = baseScore / modifier;
```

This change works because the resulting type from the math operation on the right of the equal sign (float) now matches the variable type (also float) on the left of the equal sign. This is around the time when people usually ask me – "why don't we work just with floats to make things easier"? It's a fair question, and many people, especially beginners, do exactly that – work only with floats to avoid frustrating math and variable issues.

But, this isn't always the best plan. Int variables and literals exist for a reason, and we use them (and other whole-number data types) to represent things that can't (or shouldn't) be broken down into parts or decimals. Think about this in a video game context – our game has a party, or group, of playable characters. It makes sense to have 4 characters in our party, but a group of 4.1 or 4.8 characters is a problem. We could represent the number of characters as 4.0 in a float, but this opens the door to accidentally changing it to 4.4 characters. So, the best way to represent certain variables – like the number of characters in a party – is with a whole number variable like int. It makes things a bit more complicated, but it's also the right thing to do.

You might have noticed that all of the statements in the variable examples are initializations (combined declaration and assignment). There's no reason for this other than the fact that initializations are both very common and more compact than separate declarations and assignments. Let's finish off this section with an expanded version that shows that math operations can just as easily be done using separate declaration and assignment statements:

```
int baseScore;
float modifier, finalScore1, finalScore2, finalScore3, finalScore4;

baseScore = 100;

modifier = 25.0f;

finalScore1 = baseScore + modifier;
finalScore2 = baseScore - modifier;
finalScore3 = baseScore * modifier;
finalScore4 = baseScore / modifier;

Console.WriteLine("Player 1 score: " + finalScore1);
Console.WriteLine("Player 2 score: " + finalScore2);
Console.WriteLine("Player 3 score: " + finalScore3);
Console.WriteLine("Player 4 score: " + finalScore4);
```

Order of Operations and ()

So far, we've looked at how +, –, *, and / work, we've looked at simple math expressions with both literals and variables, and we've seen what happens when we mix our data types. But all of our examples have had only one math operator and two values (or operands) on the right-hand side. There's nothing stopping us from stringing a few operations together into longer expressions, like this:

```
int result1 = 6 + 4 + 9;
int result2 = 6 + 4 - 9;
```

If you were to output the values stored in result1 and result2, you would see:

```
19
1
```

When you combine multiple math operations in a single statement, C# follows standard order of operation rules. If you've learned about order of operations before, you might have called it BEDMAS or PEDMAS (depending on whether you say brackets or parentheses). As an ultra-quick review, complex expressions are solved in this order:

1. brackets (or parentheses)
2. exponents
3. division and multiplication (left to right)
4. addition and subtraction (left to right)

In the examples above, since there is only addition and subtraction, C# computes them in order from left to right. If we make it a bit more complex by adding a multiplication:

```
int result3 = 1 + 2 * 3 + 4;
```

This will store 11 in result3 (multiplication first, then the addition operations). If we want to force the addition to be done first, we can use round brackets or parentheses () like this:

```
int result4 = (1 + 2) * (3 + 4);
```

This will store 21 in result4. Why? Because now the operations in the ()'s happen first. As long as you make sure that every open bracket (has a corresponding closing bracket), you can build your expression however it makes sense to do so:

```
int result5 = ((10 + 5) / (1 + 2)) * ((2+2) / 4);
```

Try coding and compiling that last statement (and the previous ones) and work through why the answer is the way it is (make sure to output the value in result5). Hint: it's BEDMAS – or order of operations.

A full review of BEDMAS (or PEDMAS) is outside of the scope of this level. If you're feeling rusty (or haven't seen it before), I recommend a quick internet search. Also, the examples in this section use ints for simplicity, but the ideas here would apply to floats and other number data types. Order of operations depends on the math we want to accomplish, not the data types of the literals or variables we use.

Unary Negation

The last of our "simple" operators is one that works a bit differently. We can use − (dash, or minus) as a binary subtraction operator (two values or operands), like this:

```
int subtractionResult = 6 - 4;
```

We can also use it for unary negation – turning a positive number negative and turning a negative number positive. The simplest example is to do something like this:

```
int negativeValue = -5;
```

It doesn't look like much, but this statement stores a negated 5 (or −5) in negativeValue. It works for floats too:

```
float negativePi = -3.14f;
```

We can also use it in expressions that are more complex:

```
int result = 10 + -5;
```

Again, this might look weird, but this says add negative five (−5) to 10 and store the result. As always, try coding it and outputting the result for yourself.

Unary negation can even be used with variables – in fact, this is where it becomes quite powerful. Consider the following commented example:

```
//store 25 in score
int score = 25;
//store the number of hits taken by the player
int hitsTaken = 5;
//negate the number of hits and store in penalty
int penalty = -hitsTaken;
//add the score and the penalty
int finalScore= score + penalty;
//finalScore is displayed to the console
Console.WriteLine(finalScore);
```

You could solve the problem of subtracting a penalty from a score differently, but this example shows how you can negate the value in a variable. Outside of this example, you might think this operator doesn't get used much, but in games, we often use negative and positive values to tell the direction something is traveling. This means that negating a movement variable can reverse the direction. Cool, right?

Updating Variables

Does that title make sense for this section – didn't we learn how to change or reassign variables in Level 3? Indeed, we did, and it looked something like this:

```
int numberOfPlayers;

//set the variable's initial value
numberOfPlayers = 1;

Console.WriteLine("There is " + numberOfPlayers + " player in the match!!");

//change or reassign the variable's value
numberOfPlayers = 2;
Console.WriteLine("There is now " + numberOfPlayers +
" players in the match!!");
```

Now we're going to learn how to update variables, and that's a subtle but important difference. When we update a variable, we usually make a change that depends on the value that the variable had beforehand. For example, let's assume that our hero had 55 health points, and we wanted to add 10. We could do it like this (I'll do separate declarations and assignments for practice):

```
int heroHealth, bonusHealth, heroUpdatedHealth;
heroHealth = 55;
bonusHealth = 10;
heroUpdatedHealth = heroHealth + bonusHealth;
```

In the first statement, we declare three variables – heroHealth, heroBonusHealth, and heroUpdatedHealth. In the second and third statements, we assign 55 to heroHealth and 10 to bonusHealth. In the fourth statement, we assign the sum (addition) of our hero's original health plus the bonus health to our updated health variable. This is a very common approach that new programmers take – it's very normal to create a variable for every piece of data or information that we want to account for. But now we have three variables that we have to track through the rest our game. Or, even worse, we have variables that we are using then abandoning. Let's take a look at another way we could do this:

```
int heroHealth, bonusHealth;
heroHealth = 55;
bonusHealth = 10;
heroHealth = heroHealth + bonusHealth;
```

This example, like the previous one, has four statements but only two variables – heroHealth and bonusHealth. How does this work? All of the magic is in this statement:

```
heroHealth = heroHealth + bonusHealth;
```

If I was to write out what is happening in words, it would be something like this: add the "current" value of heroHealth to the value in bonusHealth and store the result back into heroHealth. It often confuses people when they first see the same variable on both the left- and right-hand sides of an assignment (=). The trick to this is timing – the right-hand side operations happen before the assignment. When this statement executes, heroHealth is 55 – that's what we set it to originally. We add the 10 that was stored in bonusHealth to the original heroHealth value giving us a right-hand side of 65. We store the computed 65 back into heroHealth so that when the statement has fully executed, the variable has been *updated* to a new value.

Try coding these statements as an illustration of this idea:

```
int heroHealth, bonusHealth;
heroHealth = 55;
bonusHealth = 10;

Console.WriteLine("The original value of hero health: " + heroHealth);
heroHealth = heroHealth + bonusHealth;
Console.WriteLine("The updated value of hero health: " + heroHealth);
```

Try to think of it this way – you are a collector of antique game cartridges. You keep your prized cartridges in a special display container, which you then keep inside a box to keep the dust away. One of your Internet friends sends you a new cartridge for your birthday. You take the display container out of the box (access the variable), put the wonderful new cartridge inside the display container (update the value), and put the display case full of cartridges back into the box (update the variable).

Video games are full of variables that are updating constantly – it's a very important part of what makes them so dynamic. Here is an example of our hero healing more than once. Take a look at these statements and see if you can figure out the value stored in heroHealth in the end (also, I'm simplifying things a bit and using some literals here):

```
int heroHealth = 55;

Console.WriteLine("The original value of hero health: " + heroHealth);
heroHealth = heroHealth + 10;
Console.WriteLine("Your hero feels better: " + heroHealth);
heroHealth = heroHealth + 5;
Console.WriteLine("Your hero feels even better: " + heroHealth);
heroHealth = heroHealth + 12;
Console.WriteLine("Your hero feels better still: " + heroHealth);
heroHealth = heroHealth + 3;
Console.WriteLine("Your hero feels so much better: " + heroHealth);
```

We do this kind of update so often in games (and other programs) that there are special operators designed to make your code more compact and your programming life easier. Let's take a look at some of them.

Compound Assignment Operators

There is a set of operators that are designed for no other reason than to make updating variables easier. These operators, called compound operators, are +=, −=, *=, and /=. Remember the score-modifier example? Let's take another look at it, but with some small changes. We're going to have four different score variables, and they are each going to be updated according to a score-modifier value. I'll set all four scores to the same value so that it's easier to see what's happening:

```
int player1Score, player2Score, player3Score, player4Score;
int modifier = 5;

player1Score = 100;
player2Score = 100;
player3Score = 100;
player4Score = 100;

player1Score = player1Score + modifier;
player2Score = player2Score - modifier;
player3Score = player3Score * modifier;
player4Score = player4Score / modifier;
```

Before moving on, code this example for yourself and be sure to output the values of the four final player scores. Even though it's not likely something we'd do in a real game, does the output make sense given the code?

```
105
95
500
20
```

Here's what's happening to our player scores:

- Player 1 receives a bonus of 5.
- Player 2 receives a penalty of 5.
- Player 3 receives a 5x multiplier.
- Player 4 receives a 5x multiplier penalty.

Essentially, we're doing what we did before – updating the score variables using our built-in math operators. But, I promised you an "easier" way to do these operations, and it looks like this:

```
player1Score += modifier;
player2Score -= modifier;
player3Score *= modifier;
player4Score /= modifier;
```

As I mentioned at the start of this section, the compound operators are specifically used to update variables:

- += add to the variable
- -= subtract from the variable
- *= multiply the variable by
- /= divide the variable by

This compact syntax doesn't save us a lot of space or code, but it does (in my humble opinion) make it even more clear that we are updating a variable instead of carrying out some sort of other operation. Each of these statement pairs is equivalent:

```
//add 10 to hero health
heroHealth = heroHealth + 10;
heroHealth += 10;

//subtract a score penalty
finalScore = finalScore - penaltyValue;
finalScore -= penaltyValue;

//enemy strength increases 50 percent
enemyStrength = enemyStrength * 1.5f;
enemyStrength *= 1.5f;

//speed is reduced to half
mySpeed = mySpeed / 2.0f;
mySpeed /= 2.0f;
```

You can use either the long form or the more compact compound operators for updating your variables – they work the same way. I suggest using whichever format makes the operation clear to you.

Increment and Decrement (++ and --)

Learning to program is a pretty even mix of finding the language syntax very confusing and finding it really charming. The operators in this section should fall nicely into that second category, and they serve a very specific programming need – the need to add or subtract one from a variable. It feels silly to write that, but we really do add and subtract one quite often, especially when we learn to control our games with loops (Level 9).

Let's say we wanted to keep track of the enemies that appear in our game, and they are likely to appear one at a time. We could certainly do it like this:

```
//there are no enemies on the screen
int numberOfEnemies = 0;
//an enemy appears!
numberOfEnemies = numberOfEnemies + 1;
```

But, we could also use our awesome new compound operators like this:

```
//there are no enemies on the screen
int numberOfEnemies = 0;
//an enemy appears!
numberOfEnemies = += 1; //add one to our enemy counting variable
```

If you're an experienced programmer, you might be shouting at this page – "but there's an even easier way to do this", and you'd be right. I give you, the increment operator:

```
//there are no enemies on the screen
int numberOfEnemies = 0;
//an enemy appears!
numberOfEnemies++;
```

This is the shortest of shorthands that says – "add one to numberOfEnemies". So, we now have three ways of adding one enemy to our counter variable:

```
int numEnemies = 0; //there are no enemies on the screen
//an enemy appears!
numberOfEnemies = numberOfEnemies + 1;
//an enemy appears!
numberOfEnemies += 1;
//an enemy appears!
numberOfEnemies++;
Console.WriteLine("There are " + numberOfEnemies + " enemies.");
```

Each one of the bold statements above adds one to our numberOfEnemies variable – they are equivalent and perform exactly the same task. Which one you use is up to you, but you should at least be aware of ++, or the increment operator. We can do the same thing in reverse – decrementing by one like this:

```
int numEnemies = 3; //there are some enemies on the screen
//an enemy is vanquished!
numEnemies = numEnemies - 1;
//an enemy is vanquished!
numEnemies -= 1;
//an enemy is vanquished!
numEnemies--;
Console.WriteLine("There are " + numberOfEnemies + " enemies.");
```

This code works the same way as the previous example, except that each bolded statement subtracts one from our numberOfEnemies variable (we also cheated by starting with 3 enemies this time, so that we didn't have −3 enemies when we were done). The first decrement uses the long-hand version of having the variable on either side of the assignment. The second version uses the compound assignment operator (this time with subtraction instead of addition), and the final version uses the − decrement operator to remove one from the value of the variable.

Both ++ and −− are very important operators, and (as always) it's worth practicing with them so that you know what they are doing – adding or subtracting one from the value of a variable!!

Revisiting Concatenation, Addition, and Automatic Conversion

Maybe you're wondering how we can have two uses for the + operator. In this level, it means to add (mathematically) numbers, like:

```
Console.WriteLine(10 + 4);
float result = 10.1f + 22.9f;
```

But, in Level 2, we used the + operator to concatenate strings like this:

```
string name = "Aaron";
Console.WriteLine("My name is " + name);
```

How is it possible to use the same operator, +, to do two different jobs? Well, it's all in the type of operands. When the operands are numbers, we add them. When the operands are strings, we concatenate them – which, if you think of it, is like string addition, in a way. We also know, from earlier in this section, that when we mix operands the result becomes the most appropriate type.

Consider these simple literal examples (though this logic would hold if it were variables, or a mix of literals and variables):

- 1 + 2: both operands are integers, so the result (3) is an integer
- 1.0f − 2.0f: both operands are floats, so the result (−1.0) is a float
- 2 * 2.0f: one operand is an integer (2), and one is a float (2.0f) so the result is a float (4.0f)
- 2.0f * 2: same idea but we've switched the operand order
- 1 + 1 + 1 + 1: all the operands are integers so the result is an integer
- 1 + 1.0f + 1 + 1: at least one operand is a float so the result will be a float

Now, what happens when we combine strings and number data types? We've done a few examples like this:

```
Console.WriteLine("A number: " + 6);
```

This is an example of string concatenation and results in a new string that looks like this – "A number: 6". In fact, we could even do the concatenation outside of the output statement:

```
string output = "A number: " + 6;
Console.WriteLine(output);
```

Just like the mixed float and int example, if one of the operands is a string, they all get converted to strings. Here's another example:

```
Console.WriteLine("Sum: " + 10 + 1.5f);
```

The output from this example is:

```
Sum: 101.5
```

Since this expression starts with the string "Sum: ", the 10 and 1.5 are also treated like strings and are concatenated to the "Sum: ". If we wanted the numbers to be summed, we'd need to use our round brackets to force the order of operations like this:

```
Console.WriteLine("Sum: " + (10 + 1.5f));
```

Try it out! In the end, + can be used to add numbers and concatenate strings. The best way to get a feel for the difference is to try some assignment and output statements – have some strings, have some numbers, and have some fun! The more you practice, the more it will all make sense.

Math Functions

Sometimes, we want to do math that is more complex than we can easily manage with the built-in operators. This is especially true in games when we need to calculate collisions between objects, physics like gravity, and movement in 2D and 3D space. Luckily, C# (and, by extension, MonoGame and engines like Unity) have some terrific built-in functions that allow us to easily call up some cool, useful, and complex math operations. In this section, we'll very briefly look at some of the simpler (but still cool and useful) math functions that are available.

Before we dig in, we should discuss what a function is – a function is one or more statements that perform a task and (typically) return a value to us. We don't usually see the specific statements, they operate in the background, but we can "call" the function to do some work for us. Sometimes we pass data (or arguments) to the function so that it can do its job properly. That might all seem a bit confusing, but some examples are coming up.

As a quick analogy – a function is a bit like a bank machine (or ATM). We walk up to the bank machine, we press a few buttons, and we receive some cash (and maybe a receipt). We don't really see how the internal parts of the bank machine work, but we know what buttons to press, and we can collect what it gives us in return. We're going to write our own custom functions (also called methods) in Level 10, but let's look at some functions that we're actually familiar with already:

- Console.**WriteLine("some text")**; – WriteLine() is a function that is part of the Console class (we'll cover classes in Levels 10 and 11, but for now, you can think of it as a collection of functions). When we pass "some text" to it, it outputs "some text" to the console screen.

- string input = Console.**ReadLine()**; – ReadLine() is also a function that is part of the Console class, but this one takes no arguments (it doesn't need any data to work) and collects a string from the command line. Since it generates something – input from the command line – we usually put this in an assignment statement so that we can store the result.

- int convertedNumber = int.**Parse("123")**; – Parse() is a function that converts text to some other type, whether it's an int, float, char, boolean, or whatever we are looking for.

These familiar examples are here as an anchor point so that what we do next won't seem totally new – you've used functions before, we're simply going to introduce a few more. What follows are examples of math functions and their syntax. There are many math functions available in C#, but a lot of them won't apply to our examples (console or future MonoGame programming). Still, I encourage you to look up the C# Math class functions to see what is available.

Most of the examples below work with ints, floats, doubles, and decimals, as well as both literals and variables. Try them out for yourself to find out what they can – and can't – do.

```
//Max takes two number arguments and returns
//the bigger one of the two.
float maximum = Math.Max(value1, value2);

//Min takes two number arguments and returns
//the smaller one of the two.
float minimum = Math.Min(value1, value2);

//Abs takes one number argument and returns
//the absolute value (or positive version)
int absoluteValue = Math.Abs(value);

//Sqrt takes one number argument and returns
//the square root of that number.
float squareRoot = (float) Math.Sqrt(value);

//Pow takes two arguments and returns the
//result of value1 to the power value2. For
//example, if the first argument is 2 and
//the second argument is 4, the result returned
//would be 16.
float power = (float) Math.Pow(value1, value2);

//Round takes two arguments, a number to round,
//and a second argument that is the number of
//digits of precision to round to.
float round = Math.Round(value, precision);
```

If you look closely, you'll see that some of the results need to be converted with a special bit of code called a type cast – like (float) in some cases. We'll see this again in the next level, and you can read even more about it in Bonus Level 2.

As with everything else we've covered (and will cover), the more you practice with these functions, the more they will make sense when it is time for you to use them in your games and programs!

Side Quests

Want to Know More?

I've got 99 problems, but a lack of math functions isn't one of them: C# has a lot of math functions similar to the ones we looked at in the last section of this level.

Many of them have to do with trigonometry (sine, cosine, tangent, etc.), and others are used in pretty specific cases. It's good to know what's available, so search for a list of C# math functions and give it a quick look-over.

But I want to store a fridge in a shoe box (revisited): This side quest appeared in Level 3, but the idea of casting and type conversions has reappeared at the end of this level. We'll talk about this a bit more in Level 6 and again in Bonus Level 2, but you can find more examples – online or in other books – of casting and type conversions in C#.

Want to Do More?

Let the computer do the math: I wasn't a very good math student in school. I always found it to be my most challenging subject. When I learned to program, I discovered that the computer could do the math for me – not in a cheating sort of way, but in a way that helped me to better understand many math concepts by coding them. Find some math problems of medium complexity online, or better yet, in some books or notes from your math classes. See if you can get C# to solve the problems and give you accurate answers.

Functional practice: Try some more of the C# math functions, even the ones you think you won't use often. It's really good practice to see what these functions can do, what kinds of arguments they need to do their job, and what types of results they give you in return. Keep the math library documentation handy in case you get stuck.

Code Reward – The Amazingly Silly Score Calculator

Let's take stock of what we've learned so far. We know about data types, literals and variables, user input, and now some of the basic math operations and functions. We're still missing a few key pieces before we can make simple console games, so in this program, we're going to practice what we know by writing a working, but somewhat silly, score calculator. The program will have a single input for the user to enter the player's base score, but then we're going to update that score through a series of hard-coded math operations. The score will change depending on the value input by the user, but the operations will always be the same. My solution uses integers (as scores are often whole numbers), but you can change it to work with floats. Feel free to modify or extend this program into something that is more interesting to you!

Here are the steps to create this program:

- Write a quick introductory output statement letting the player or user know what the program is about (this is always a fun, and helpful thing to do).
- Prompt the player to input their base score. My version is expecting an integer. Assume the player/user will enter a good value – something that can be properly parsed as an integer (or other number type if you decide not to use integers).
- Collect and store the player's base score. This is one of only two variables in my solution – I update this variable after each math operation (below). All the other values are literals.
- Here are the math operations to apply to the base score. After each operation, show the updated score:
  - Increment the score by 1.
  - Multiply the score by 3.
  - Add 5 to the score.
  - Divide the score by 2 (let integer division remove any decimals here, but make a note of it).
  - Decrement the score by 1.
- Challenge: Compute and display the smaller number between the player's score and 100 (hint: use a Math function for this). For example, if the player's final score is 53, the program should display 53. If the player's final score is 110, the program should display 100. This is where I use my only other variable in this program – a variable that stores the smaller of the score or 100.
- End the program.

Try this Code Reward for yourself. If you get stuck, peek at my solution for a hint.

```
/*
This is a simple math example. The player enters a base score, and this
program runs through some math operations to print an updated score.

This program is the Code Reward for Level 5.
Author: Aaron Langille
*/


//Welcome message followed by a blank line.
Console.WriteLine("Welcome to the (Silly) Score Calculator.");
Console.WriteLine();


/*
When we collect input, particularly numbers, the program can crash if the
user enters input that can't be properly parsed.
Assume the user enters meaningful and parse-able input. Bonus Level 3 has
more information.
*/


//Prompt the user to enter their score.
Console.Write("Enter your base score: ");

//Store the player score in a new variable called baseScore.
int baseScore = int.Parse(Console.ReadLine());

//Spacing and helpful output.
Console.WriteLine();
Console.WriteLine("Here we go … ");

baseScore++;               //increment the score and display
Console.WriteLine("Incrementing the score by 1: " + baseScore);

baseScore = baseScore * 3;     //multiply the score and display
Console.WriteLine("Multiplying the score by 3: " + baseScore);

baseScore += 5;               //add to the score and display
Console.WriteLine("Adding 5 to the score: " + baseScore);

baseScore /= 2;               //divide the score and display
Console.WriteLine("Dividing the score by 2: " + baseScore);

baseScore--;               //decrement the score and display
Console.WriteLine("Decrementing the score by 1: " + baseScore);

//Use Math.Min() to determine which value is smaller – baseScore or 100

int smallestValue = Math.Min(baseScore, 100);

Console.WriteLine("Which value is smaller – 100 or " + baseScore + ": " +
smallestValue);
```

12

Code Quest 5: Tiny Tournament Stats

Before proceeding with this quest:

- review Level 5
- complete Code Quest 4 (optional)
- create a new Visual Studio Console project. If you need a refresher, detailed instructions can be found at the beginning of Code Quest 1.

In this Code Quest, we're going to practice some of the built-in math operations and call some of the C# math functions. To give our practice some context – imagine we have been asked to write a program that computes some stats from a player's scores in a tournament. We're a bit limited in how complicated we can make this program, so the player will only play two matches! Don't worry, most of what we're doing here would apply to more than two matches, but without if-statements (Levels 7 and 8) and loops (Level 9), we'll have to limit our tournament to a pair of scores for now.

Main Quest – Tiny Tournament Stats

The code in this quest should accomplish the following tasks:

1. Prompt and collect an integer from the player – this is their first game's base score.
2. Prompt and collect any penalties earned by the player in their first game. A penalty is an integer amount that is subtracted from the player's base score.
3. Repeat Steps 1 and 2 for the player's second game score. Remember, we are trusting the user to enter positive integer values that can be properly parsed. If they enter something unexpected, the program may crash, and that's ok.
4. Using built-in math operators and/or C# Math functions, compute and display the following:

DOI: 10.1201/9781003348481-12

    a. The player's adjusted first and second scores (any penalties are subtracted from each of the base scores).

    b. The total points earned by the player (both adjusted scores added together).

    c. The average points earned by the player (total points divided by number of games played – 2 in this case. Be careful, a proper average can be a decimal number.)

    d. The maximum score earned by the player. Use the appropriate built-in math library function here.

    e. The minimum score earned by the player. Use the built-in Math library function here.

    f. Hint: For Steps 4a through 4e, you'll need to decide when to create a new variable and when to update existing variables. Try a few different approaches.

Here is the output from my version of this quest (Figure 12.1).

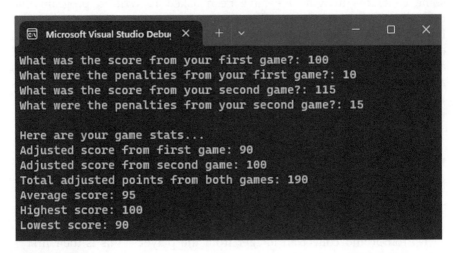

FIGURE 12.1
Try duplicating the tiny tournament stats program and using the numbers shown here as input. This will help you to see if your math operations and functions are working properly.

Remember, when we collect user input, our programs become more dynamic and the output changes when the input changes (Figure 12.2).

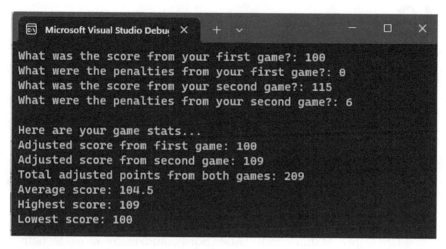

FIGURE 12.2
Here is another run with different input. Check the output very carefully and if yours doesn't match, check for some of the common math issues like integer division.

Side Quests

Less code, same output: Can you eliminate two variables by updating the base score to include the penalty values instead of storing them separately? For an extra challenge, use the compound operator -= in your solution.

Bonus points: Add a prompt and the necessary statements so that the player can enter any bonus points they've earned as well as any penalties. Bonus points work like penalties except they are added instead of subtracted.

Mega-multiplier: Similar to the "Bonus points" Side Quest – but add a score multiplier!! If the player enters 2.0 for the multiplier, the base score is doubled. If they enter 0.5, the base score is cut in half. It should work for any positive decimal value (but don't be surprised if the output gets a bit messy. Remember, if the value is going to be decimal, you'll have to store this result in an appropriately typed variable).

13

Level 6: A Random Opportunity

Level 5 Recap:

- Built-in math operators like +, −, *, /, ++, and −−, allow us to calculate most of the awesome mathematics that make our games and programs exciting.
- C# also provides a library of math functions like Math.Max(), Math.Min(), Math.Round(), Math.Sqrt(), and many more to help us with some of the more complex calculations.
- Compound assignment operators including +=, −=, *=, and /= make it easy to update variables.

Video Games Use Random Numbers

In video games, randomness is that glimmer of hope that we can win the race, even when we're far behind our friends. It powers the anticipation behind our loot drops. It gives our non-player characters (NPCs) variety in their dialog when we pester them repeatedly. It energizes our coin flips, our dice rolls, and our card shuffling. Randomness sprinkles unpredictable excitement into situations that would be predictable without it.

Randomness is also that last-second realization that something could still stop us from making it to the flag. It makes clay pots, question mark boxes, and treasure chests spit out things we don't really want or need. It makes our NPCs seem a bit scattered and unorganized when we pester them repeatedly. It sinks our hopes with tails when we need heads, a one when three or more would defeat the boss, and base cards when we need power ups. Randomness is the dasher-of-hopes when everything is on the line.

If variables and input give our games interactivity, and if math brings our games to life, it's random number generators – or RNG – that bring the fun and frustration! There is so much hope and heartbreak in random numbers, and they are easily misunderstood and poorly applied. How many times have you thanked your "lucky stars" for the last-minute power-up that pushed you across the finish line first? Or, how many times have you cursed the "blasted RNG" for spoiling your speed run?

DOI: 10.1201/9781003348481-13

In game design, randomness is the opposite of skill – with skill, we are in control of the situation, and our expertise determines our success. With complete randomness, our fate is out of our hands. This is why so many great games strike an important balance between player skill elements (knowledge of the game, quick reflexes, executing combos) and random elements (loot drops, spawn locations, hero and enemy stat modifiers). Skill elements make us feel like we're good at the game, but randomness keeps it fun and interesting.

In this level, we're going to look at how to create random numbers in C#. We won't do many of the things described in this intro – yet. But as we make our way through the coming levels, we'll keep working randomness into our examples and exploring fun ways to surprise our players and keep them on their toes. Also, watch for some examples of casting (manually changing from one data type to another) toward the end of this level.

Now, without further delay, let's get a bit random!!

Setting Up a Random Number Generator

So far, all of our declarations have looked something like this:

```
int playerScore;
float playerStrength;
string playerName;
```

... and so on. Declaring a random object is similar:

```
Random rng;
```

But it's also different. For one thing, we are introducing a new type. It's not one of our built-in types – it's called an object type. We're going to write our own custom objects starting in Level 10, but Random is a great introduction to the idea of C# object types. Even though the declaration of a Random object seems similar to our built-in type declarations, things look a bit different when it comes to assignment:

```
playerScore = 125;
playerStrength = 10.9f;
playerName = "Chell";
rng = new Random();
```

Hm – that's definitely something new (pun intended, because it says new). The syntax of our built-in type assignments should be familiar to you, but our random object might need a bit of explanation. Let's put our Random object declaration and assignment together like this:

```
Random rng;
rng = new Random();
```

In the declaration we are saying – "create a variable of type Random named rng". This part is the same as our built-in type declarations, except now we're using type Random. In the assignment, we are saying "associate a new Random object with our variable". This part is different for two reasons. First, we use the keyword new and add round brackets at the end because Random is an object type, not a built-in data type. We'll learn more about this in Levels 10 and 11. Second, a Random object is a bit more complex than our built-in types. Remember in Level 1 when we talked about the built-in types being like the individual building blocks for a model? Well, a Random object is more like a small model itself – it is made up of smaller pieces, but we get to use the completed object to do cool things in our games and programs. Before we move on to some of those cool things Random can do, it's worth pointing out that we can initialize (declare + assign) a Random number object like this:

```
Random rng = new Random();
```

Once we have a properly declared and assigned (or initialized) Random object, we can get to work creating random numbers! Read on to learn how.

Generating Random Integers

As we saw in the last section, before we can generate any random numbers, we need to create a Random number object, like this:

```
Random rng = new Random();
```

When that's done, we can ask our Random number object to create a random integer for us like this:

```
int myRandomInt = rng.Next();
```

In this case, .Next() is a special method (or function) that asks our Random object – named rng – to give us the next Next() random integer. Think of our Random object like a candy dispenser that hands out randomly-flavored candies (or in our case numbers with values that we can't predict) one at a time. A simple program to illustrate how this works might look like this:

```
Random rng = new Random();
int myRandomInt = rng.Next();
Console.WriteLine("This is random: " + myRandomInt);
```

If I were to run this program three separate times I *might get* the following output:

```
This is random: 1472214941
This is random: 200712395
This is random: 1661321354
```

There we have it, three really big random numbers. I said "might get" above, because if I were to run this program three more times, the numbers would be different. If you code and run these statements for yourself (and you should absolutely do that), you're very likely going to get three numbers that are completely different from mine.

According to the official C# documentation, calling.Next() like this produces "an integer from 0 to a maximum value (Int32.MaxValue – 1)". Cool. Do you remember from Level 1 what the maximum integer value is? Hint: it's a little over two billion. This is why our example random numbers are so big – they are between 0 and (roughly) two billion. Before we look at other ways of generating (less gigantic) random numbers, we should make it clear that once you've created a Random object, you can reuse it many times – like a hammer that can hit more than one nail or a wand that can cast more than one magic spell. We can absolutely do this:

```
Random rng = new Random();
int myRandomInt1 = rng.Next();
Console.WriteLine("This is random: " + myRandomInt1);
int myRandomInt2 = rng.Next();
Console.WriteLine("This too is random: " + myRandomInt2);
int myRandomInt3 = rng.Next();
Console.WriteLine("This is also random: " + myRandomInt3);
```

Notice how there is only one initialization of our Random object (the first statement), but we used it to create three different random numbers. Code this example, run it a few times, and then adventure onward.

What can we do if we don't want giant random integers? We control how.Next() "behaves" by putting some values – called arguments – inside the round brackets (). For example, let's modify our code like this:

```
Random rng = new Random();
int myRandomInt1 = rng.Next(1);
Console.WriteLine("This is random: " + myRandomInt1);
int myRandomInt2 = rng.Next(10);
Console.WriteLine("This too is random: " + myRandomInt2);
int myRandomInt3 = rng.Next(100);
Console.WriteLine("This is also random: " + myRandomInt3);
```

See the bold numbers inside the round brackets? Here is the output from running the program twice:

```
This is random: 0
This too is random: 6
This is also random: 92

This is random: 0
This too is random: 8
This is also random: 51
```

Can you tell what has changed in our output? The argument we gave to.Next() caused it to produce "an integer between 0 and a specific value", in this case, 0–1, 0–10 and 0–100. *There's a big LOOK OUT here* – when the documentation says between 0 and a specific value, it means "between 0 and a specific value, exclusively", which is a fancy way of saying that the specific value is not actually included. When I put 1 as an argument, it means between 0 and 1, but the 1 isn't included, so it's actually between 0 and 0 – so helpful. When I put 10, technically, it will only produce values from 0 to 9 and with 100 as the argument, we will only ever get values between 0 and 99. It's a strange thing that many random number objects do, but it's worth noting that if you really want 0–1 you should put 2 as the argument and for 0–10 or 0–100 the values should be 11, and 101, respectively.

There's another version of .Next() that is pretty handy. This time, we'll put two arguments (and a comma) instead of just a single argument:

```
Random rng = new Random();
int myRandomInt1 = rng.Next(1,5);
Console.WriteLine("This is random: " + myRandomInt1);
int myRandomInt2 = rng.Next(-10,10);
Console.WriteLine("This too is random: " + myRandomInt2);
int myRandomInt3 = rng.Next(100,10000);
Console.WriteLine("This is also random: " + myRandomInt3);
```

In this updated code, we have put a minimum and maximum limit on the random number that .Next() will generate for us. The minimum is inclusive (meaning it can be included) and the maximum is still exclusive (like the last example), so these examples will produce random integers from 1 to 4, from −10 to 9, and from 100 to 9,999. Adding 1 to each of the second arguments would give us the range that we (probably) want. Regardless, this example shows that we can coax our .Next() method to give us random numbers between a minimum and maximum range. Here are three sample outputs from this code (but keep coding them for yourself too):

```
This is random: 3
This too is random: -5
This is also random: 7382

This is random: 4
This too is random: -8
This is also random: 3609

This is random: 2
This too is random: 2
This is also random: 2875
```

Here's a short recap of what we've looked at, so far, in this section.

- Initialize your Random object using a statement like Random rng = new Random();
- Use your new rng object like a tool to dispense (or hand out) random integers using the .Next() function
- .Next() with no arguments creates a random number between 0 and the maximum positive integer (around two billion)
- .Next(maximum) creates a random number between 0 and maximum minus one
- .Next(minimum, maximum) creates a random number between minimum and maximum minus one

Now go forth and create some awesome random integer chaos!!! Or read the next section to see how to create your own fake C# "dice".

Simulating Dice

This would make a great code reward, but I'm just too excited to show you a practical use for random integers.

Picture, in your mind, a standard die (singular of dice) that has six sides. On its sides are representations (numbers or dots called pips) of 1, 2, 3, 4, 5, and 6. How can we use what we learned in the previous section to create a code-based standard six-sided die (or d6) in our games? It turns out, it's pretty easy, and it's done like this:

```
Random rng = new Random();
int myD6 = rng.Next(1, 7);
```

In the first statement, we initialize a Random object – always very important. Then, we call .Next() using our random number object (named rng). But the part that makes this like a d6 is the arguments we pass to .Next(). The 1 says the lowest number should be 1, and the 7 says the highest number should be 6 (I know it's awkward, but you do get used to it after a while). With this little bit of programming magic we have a simulated d6! Let's push this example a bit further by adding another simulated die to our program. A lot of games, especially board games, use two dice to give a wider range of values for players:

```
Random randGenerator = new Random();
int die1 = randGenerator.Next(1, 7);
int die2 = randGenerator.Next(1, 7);
int sumOfDice = die1 + die2;
Console.WriteLine("Die 1 = " + die1 + ", Die 2 = " + die2
   + ", Dice sum = " + sumOfDice);
```

Here is sample output from five separate runs of the code above:

```
Die 1 = 1, Die 2 = 3, Dice sum = 4
Die 1 = 3, Die 2 = 5, Dice sum = 8
Die 1 = 5, Die 2 = 3, Dice sum = 8
Die 1 = 4, Die 2 = 6, Dice sum = 10
Die 1 = 6, Die 2 = 6, Dice sum = 12
```

As always, if you code and run this example for yourself, expect to see different values because that's exactly how Random objects work!

Maybe you're not a board game player – maybe you're more of a tabletop role-playing game person. Do you need a d20 (20-sided die) for a critical roll in your campaign but you accidentally left your lucky bag of dice at home? How would you modify the d6 example above to simulate 20 sides instead of 6? Where, in the code, did we tell the program that we wanted values between 1 and 6? How would you change this to produce values between 1 and 20 instead? You can do this! I believe in you. As a mini practice side quest, modify the previous example to roll two d20s instead of two d6s. If you get stuck, I'll post an example program at the end of this chapter.

Not every situation is well served with random integers. Sometimes, a random decimal number is most appropriate and useful. In the next section, we'll see how to create random decimal values and explore the idea of casting to manually convert from one type to another.

Generating Random Decimals and Casting

Creating random decimal numbers starts the same way as creating random integers, with the initialization of a Random number object:

```
Random rng = new Random();
```

Once we have our generator, we can call the .NextDouble() method, instead of .Next() like this:

```
Random rng= new Random();
double myRandomDouble1 = rng.NextDouble();
Console.WriteLine("This is random: " + myRandomDouble1);
double myRandomDouble2 = rng.NextDouble();
Console.WriteLine("This too is random: " + myRandomDouble2);
double myRandomDouble3 = rng.NextDouble();
Console.WriteLine("This is also random: " + myRandomDouble3);
```

Some sample (random) output might look like this:

```
This is random: 0.17233100839584048
This too is random: 0.7492792532353303
This is also random: 0.18807490685073536
```

Here's another run of the same code:

```
This is random: 0.22621455361016685
This too is random: 0.6153583470354564
This is also random: 0.05216791839142576
```

There is a trio of things to note here in the code and the sample output:

1. we call .NextDouble(), instead of .Next() (which is for integers)
2. the values returned by .NextDouble() are between 0 and 1 (exclusive of 1, meaning we might have a random 0, but we'll never have a random 1)
3. .NextDouble() gives us a double, not a float

The first point is probably the simplest – for random integers, we use Next (), and for random decimal numbers, we use NextDouble(). For the second point, NextDouble() gives us a random decimal number between 0 and something like 0.99999999999ish (thanks to that "exclusive of 1"). Finally, NextDouble() gives us a double value, not a float. In Level 1, I recommended we use floats in our programs instead of doubles. I made this suggestion because game engines, like Unity, use floats as their default decimal data type and, when you're ready, I want you to feel comfortable moving from C# + MonoGame to C# + Unity (or a similar game engine) as your adventure continues beyond these books. Why am I not showing you the handy NextFloat() method for creating random floats – because it doesn't exist. It might seem silly, but the only way to create random decimal values in C# is to use NextDouble(). But there's a handy "trick" that allows us to change from one type to another. Here's how it works:

```
Random rng = new Random();
float myRandomFloat1 = (float) rng.NextDouble();
Console.WriteLine("This is random: " + myRandomFloat1);
float myRandomFloat2 = (float) rng.NextDouble();
Console.WriteLine("This too is random: " + myRandomFloat2);
float myRandomFloat3 = (float) rng.NextDouble();
Console.WriteLine("This too is random: " + myRandomFloat3);
```

This produces output similar to:

```
This is random: 0.9122558
This too is random: 0.65022933
This is also random: 0.898551
```

These statements are almost identical to the previous example, except for two small changes. First, our variables (myRandomFloat1, myRandomFloat2, and myRandomFloat3) are floats, not doubles. Second, in order to make the NextDouble() values fit in our variables, we use a technique called casting to manually convert from double to float. To cast our double down to a float, we put (float) in front of rng.NextDouble() – we lose a few decimal places of precision by doing this, but we save half the memory (doubles take twice the memory space of floats). If you don't need "lots and lots" of precision, this is a good trade-off!

Casting is an important tool in our programmers toolbox, but it's only needed in specific cases. Rather than distracting you from all the random fun we're having in this level, you can read a more detailed explanation of casting and see more examples in Bonus Level 2.

Unfortunately, there's no "easy" way to create a range of random decimal values between a minimum and maximum – we can't simply put one or two arguments in NextDouble() like we did with Next(). If you want values between 3.5 and 9.1, or between –3.14159 and 3.14159, you need to do a bit of math to convert the default output (0 to 1) to something more useful. Officially, according to C# documentation, the math looks like this:

```
Random.NextDouble() * (maximum value - minimum value) + minimum value
```

That might look a bit complicated, but here are some examples:

```
Random rng = new Random();
//minimum value 3.5, maximum value 9.1
float myRandomFloat1 = (float)(rng.NextDouble() * (9.1f - 3.5f) + 3.5);
Console.WriteLine("This is random: " + myRandomFloat1);
//minimum value -3.14159, maximum value 3.14159
float myRandomFloat2 = (float)(rng.NextDouble() * (3.14159 - -3.14159) +
-3.14159);
Console.WriteLine("This too is random: " + myRandomFloat2);
//minimum value 100.0, maximum value 1000.0
float myRandomFloat3 = (float)(rng.NextDouble() * (1000.0 - 100.0) + 100.0);
Console.WriteLine("This is also random: " + myRandomFloat3);
```

It takes a bit of getting used to, but once you have the hang of it, you'll be making wonderful random decimal numbers for all your random decimal number needs! Try this code out for yourself and put some more interesting values in for max and min. Remember – all of this code would also work if we were using variables instead of literals. Always keep that in mind!

It may not be obvious yet, but we've now unlocked the key to many of the ideas introduced at the start of this level. With our new knowledge, we'll be able to spawn game elements at random locations on our screen or in our levels. We'll be able to dispense common loot often and legendary loot rarely. We'll be able to simulate dice rolls, card shuffles, and coin flips. We'll be able to mix up our NPC dialog prompts. As we move forward through the next few levels, random numbers will work their way into our examples, code quests, and side quests. So, be on the lookout for interesting ways to add some fun that surprises, or even frustrates, your players!

Review the Code Reward below, try the next Code Quest, and when you're ready, meet me at the start of Level 7!

Side Quests

Want to Know More?

Games use random: This level is shorter than the others, and until we learn about if-statements, loops, and even MonoGame (in the next book), there's not really a lot we can do with our random numbers. While you're waiting to get to those awesome topics, do a bit of digging on the internet and find some articles that talk about how video games use randomness. There are also some great books on this subject as well.

Random is in your games: It's true – aside from games of pure skill, randomness is in almost every game we play. The next time you play a board game or a video game, try to figure out where the randomness is – is it in the dice, the cards, a loot crate, a power-up, or somewhere else? Also, think a bit about how the randomness affects your experience of the game – both positively and negatively.

Want to Do More?

Random "homework": Okay, maybe homework isn't the best word, but if you skipped any of the examples from the level, go back and code them for yourself. Run them a few times to convince yourself that the output is, in fact, random.

Old examples are new again: In Level 4, we learned about user input – a great way to make our programs interactive and fun. In some cases, we can substitute randomness for user input – instead of asking the user to enter a value, we can generate one for them. Revisit some of the previous levels and code quests to see if there are places where a random number generator might make the program more interesting than using hard-coded values or even user input.

Code Reward – The Higher Roll

You've been asked to code a small program to support a tabletop role-playing game (or RPG) for your friendly game master (or GM). They've asked you to simulate two dice and output the higher of the two values – this way, they can easily tell which of the two rolls to apply in the game. To make the program more useful, they want the user to be able to input the number of sides that both dice have. Whether you have experience playing tabletop RPGs or not, there should be enough information for you to attempt this program! Here it is broken down a bit more clearly:

- Write a quick introduction or welcome output line.
- Prompt the player to input the number of sides on both dice (hint: for this program, they both have the same number of sides, so you only need to collect this value once).
- Collect and store this input as a variable, I recommend int as the type.
- Generate two random numbers between 1 and the number of sides input by the player (that you stored in a variable in the previous step). Store both random values in separate variables. Be careful here. If the player wants 12 to be the highest roll on a single die, you need to account for that when you generate your random number.
- Output the values of the variables storing your random numbers to the console.
- Determine which value of the two is highest and output that to the console too.
- End the program.

Try this code reward for yourself. If you get stuck, peek at the solution for a hint.

```
/*
This is a small program that simulates two dice rolls using random integers.
The program also calculates and displays the maximum of the two simulated
dice.

This program is the Code Reward for Level 6.
Author: Aaron Langille
*/


//Declare some int variables that we'll need
int die1, die2, numberOfSides, maximumValue;

//Initialize our random number object
Random rng = new Random();

//A quick intro/welcome to the program.
Console.WriteLine("Welcome to the amazing Max Roll program!");
Console.WriteLine(); //a blank output line for nice spacing

/*
When we collect input, particularly numbers, the program can crash if the
user enters input that can't be properly parsed. Assume the user enters
meaningful and parseable input. Bonus Level 3 has more information.
*/

//Prompt and collect input for the number of sides on the two dice.
Console.Write("How many sides are on your two dice: ");
numberOfSides = int.Parse(Console.ReadLine());

//Use our Random object (called rng) to assign values to our fake dice.
die1 = rng.Next(1, numberOfSides + 1);
die2 = rng.Next(1, numberOfSides + 1);

//Output the results with some dashes for spacing.
Console.WriteLine("------------");
Console.WriteLine("Die 1 value: " + die1);
Console.WriteLine("Die 1 value: " + die2);
Console.WriteLine("------------");

//Use Math.Max (found in Level 5) to figure out which value is the highest.
maximumValue = Math.Max(die1, die2);

//Output the maximum value.
Console.WriteLine("The maximum of these two dice is: " + maximumValue);
```

14

Code Quest 6: A Random Encounter (Part 1)

Before proceeding with this quest:

- review Level 6
- complete Code Quest 5 (optional)
- create a new Visual Studio Console project. If you need a refresher, detailed instructions can be found at the beginning of Code Quest 1.

In this Code Quest, we're going to practice generating random numbers. We're going to stick to integers for now because they're more interesting and practical for this example. Let's code a program that would be useful in a few scenarios – a tabletop RPG, a card-based RPG, or a video game RPG. We're going to use some of the built-in math operations, which might make this feel a bit like Code Quest 5 – but we're going to leave some of the values up to random fate – after all, games are full of random encounters, both good and bad. This program will prompt the user to enter their hero's current health value. Then we're going to run our hero through a few "hard-coded" events and see how "healthy" they are in the end. Ready? Let's do this.

Main Quest – A Random Encounter (Part 1)

The code in this quest should accomplish the following tasks:

1. Prompt the user and collect a single integer that is the hero's starting health value. Ask the user to enter a value between 0 and 100, just so the rest makes sense. Assume the user will enter a value that can be parsed and makes sense for the program.
2. Our hero encounters a deadly zombie. The zombie deals between 10 and 30 damage. Generate and store (in an appropriate variable) the zombie damage value using a random number generator, and deduct the value from the hero's health.

DOI: 10.1201/9781003348481-14

3. Our hero finds a health potion. The health potion adds between 25 and 45 health points. Generate and store (in an appropriate variable) the random number for this event, and add it to the hero's health.

4. Our hero falls into a deadly trap and loses between 20 and 60 health. You know what to do (just like Steps 2 and 3)!!!

5. For each of Steps 2, 3, and 4, display a line of text telling the user what happened to the hero and showing them the value that was either added or subtracted from the hero's health.

6. Finally, show the hero's final health value.

Here is the output from running my version of this quest two separate times (Figures 14.1 and 14.2).

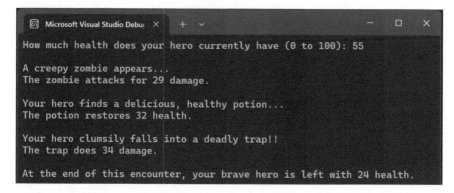

FIGURE 14.1
Here are some example inputs and outputs to help guide you through this quest.

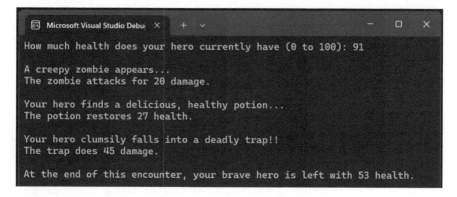

FIGURE 14.2
Here are some more example inputs and outputs to help guide you through this quest.

In my solution, I have used variables for the hero's health and one for each of the random events that our hero experienced.

Side Quests

More code, more control: Not all games would handle the events the same way. For each event, prompt the player to enter the minimum and maximum values that event could generate. For example, prompt the player for a minimum zombie damage amount and a maximum zombie damage amount. Use the player-input numbers to generate your random values.

Make it your own: Do you find my output uninteresting or uninspiring? Do you prefer post-apocalyptic games? Do you prefer cooking games? Do you prefer post-apocalyptic cooking games? Change the event text and the variables to make this Quest more fun for you!!

15

Level 7: A Fork in the Road

Level 6 Recap:

- Randomness makes our games and programs more dynamic and often, more fun.
- In C#, random numbers are generated using a Random object.
- Random objects have a .Next() method that can be used to create random integers and a .NextDouble() method that can be used to create random decimal numbers.
- Casting is a way to manually change one data type to another – like changing a double to a float so that a double value can be stored in a float variable.

Video Games Use Simple Decisions

Your friend sends you a message in the middle of the afternoon – there's a new video game that you absolutely have to try! You find and install it on your favorite platform. As soon as the game loads, a charmingly dressed character starts running across a grassy landscape. There are obstacles, enemies, and other cool game things in the scene, but the character simply runs through them as if they weren't there at all. You push keys on the keyboard – and nothing changes, just more running in a straight line and at a constant speed. You try a controller. No change. After 2 full minutes, a message flashes across the screen saying "You win!" and the game shuts down. Confused, you load the game again, and the same thing happens – 2 minutes of full speed, unimpacted running, and game over.

This game, if we can even call it that, probably won't be topping any sales charts. Here are some ideas to improve it:

- When the game loads, ask the player to press "start" when they're ready. **If** the player indicates they are ready, start the game.
- Most games begin with the player character not moving – **if** the player presses the appropriate keyboard keys or controller input, the character moves.

DOI: 10.1201/9781003348481-15

- The player also decides how fast and in what direction the character moves. **If** the player presses the turbo button, the character charges ahead. **If** the player drifts right, their path is different than **if** they drift left.
- **If** the player collides with an enemy or an obstacle, something should happen to the player (lose some health, stop running, change directions, earn points, etc.) and maybe something should happen to the enemy or obstacle too.
- **If** the player reaches the end of the level in time and with some health remaining, the game says "You win!" But **if** the player loses all their health or they don't find the end of the level in time, the game should probably encourage them to try again.
- Finally, most games don't simply shut down at the end of a level – they shut down **if** and when the player asks to quit.

Most of us prefer when our games respond to certain conditions, like the ones listed above. Notice that each of our improvements involves an "if" condition – if the player does something, if there is a collision, if something interesting happens, and so on. Each of these conditions is like a small decision that changes the flow of our game in a way that makes it far more interesting.

You are at a fork in the road, brave adventurer. If you push forward, Level 7 will show you how to control the flow of your code using simple if and if-else statements. You'll also see how if-statements often introduce a new type of coding error – logic errors. If you turn back now the wonders and joys of conditional execution will be forever lost to you – unless you decide to come back and tackle this challenge later. Which is also cool.

Conditional Execution

Until now, our programs have run from start-to-finish with no chance of deviating. Consider this short example:

```
//initialize our simulated 20-sided die variable
int d20 = 0;

//initialize a random object called rng
Random rng = new Random();

//assign d20 a value between 1 and 20
d20 = rng.Next(1,21);

//output the roll value
Console.WriteLine("You rolled: " + d20);
```

This program starts running at the beginning and goes straight through to the last statement. Since we're using a Random object, we'll get different values when we run this program, but it will always run from start to end – with no deviation – every single time. If we were to draw a diagram of the flow of this program, it would look something like this (Figure 15.1).

But what if we want the program to do something different based on the value stored in our simulated die – maybe we want to display a message of congratulations on a good roll? To do that, we need to change the flow of the program like this (Figure 15.2).

These illustrations, called flowcharts or flow diagrams, are meant to show how our code can execute "conditionally" – we only output "Great roll!" on condition that the value stored in d20 is greater than or equal to 17. If the value in d20 is less than 17, we don't display that message at all – that part

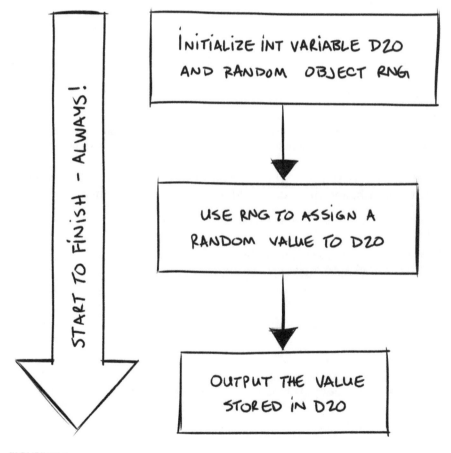

FIGURE 15.1
Flowcharts, like this one, can help illustrate how our code "flows" from the start of the program (or section of the program) to the end.

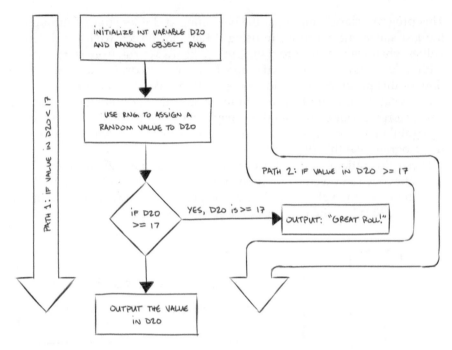

FIGURE 15.2
Here, we see that the code flows differently depending on the value stored in variable d20. If it's less than 17 we go one way, if it's greater than or equal to 17 we go another way.

of the code gets skipped. The decision to display "Great roll!" or not is called a branch, and the code would look something like this:

```csharp
//initialize our simulated 20-sided die variable
int d20 = 0;

//initialize a random object called rng
Random rng = new Random();

//assign d20 a value between 1 and 20
d20 = rng.Next(1, 21);

//IF the value stored in d20 is greater than
//or equal to 17 …
if (d20 >= 17)
{
  // … display this positive message!
  Console.WriteLine("Great roll!");
}

//output the rollvalue
Console.WriteLine("You rolled: " + d20);
```

Using programming structures like if-statements (Level 7 and Level 8, as well as loops in Level 9, and switch statements in Bonus Level 4), we can direct our program to run certain lines of code and to skip others depending on conditions that matter to us. Let's take a closer look at how this is done.

Simple Ifs (or Nothing but the Truth)

In order to control the flow of our program or make simple decisions based on conditions, we need a new programming "structure" called an if-statement. Here is the general idea:

```
if(some condition to check is true)
{
        some cool code that runs if the condition is indeed true
}
```

The structure of an if-statement is a bit more complex than many of our other single-line statements. It has two parts – a condition that needs to be checked, and one or more statements that are executed if the condition is true. To be very clear, the statement(s) inside the curly braces will only run if the condition is true. If the condition is not true, the statements inside the curly braces will be skipped! This is the decision-making power of an if-statement. Let's take a look at a specific, but simple (no variables, no input, no random numbers) example:

```
if(1 < 2)
{
        Console.WriteLine("1 is less than 2");
}
```

This example might seem silly, but it shows all the pieces we need for a working if-statement. When C# is executing our code and reaches an if statement, it evaluates the condition inside the round brackets (parentheses). If that condition evaluates to true, the statements inside the curly braces get executed. This can be a bit confusing at first, but think of it this way – the condition inside the round brackets must be a question with a true or false answer. In our example, the question is – 1 is less than 2? The answer to that simple question is true (or yes) – 1 is less than 2. Before moving on, code this example for yourself. You should see "1 is less than 2" as output. We'll see more of these simple true or false questions in all of our if-statement examples.

What happens if we change the condition, like this:

```
if(2 < 1)
{
        Console.WriteLine("1 is less than 2");
}
```

Now, we have a different situation. The question we are asking (or the condition we are checking) is whether 2 is less than 1. The answer to this is now false (or no). If you try to run this code, you'll see no output at all. The statement inside the curly braces is skipped because the condition is false.

As always, where there are literals in our code, we can use variables instead. Here's a similar, but more interesting example for our future games:

```
int playerScore = 110;
if(playerScore > 100)
{
    Console.WriteLine(playerScore + " is a great score!!");
}
```

There are a couple of things to notice in this example – we've initialized a variable before the if-statement and we've used it in the if-statement condition. Remember, whenever C# sees a properly declared and assigned variable in the code, it will substitute the value stored inside. If you run this code, you should see that our player has a great score. The variable playerScore holds a value of 110 which is greater than 100 – as such, the condition is true and the message displays. Try changing the value of playerScore to be 75, 50, or 10 – in these cases the condition will be false and the message will be skipped. This example could also use user input like this:

```
Console.Write("What is your score: ");
int playerScore = int.Parse(Console.ReadLine());
if(playerScore > 100)
{
    Console.WriteLine(playerScore + " is a great score!!");
}
```

Notice how the if-statement doesn't really know, or care, where the value of playerScore comes from. As long as the value in playerScore is an integer and the condition in the round brackets can be evaluated to be true or false, it won't matter. Take a moment to code this example and try it with a few different input values.

We can also have more than one statement inside the curly braces:

```
//initialize a Random object named rng.
Random rng = new Random();

//set a random player score between 1 and 150
int playerScore = rng.Next(1, 151);

//set the current high score to 100
int highScore = 100;
```

```
//if the player's score is greater than the current
//high score, update the high score
if(playerScore > highScore)
{
    //the player's score is the new high score
    highScore = playerScore;
    Console.WriteLine("We have a new high score: " + highScore);
}

//the program is finished
Console.WriteLine("Game over!");
```

This example is our most "complete" program so far in this level – read the code and comments carefully. Here we are using a random number to simulate the player's score. If the player's random score is greater than the current high score – update the high score to the player's score and also display a message. It's very important to note that in most cases, you'll have code that goes before the if-statement, code that is part of the if-statement, and code that is after the if-statement. The details of each specific case are different, but here are some general guidelines:

- *Before:* make sure that any variables that the if-statement needs are declared and have assigned values
- *During:* this is where the if-statement will check the condition and execute any statements if the condition is true
- *After:* this is any code that runs after the if-statement has completed

Here is an example that has two if-statements in the same program. One checks to see if a simulated 20-sided dice roll is very high, and the other checks if the roll is very low. See if you can identify the before, during, and after parts of each if-statement.

```
//initialize d20 with a value between 1 and 20
int d20 = rng.Next(1,21);

//if it's a high roll …
if(d20 > 17)
{
    Console.WriteLine("That's a great roll!!");
}

//if it's a low roll …
if(d20 < 3)
{
    Console.WriteLine("Ouch, that's a tough roll!!");
}
//output the roll value
Console.WriteLine("You rolled: " + d20);
```

Try this code out for yourself. Be sure to run it a few times to see the range of output possibilities. In this program, we are checking the value of d20 for two possible conditions. In the first if-statement, we are checking to see if it has a value of 18, 19, or 20 (all values greater than 17). If the condition is true, we display a positive message. In the second if-statement, we are checking to see if the value in d20 is less than 3 (2 or 1) and displaying a sympathetic message if the condition is true. What happens if the value in d20 is between 3 and 17? Nothing much. We display the value that the user (or player) rolled, but we don't comment any further. Outputting the value stored in our d20 is outside of either of the if-statements, so it runs no matter what value d20 receives.

So far in this level, all of our examples do something if a checked condition is true, but we don't take any action if the condition is false. A player with a high score is a great use of this kind of if-statement – if the player earns a score greater than the current high score, we update the high score to the player's score. If the player's score is less than the current high score, what should we do? I'd argue that we should do nothing – there's no action needed if the player didn't beat the high score. There are lots of similar take-action-or-ignore cases in games:

- If the player collides with an enemy they lose health, otherwise the player's health stays the same.
- If the player presses the A-button on their controller, their hover-craft should accelerate forward, otherwise it should stay where it is.
- If the player presses any key the game should begin, otherwise it should stay on the title screen.

There are also many examples of conditions that have both a true and a false consequence, so let's take a look at how to handle those cases.

Else Handles the False Case

I assume you want to be able to run code if an if-statement condition is false? Here's how it's done. First, we need to be aware of the "else clause" which looks something like this:

```
if(some condition to check is true)
{
        some cool code that runs if the condition is true
}
else
{
        some other cool code to run if the condition is false
}
```

An else clause is added when we want to take action if the condition is false. Without an else, we ignore the false case and take no action, but when we add the else our code will respond to a false condition. Here is one of our previous simple examples revisited:

```
if(1 < 2)
{
        Console.WriteLine("1 is less than 2");
}
else
{
        Console.WriteLine("2 is NOT less than 1");

}
```

If you were to write, compile, and run this code (highly recommended), you would see that the if statement is still true (like it was when we saw this code at the start of this level) and "1 is less than 2" is printed. But if we were to change the condition:

```
if(2 < 1)
{
        Console.WriteLine("1 is less than 2");
}
else
{
        Console.WriteLine("2 is NOT less than 1");
}
```

This new condition (2 < 1) is false and the else does its job and outputs "2 is NOT less than 1". This example isn't very useful outside of illustrating how else works, so let's push forward with a more interesting example:

```
//hard code a secret number
int secretNumber = 47;

//prompt the user for an integer between 1 and 100
//this is their guess

Console.Write("I'm thinking of a number between 1 and 100, your guess is: ");

int playerGuess = int.Parse(Console.ReadLine());

//if the playerGuess is equal to the secretNumber
if(playerGuess == secretNumber)
{
   //they did it!
   Console.WriteLine("Amazing!!! You actually guessed it!");
}
else
{
```

```
    //they didn't do it.
    Console.WriteLine("Sorry, better luck next time.");
}

Console.WriteLine("Game over.");
```

In this very, very tough guessing game, we have hard-coded a variable to have the "secret number" 47. We then prompt the user to guess the secret number and use an if-else statement to tell them whether or not they were successful. It's a pretty tough game since the player probably doesn't know that the secret number is 47, but a good illustration of if-else. The == (equal to) comparison operator is handy here. We'll take a closer look at it and other comparison operators in the next section.

In the meantime, let's end this section with an example that combines almost everything we've learned so far in one relatively short but interactive example. Read the code (without comments) before reading the program description below:

```
Console.Write("Enter your hero's health: ");
int heroHealth = int.Parse(Console.ReadLine());

Random rng = new Random();
int randomChance = rng.Next(1, 101);

if(randomChance < 50)
{
        Console.WriteLine("Your hero finds a health potion lying on the
        ground!!");
        heroHealth += 10;
}
else
{
        Console.WriteLine("Your hero steps into a dangerous trap!!");
        heroHealth -= 15;
}

Console.WriteLine("In the end, your hero has " + heroHealth + " health.");
```

Our program starts by prompting the user and collecting a hero's health value. Then, we initialize a Random object named rng and use it to generate a value between 1 and 100. Now, our if-else kicks in. If the random number we generated is less than 50, the hero finds a health potion and is healed for 10 health points. If, on the other hand, the random number we generated is 50 or greater, the hero steps into a trap and loses 15 health points. We've created a 50/50 random chance of our hero healing or taking damage!! After all the action is done, we display the hero's final health value. Again, pay attention to what happens before the if-statement, what happens during (including the else), and what happens after. The variable(s) used in our condition need to be declared and assigned before the if-statement. During, we display some helpful messages to the player and make some variable updates. After, we output the final result.

So far, we've used three comparison operators: < less than, > greater than, and == equal to but there are a few more that you might find useful in your games and programs. Let's take a look at what they are and try out some more if and if-else examples while we're at it.

Comparison Operators

We know from previous levels that games are full of numbers – mostly ints and floats for us. C# has several built-in comparison operators that allow us to compare numbers and ask simple true or false questions:

- x < y: use this operator to ask if x is *less than* y.
- x > y: use this operator to ask if x is *greater than* y.
- x <= y: use this operator to ask if x is *less than or equal to* y. Be careful here – the operator is <=, not =< or < = (those last two are syntax errors).
- x >= y: use this operator to ask if x is *greater than or equal to* y. Be careful here – the operator is >=, not => or > = (those last two are syntax errors).
- x == y: use this operator to ask if x is *equal to* y.
- x!= y: use this operator to ask if x is *not equal to* y. Be a bit careful with this one – it's true when x and y are not equal and false when they are. It's the logical opposite of == (equal to).

Here's an example program that tests all the built-in number comparison operators. Pay close attention to how each one is used and the output it produces. Try coding this multi-if example for yourself and running it with some different values for playerScore and highScore. Don't be surprised if more than one if-statement is true when you run this program. Take some time to look at the code so that you understand when each separate if-statement condition is true:

```
int playerScore = 0;
int highScore = 0;

Console.Write("Player score?: ");
playerScore = int.Parse(Console.ReadLine());
Console.Write("High score?: ");
```

```
highScore = int.Parse(Console.ReadLine());
if(playerScore < highScore)
{
     Console.WriteLine("Player score is less than the high score.");
}
if(playerScore > highScore)
{
     Console.WriteLine("Player score is greater than the high score.");
}
if(playerScore <= highScore)
{
     Console.WriteLine("Player score is less than or equal to the high
     score.");
}
if(playerScore >= highScore)
{
     Console.WriteLine("Player score is greater than or equal to the high
     score.");
}
if(playerScore == highScore)
{
     Console.WriteLine("Player score is equal to the high score.");
}
if(playerScore != highScore)
{
     Console.WriteLine("Player score is NOT equal to the high score.");
}
```

Remember, many of these examples use ints to keep things simple (and because we use ints often in games), but they'll also work with other number data types including floats. Some of the built-in comparison operators even work on strings and characters – let's take a look at which ones.

Comparing Strings and Characters

When writing games, most of our comparisons are between number data types. This makes sense since our game data is mostly numbers – score, speed values, screen positions, health and other player stats, enemy count, time remaining, and so on. But there are also times when it is helpful to be able to compare strings and keyboard characters. Most of our string and character comparisons will be done in our console examples, and you won't see them as much if you decide to continue your journey with MonoGame. But if you do write your own games and programs in MonoGame, Unity, or some other engine or framework, you might find this information useful.

In C#, comparing strings and characters for equality (==) or not equality (!=) is done the same way as comparing number types. For example:

```
Console.Write("Your hero picks up a helpful item (what is it?): ");
string pickUpItem = Console.ReadLine();
if(pickUpItem == "health potion")
{
    Console.WriteLine("Your hero feels healthier already!!");
}
else
{
    Console.WriteLine("I'm sorry, I can't use a " + pickUpItem + " at this
    time.");
}
```

In this example, we ask the user to enter an item that the hero has picked up on their journey. We store the user input in a string variable and use == to compare the user input (pickUpItem) with the hard-coded string literal "health potion". If the user enters the text "health potion", we output a healing message (and we could have also increased the player health if that was part of our program), but if the user enters anything else, we simply output a "can't use that" message – it is a simple example, after all. Try to code this example and enter a few common and bizarre items that your hero might have picked up. As you try some different inputs, you might find that this if-statement is a bit sensitive. For example, if you enter "Health Potion", or "healthpotion", or "healthy portion", the comparison is false, and the else kicks in – it's only true if you enter exactly "health potion". Take a look at Bonus Level 3 to see some helpful tips on how to make this kind of comparison less sensitive to minor differences in the strings.

Although we didn't cover the char built-in data type as thoroughly as we did other data types in Level 2, they can be quite helpful – particularly in our console programs. Here's a quick overview on the char data type:

- char is a single character – remember strings are made up of characters
- a char literal is placed in single quotes like this: 'A', '3', or ' (space) '
- you can parse characters from the console using char.Parse()

And here's an example that shows char in action:

```
Console.Write("Are you enjoying your coding adventure so far (y/n): ");
char userResponse = char.Parse(Console.ReadLine());
if(userResponse == 'y')
{
    Console.WriteLine("I'm so glad to hear that!!");
}
else
{
    Console.WriteLine("Hm, keep going. More exciting topics are
    coming!");
}
```

In this example, we're asking the user to enter a single y or n character in response to the prompt. Our if-statement compares the user input, with a hard-coded 'y' char literal. If the user inputs a 'y,' the if-statement is true, and we're thrilled to see a happy coding adventurer. The false case is a bit of a cheat in this example – anything other than lowercase y results in a false! We say in the prompt y/n – this is a standard yes or no prompt – but we actually mean "y or anything else". Like our string example above, this char example is sensitive – capital Y doesn't count here. Head over to Bonus Level 3 to see how to make this a bit more robust.

Before we continue our journey in the next section, it's worth pointing out that I didn't show any examples of <, >, >=, or <= with strings or chars. When we use == or != with strings or chars the question we are asking is pretty clear – are these strings or chars equal or not? When we ask is "this string less than that string", or "is this char greater than one", the question is less clear. We might be talking about alphabetical or (apple comes before zebra), but we could also be talking about length (app comes before apple), or some other property of strings (or characters). For this reason, the built-in comparison operators such as <, >, >=, or <= don't work with strings and (probably) don't work the way you might think they should with chars. I'll post some more information in the side quests below, but we won't be doing string or char comparisons other than == or != in this book. And with that, let's journey-on!

Introducing Logic Errors

In Level 1, we introduced the idea of syntax errors – errors that prevent your program from compiling and running. If you're like me, you've probably made a few (or many) syntax errors in trying out our examples. Don't worry, syntax errors are a very normal part of coding. But have you written any programs that compiled properly and ran ... improperly? That might seem like an odd question, so let me clarify – sometimes we write a program and expect a certain result or output, but what we get is something unexpected. Has this happened to you? If it hasn't happened yet, it certainly will, and adding if-statements to your code is only going to increase the chances of adding logic errors.

Logic errors are errors in our code, but unlike syntax errors, logic errors are not detected by the compiler. Take a look at this example (be sure to read the comments):

```
//player's starting score
int playerScore = 75;

//ADD 25 to the player's score
playerScore -= 25;

//display the score
Console.WriteLine("Final score: " + playerScore);
```

Can you see the error in this code? Try running it for yourself to see what the final output shows. There's no if-statement in this example, but there is a logic error. In the first statement, we initialize a playerScore variable with a starting value of 75. Then, in the next statement, we subtract 25 from the player score – even though the comment says we want to ADD 25. Finally, we display the final score. We are expecting an output of 100 (75 + 25), but we actually see an output of 50 (75 – 25). The compiler doesn't catch this error – syntax-wise, everything is fine. We simply put the wrong math operation and introduced a logic error to our code. Logic errors, like syntax errors, are a very normal part of programming. What makes them a bit trickier to handle is that the compiler tells us when we have a syntax error – and usually gives us a sense of how to fix it. There is no such support for logic errors.

What does this have to do with if-statements? If-statements are logic structures that control the flow of our code, and it's all-too-easy to make small mistakes that have big and sometimes unfortunate impacts on our program. Take a look at this familiar code:

```
Console.Write("Please enter you hero's health: ");
int heroHealth = int.Parse(Console.ReadLine());
if(heroHealth >= 0)
{
     Console.WriteLine("I'm sorry, but your hero has perished.");
}
else
{
     Console.WriteLine("Your hero seems healthy enough to continue!");
}
```

Can you find the logic error? Take a moment to really look at this code, or better yet, write, compile, and run it. This example is identical to our last hero health checker, except for one small change – if(heroHealth <= 0) from the original code has been changed to if(heroHealth >= 0). This very small, and hard to see, change flips the logic of our program – now we are saying that any hero with health points has perished and only heroes with negative health (zombie heroes?) are healthy enough to continue. If you caught that error on your own, awesome! If you didn't, don't be discouraged – it takes a while to be able to find those types of small, and frustrating, logic errors. Here's one more example with the same small program:

```
Console.Write("Please enter you hero's health: ");
int heroHealth = int.Parse(Console.ReadLine());
if(heroHealth < 0)
{
    Console.WriteLine("I'm sorry, but your hero has perished.");
}
else
{
    Console.WriteLine("Your hero seems healthy enough to continue!");
}
```

Do you see the error this time (hint: it's in the same place). This time we have the logic "almost" correct. We are checking to see if the hero's health is below 0 to pronounce them perished. But by leaving the = off the comparison operator, we're allowing zero-health heroes to continue adventuring when they should really be resting (at the very least). Again, if you didn't catch the error, don't give up! The goal of this section is to show you how easy it is to introduce logic errors with if-statements, and to introduce the idea of logic errors in general. In Cutscene 3 (coming up soon), you'll find some tips on "debugging" – finding bugs and errors – your code, especially when your if-statements become more complex, and we add loops (Level 9) to our programs.

A Few Last Words on Simple Ifs

Now that you know how to create simple if and if-else statements, let's finish by answering a few questions you may (or may not) have thought of while bravely battling your way through this level.

Why Aren't There More Examples of How to Do (Some Cool Thing) in Games?

There are so many great things you could do with if-statements in games – if we even tried to cover all them, this would be a zillion-book series! The examples in this level are designed to introduce you to if and if-else syntax and to give you a sense of how and when they are used. Also, we'll see many more if and if-else examples in every level going forward (and in the next book, because if-statements work in MonoGame too).

These If and If-Else Statements Are Pretty Simple. Can We Write More Complex Logic for Our Games and Programs?

Absolutely! Watch out for Level 8, when we'll take what we've learned here and build even cooler if-statements to handle more complex logic.

Are the Curly Braces Really Necessary?

The answer to this question is both yes and no. The way I have styled the examples in this level (see Cutscene 3 for more on programming style), the if and else clauses take up a lot of space. If you've been coding these examples with me, you've probably noticed that this is the same style that Visual Studio uses. Can you remove the curly braces ({ }) to save some space in your programs? Yes – but only when your if or else has a single statement that is to be run. For example:

```
if(1 < 2)
{
        Console.WriteLine("1 is less than 2");
}
else
{
        Console.WriteLine("2 is NOT less than 1");

}
```

could be written as:

```
if(1 < 2)
        Console.WriteLine("1 is less than 2");
else
        Console.WriteLine("2 is NOT less than 1");
```

The second version of this example works because both the if and else have only one statement each. When you remove the curly braces, C# will automatically run the next single statement after the if or else. Personally, I prefer the second version of this example because it does save me a bit of space and coding time. But I also have 30(ish) years of experience and can (usually) remember when it's ok to remove the curly braces or when I need to add them. If you have more than one statement in your if or in your else, you **must** include the curly braces, or the code will not run properly – you'll end up with either a syntax error or a logic error depending on the situation.

When in doubt (and I recommend this for all beginners) include the curly braces!

Why == and not =?

Why is the equality comparison == and not simply =? The answer to this is simply – because = is already used. The = operator is assignment as in:

```
playerScore = 100;
```

We can try to put a single equals in our if-statement conditions:

```
if(playerScore = 100)
```

C# reads this as an attempt to store 100 into the variable playerScore – which is not compatible with an if-statement. To get around this we need a new operator to check for an "equality" condition, and that operator is ==. It's really common for beginners to try and put a single = in an if-statement, in part because we are used to that symbol as equals outside of programming. Don't worry, C# will tell you when you've used = instead of == in an if-statement – it's a syntax error.

Can I Have an Else Without an If?

We started this level with examples of if-statements that had no else – these if-statements ignored the false case. It's reasonable then to ask if we can have an else without if? The answer to that is – nope. The reason for this is that an else has no condition – it asks no question. The if-statement is the part that has the condition (or question) and the else is the part that executes code if the condition is false. An else without and if doesn't ask anything and is considered a syntax error.

Is There Anything Else You Think I Should Know?

This is a challenging level for many beginners. There is a specific way of thinking that needs to be nurtured when introducing if-statements. It's the beginning of a very logic-driven way to solve problems. Some people pick it up quickly, others need more time and practice to feel comfortable. If you find yourself a bit (or a lot) confused by the examples and ideas in this level, be patient with yourself. This adventure is more of a marathon than a sprint and if you stick with it – and practice – it will start to make sense.

Side Quests

Want to Know More?

Strings are tricky to compare: As I mentioned in the level, comparing strings with == and!= in C# is easy, but the other built-in comparison operators don't work. If you find yourself needing to compare strings beyond simple equality, you'll want to look up the String.Compare() method. It's like

Console.WriteLine() or Math.Max() except that it will help you with your string comparisons.

Characters are tricky to compare: As I mentioned in the level, comparing strings with == and!= in C# is easy, and the other built-in comparison operators do work, but maybe not the way you expect them to. The char data type actually stores characters as numbers and when we use <, >, <=, and >= we are comparing the number-version of our chars. This comparison actually works pretty well to tell us that "a" is less than "b" and that "z" is greater than "s", but it gets trickier when we try to compare lowercase characters to uppercase, numbers to letters or punctuation, and so on. If this all sounds confusing, that would be the reason we only cover == and!= for characters in this level. If you're curious about the char data type and the built-in comparison operators, there are lots of websites and other resources that will more thoroughly explain what I've only briefly mentioned here.

Want to Do More?

Make the guessing game more difficult: Change the guessing game example to have a random number between 1 and 100 instead of the hard-coded value of 47. Try the guessing game a few times – if you win, I'm sending you a virtual high-five!

A small change with a big impact: Go back to the example where we asked if you were enjoying your coding journey so far. Change this logic:

```
if(userResponse == 'y')
```

to:

```
if(userResponse != 'n')
```

What impact, if any, does this have on the program? Be sure to test it with a few different input options.

Code Reward – A Simple Encounter

In this level, we learned that if-statements can make our games and programs more interesting by conditionally running – or not running – parts of our code. Let's put this new knowledge to work with what we learned in previous levels by writing an interactive character encounter program – with a twist. Not only will our character encounter a monster, they might also be poisoned as well! Here's what I've written for this code reward – try it out for yourself and take a look at my code if you get stuck:

- Prompt the user to specify what sort of monster currently stands in their way. Collect and store this input as a string. The kind of obstacle doesn't really matter, it's just part of our game's story. Write an output statement that confirms your hero's obstacle.
- Next prompt the user for the hero's current health. Store this in an appropriate variable.
- Prompt the user for the amount of damage the monster does – again, store this in a variable.
- Finally, prompt the user to say whether the hero is currently poisoned. There are a few ways to store this input – my solution uses a char to store the input for a "is the hero poisoned" prompt.
- Now we process all the input we've collected:
  - Subtract the monster damage from the hero's health and output the hero's new health.
  - If the user said that the hero was indeed poisoned, subtract 10 more health and output an appropriate message. If the user said no to poisoning, simply output an appropriate message.
  - If the hero's health at this point (maybe poisoned, maybe not) is less than 0, output a message that the hero has died. Otherwise, output a message that the hero can journey on!!
- Output a final message that the game (or program, if you prefer) is done.

If that seems like a lot to do, remember, we're already on Level 7! We've covered a lot of awesome coding topics, and our games and programs are getting more complex – and fun. There are many ways to approach this code reward and to complete it successfully, but I recommend taking your time, working on one part of the program at a time, and testing often. If you get stuck, head to my solution for a hint.

As always, if you're not a big fan of the story in my example, change it to something that you find more interesting. The code in this program would work just as well if it was set in space, on a farm, or in an underground lair populated by talking insects (just saying).

```
/*
This is a small program that simulates a simple RPG-style hero encounter.

This program is the Code Reward for Level 7.
Author: Aaron Langille
*/

//let the user specify the kind of obstacle or monster our hero is facing
Console.Write("What type of monster is hero facing: ");
string monsterType = Console.ReadLine();

//print out the encounter type
Console.WriteLine();
Console.WriteLine("Your hero is confronted by a vicious " + monsterType
+ ".");
Console.WriteLine();

//let the user specify how healthy the hero is, parse and store this input
Console.Write("How many hit points does your hero have: ");
int heroHealth = int.Parse(Console.ReadLine());

//how much damage does the obstacle/monster do
Console.Write("How much damage does the " + monsterType + " deal: ");
int damage = int.Parse(Console.ReadLine());

//let's check the poison state of our hero.
Console.Write("Is your hero currently poisoned (press y if yes, anything
else for no): ");
char poisoned = char.Parse(Console.ReadLine());

//just a line of dashes to separate the input section from the business
section
Console.WriteLine("-------------------");

//if the monster did damage, use our math operator to subtract it from the
health
heroHealth -= damage;
Console.WriteLine("Hero's health after " + monsterType + " attack: "
+ heroHealth);

//if the user said y to poison, take off 10 health points, otherwise don't.
if(poisoned == 'y')
{
        heroHealth -= 10;
        Console.WriteLine("Hero's health after poison damage:
" + heroHealth);
}
else
{
        Console.WriteLine("Your hero is not poisoned - no poison damage
recorded".);
}
```

```
//if between damage and poison the hero's health is less than 0, the hero is
dead.
//display a message.
if(heroHealth < 0)
{
        Console.WriteLine("Your hero has died.:X ");
}
else
{
        Console.WriteLine("Your hero lives to fight another day (or another
turn at least)! ");
}

//This is the end of our program.
Console.WriteLine("End of Program");
```

16

Code Quest 7: A Random Encounter (Part 2)

Before proceeding with this quest:

- review Level 7
- complete Code Quest 6 (required)
- create a new Visual Studio Console project. If you need a refresher, detailed instructions can be found at the beginning of Code Quest 1.

This quest starts where Code Quest 6 ended. What we're going to do is make our character encounter more interesting by adding some simple if and if-else statements. This way, we can add the possibility that our zombie is replaced by a vampire, and we can give our hero a health potion – but only if they really need it. We can also determine if our hero survived the encounter or perished.

If you haven't completed Code Quest 6, go back and complete it before charging forward with this challenge.

Main Quest – A Random Encounter (Part 2)

The code in this quest should accomplish the following tasks:

1. Complete Code Quest 6 as it is described. You should have a functioning zombie attack, health potion pick-up, and deadly trap.

2. Add an if-else statement so that our hero is attacked by either a zombie or a vampire. To do this, generate a random number between 1 and 100. If the number is less than 51, our hero is attacked by the zombie (you should already have this code). Otherwise (or, else), our hero is attacked by a vampire. A vampire attack is similar to a zombie attack, but it does between 15 and 25 damage.

3. We're only going to give our hero a health potion if their health points are less than 40. I know this sounds mean, but I want you to practice writing an if-statement with no else. That's what you can

use for this task – if the hero's health is less than 40, give them a health potion otherwise, ignore their health status.

4. Finally, let's figure out if our hero has perished or survived. If their health is 0 or less, output a message of condolences. Otherwise, show the player how healthy their hero is now that the encounter is over!

5. Remember, if you have completed Code Quest 6, you have a lot of this code already! Oh, and leave the trap code in place from Code Quest 6 - heroes are known to be pretty clumsy.

Here is the output from running my version of this quest two separate times (Figures 16.1 and 16.2).

There are a lot of random factors in this program, and I'm only showing output from two runs. Be sure to test your program to make sure that all three

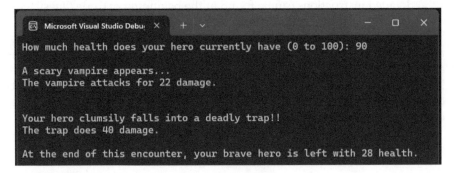

FIGURE 16.1
This is my hero trying to survive a random and deadly encounter.

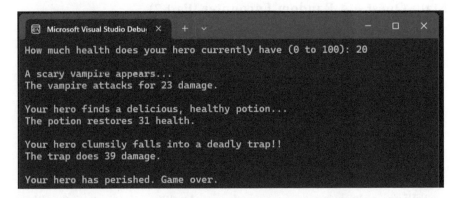

FIGURE 16.2
This is my hero trying to survive another random and deadly encounter.

of your if-statements – zombie vs. vampire attack, health potion if needed, and dead-or-alive – are working properly.

Side Quests

More encounters, more fun: This program only has three events – but there could be more! Add some more events and make them more interesting by wrapping them in if-statements.

Dead heroes don't drink health potions: As you can see in my second output screen, my hero technically perished after the vampire attack – they saved themselves with that VERY handy health potion only to perish (again) in the deadly trap. What an unlucky hero. The main reason for this is that we are only checking for hero-death at the very end of the program. Can you think of a way to rewrite the logic to make sure that once the hero perishes, they can't come back to life?

Make it your own: Do you find my output uninteresting or uninspiring? Do you prefer games with aliens? Do you prefer games with steampunk technology? Do you prefer alien steampunk technology games? Change the event text and the variables to make this quest more fun for you!!

17

Level 8: Decisions, Decisions

Level 7 Recap:

- If-statements control the flow of our code based on a condition that can be true or false.
- If the condition is true, the attached statements, the ones in the curly braces, are run. If the condition is false, the statements are ignored.
- An else clause can be used to run different statements if the condition is false.
- Conditional operators like >, <, >=, <=, ==, and != can be used to compare number variables and literals.
- ==, and != can also be used to compare strings.

Video Games Use "Complex" Decisions

There are many questions in video games that can be answered with a simple true or false:

- Did the player beat the current high score?
- Is the player character still alive?
- Is it time to start the next wave of enemies?
- Does the player want to quit the level?

But there are also many times where our games need to check trickier conditions:

- How much health does the hero have after all the current buffs (positive bonuses) and debuffs (negative penalties) are applied?
- Which of the many enemies in the current scene is going to attack next?
- The path in front of the player branches off in three directions – which path will be easy, which one is neutral, and which one is extra challenging?
- What is in that fancy loot box?

  DOI: 10.1201/9781003348481-17

In Level 7, we looked at how to write if-statements that would check a single condition and respond one way if the condition was true and another way if the condition was false. This logic is enough to handle the first set of questions above, but how do we start to work more complex conditions into our games and programs? The answer to that question is Level 8, where we'll learn how to write if-statements that have more than one or two outcomes. We'll also look at ways to ask more than one question (or check more than one condition) by "nesting" if-statements and combining them with special logic operators. We'll end this level with some examples of if-statements that check user input, and we'll look at how to use boolean variables as flags that help control the logic of our games.

Are you ready to continue the journey? Whether your answer is a simple yes or no, or something more complex, I'll be waiting in the next section.

If-Else-If (More than Two Paths)

Let's build an example that starts with some things we know how to do and ends with something new. We're going to begin with a simple program that gives our hero a 25% chance of earning a health bonus. As always, review the following code (and comments) carefully or test it out for yourself before moving on:

```
//Ask the user for the hero's current health.
Console.Write("What is your hero's current health: ");
int heroHealth = int.Parse(Console.ReadLine());

//Create a Random object and use it to get a value between 0 and 100
Random rng = new Random();
int randomValue = rng.Next(0, 101);

//If the random values is less than 25 out of a possible 100 (25%), the hero
//finds a health potion and gains 10 health points.
if(randomValue <= 25)
{
    Console.WriteLine("Your hero finds a health potion and feels refreshed!");
    heroHealth += 10;
}
//Finish with a helpful update.
Console.WriteLine("Your hero continues their journey with " + heroHealth +
" health.");
```

This is a program that uses lots of coding elements that we've covered in earlier levels – variables, literals, user input, random number generation, and even a simple if-statement. If you run this program a few times, every once in a while (about 25% of the time), your hero will gain 10 health points, and the rest of the time they'll continue their journey with the health points they started with. To be clear, 75% of the time this program would seem to be doing nothing – this is because our program responds to the true case of our if-statement condition and ignores the false case since there is no else. Let's extend it a bit by adding an else like this:

```
//Ask the user for the hero's current health.
Console.Write("What is your hero's current health: ");
int heroHealth = int.Parse(Console.ReadLine());

//Create a Random object and use it to get a value between 0 and 100
Random rng = new Random();
int randomValue = rng.Next(0, 101);

//Let's add a bit of story to this program.
Console.WriteLine("Your hero enters a room and rummages around in the
darkness …");

//If the random values is less than 25 out of a possible 100 (25%), the hero
//finds a health potion and gains 10 health points. Otherwise, the hero finds
//an empty room.
if(randomValue <= 25)
{
     Console.WriteLine("Your hero finds a health potion and feels
refreshed!");
     heroHealth += 10;
}
else
{
     Console.Write("The room is empty. Utterly empty.");
}

//Finish with a helpful update.
Console.WriteLine("Your hero continues their journey with " + heroHealth
+ " health.");
```

This extended version of our program (including a bit of riveting narrative) now tells the player what happens in either case – if the value in randomValue is less than 25, our hero receives a refreshing health reward; otherwise, we notify the player that the hero found nothing in the room. This version feels a bit more complete. But what if there's a third option that we want to include – what if there is a secret trap hiding in the darkness?

```
//Ask the user for the hero's current health.
Console.Write("What is your hero's current health: ");
int heroHealth = int.Parse(Console.ReadLine());
```

```
//Create a Random object and use it to get a value between 0 and 100
Random rng = new Random();
int randomValue = rng.Next(0, 101);

//Let's add a bit of story to this program.
Console.WriteLine("Your hero enters a room and rummages around in the
darkness …");

//If the random values is less than 26 out of a possible 100 (25%), the hero
//finds a health potion and gains 10 health points. If the random number is
//> 89 the hero finds a trap. Otherwise, the hero finds an empty room.
if(randomValue <= 25)
{
     Console.WriteLine("Your   hero   finds   a   health   potion   and   feels
refreshed!");
     heroHealth += 10;
}
else if(randomValue >= 90)
{
     Console.WriteLine("Your hero steps on a rusty nail. It really, really
hurts.");
     heroHealth -= 10;
}
else
{
     Console.Write("The room is empty. Utterly empty.");
}

//Finish with a helpful update.
Console.WriteLine("Your hero continues their journey with " + heroHealth + "
health.");
```

As promised, we started with what we knew – the first two versions of this program use simple if statements – and we ended with something new! This final version adds what is called an if-else clause and it allows us to have more than two paths in our if-statement. Here's how it works:

- Our program collects the user input, creates a random number object, and sets all the appropriate variables.
- When the program arrives at if(randomValue <= 25), it checks to see if the condition is true. Because we're using random numbers, we don't really know (and maybe don't really care) what the value is, but the logic says if randomValue is <= 25 give the hero some extra health. If this happens, the program prints the refreshed output, gives the hero the extra health points, and then jumps right to the final output of the program.
- If randomValue is not <= 25, the program goes to the next condition – in this case, randomValue >= 90. If this condition is true, we print the

rusty nail (or trap) output and we remove some health points. After that, we jump to the final output of the program.

- If randomValue isn't <= 25 and it also isn't >= 90, the program runs the else part. We tell the player the hero's room is empty and then proceed to the end of the program.

In other words, when we have multiple conditions using the if-else-if structure and the program checks one condition at a time. As soon as it finds a true condition, it executes that code and then leaves the if-else-if. Only one branch of an if-else-if will ever be run – and that's by design. If all of the conditions are false and you have written an else clause (which is optional but highly recommended), then the else statements will run. Try running this program a few times to get a feel for what is going on in the code. It might be helpful to print the value of randomValue so that you can make sure the program is working the way you expect it to. There are ideas on extending this program even further in the side quests at the end of this level.

Now, let's revisit a program from Level 7 – our "almost-impossible" guessing game. In the original version, we asked the player to guess the secret (but hard-coded) number. What makes this little game so challenging is that we only give the player one chance to guess the number (don't worry, we'll give them multiple chances in Level 9), and we don't give them any clues as to whether their guess was too high or too low. We can fix that with an if-else-if like this:

```
//hard code a secret number
int secretNumber = 47;

//prompt the user for an integer between 1 and 100
//this is their guess
Console.Write("I'm thinking of a number between 1 and 100, your guess is: ");
int playerGuess = int.Parse(Console.ReadLine());

//if the playerGuess is equal to the secretNumber
if(playerGuess == secretNumber)
{
  //they did it!
  Console.WriteLine("Amazing!!! You actually guessed it!");
}
else if(playerGuess < secretNumber)
{
  //they didn't do it.
  Console.WriteLine("Your guess was too low.");
}
else
{
  //they didn't do it.
  Console.WriteLine("Your guess was too high.");
}
Console.WriteLine("Game over.");
```

With the new code (the original example is back in Level 7), we are able to respond to the three possible cases when the player guesses – they guess the secret number correctly (playerGuess == secretNumber), they guess a number that is too low (playerGuess < secretNumber), or they guess a number that is too high (playerGuess > secretNumber). As with the previous examples, only one of these three logic branches will run. Take some time to try this little guessing game before moving on to our last example of this section, where we'll put a twist on our hero builder examples:

```
//let's name the hero
Console.Write ("Hero name: ");
string heroName = Console.ReadLine();

//let's figure out what the hero does
Console.Write ("Hero profession (fighter/magician/bard): ");
string heroProfession = Console.ReadLine();

Console.WriteLine();

//variables for our hero's stats

int heroHealth = 0;
int specialSkillPoints = 0;

if (heroProfession == "fighter")
{
        //is this a good starting setup for a fighter?
        heroHealth = 100;
        specialSkillPoints = 5;
}
else if (heroProfession == "magician")
{
        //is this a good starting setup for a magician?
        heroHealth = 55;
        specialSkillPoints = 15;
}
else if (heroProfession == "bard")
{
        //is this a good starting setup for a bard?
        heroHealth = 75;
        specialSkillPoints = 10;
}
else
{
        Console.WriteLine("Sorry, that profession isn't available.");
}
```

```
string output = heroName + ", a " + heroProfession
    + ", has entered the battle with " + heroHealth
    + " health, " + specialSkillsPoint
    + " skill points for the journey.";

// ... and output our string
Console.WriteLine(output);
```

In this example, we're using an if-else-if structure to determine the starting stats of a hero character based on user input. Each of our possible hero configurations depends on the profession that is input by the user – fighter, magician, or bard (a kind of heroic musician). A final else clause helps to catch any professions that the user enters that we might not be set up to handle right now – like pirate, space marine, or professor (those professions might be introduced in a later update, like DLC).

Things to Think About with If-Else-If

Here are some things to keep in mind when using if-else-if statements in your games and programs:

- *No limit on number of conditions or branches:* Most of the if-else-if examples have three conditions, or branches, while the hero stats and profession example has four. They are all small-ish to make them easier to understand, and so they fit nicely within the pages of this book, but there is really no practical limit to how many conditions or branches your if-else-if can have. Need five branches? No problem. Need 10 branches? Ok! Need 100 branches? Doable, but pay very close attention to the logic, because that many branches will be hard to keep track of.
- *Only one branch will execute:* This is a really, really important point and is a key feature of if-else-if statements. As soon as your program finds a condition that is true, those statements will run, and the rest of the if-else-if will be skipped. If all the conditions are false and you have an else clause, that will run instead. If all the conditions are false and you don't have an else clause, then nothing will run (like a simple if-statement that has no else). Code and run any or all of the examples from the previous section and see if you can find input values that will force more than one condition or branch to run (hint: you won't be able to).

- *Conditions shouldn't overlap or have gaps:* When we write simple if-else statements, there are only two options for our logic – either the condition is true or it's false. But when we write if-else-if statements, it is possible for us to overlap our conditions or even to have conditions with gaps that don't catch certain values. Both of these are types of logic errors that are found only through careful testing of our if-else-if conditions.

- *You don't need a final else, but you should probably have one:* All of the examples in the previous section end with an else clause. It's common to use an else clause as your final "condition". In the hero health example, the else handles the "empty room" case. In the very difficult guessing game, the else handles the "too high" guess. In many cases, an else clause is something of a safety net – if there are any gaps or errors in your if-else-if logic, an else clause can help you find them. Often, the else clause of my if-else-if statements is simply an output statement like "something unexpected has happened". Try adding an else branch if you're seeing strange if-else-if behavior.

Nested Ifs

So far, we've looked at ways to code multiple outcomes from a single question or condition like what happens when my hero enters the room, or how did the player's guess compare to the secret number, or how should I set my hero up given their chosen profession. Sometimes, we want to ask more than one question or check more than one different condition. In some cases, we might use more than one if-else or if-else-if statements in a row. For example, if our hero visits three different rooms, we might have three separate if-structures to deal with each room – one at a time.

In other cases, we might want to check more than one condition at the same time. Let's say your game has a magic user that can cast a lightning spell, but they need to be at least magician level 9 (because that's when you get to learn the lightning spell) and they need to have some mana points left. Mana points are the magic equivalent of health points – no mana, no spells. How can we express this in code? One way is to nest one if-statement inside of another, like this:

```
int level = 9;
int manaPoints = 3;
Random rng = new Random();
int lightningDamage = 0;
```

```
if(level >= 9)
{
        if(manaPoints > 0)
        {
                lightningDamage = rng.Next(10,21);
                manaPoints--;
                Console.WriteLine("Lightning streaks across
                the room for " + lightningDamage + " damage!");
        }
        else
        {
                Console.WriteLine("No mana points - can't cast lightning.");
        }
}
else
{
        Console.WriteLine("Sorry, I need to level up first.");
}

Console.WriteLine("That's all for now.");
```

In this code, we have an if-statement that checks to see if our magic-user has leveled up enough to cast a lightning spell. If they are below level 9, this condition is false, and we drop to the else that says our character needs to level up. However, if they are at level 9 (or more), the condition is true, and we proceed to the next condition – check that they have more than 0 mana points. If there are no mana points to spare, we print a no-mana apology and leave both if-statements. If our magic-user does have some mana points then we execute a powerful (and crackly) lightning strike with a bit of randomness for extra flair. Don't forget to subtract a mana point for the successful spell that was cast.

For some of you, this example might seem perfectly reasonable, and for others, it might seem as though our code has become a lot more complicated? In a way, everyone is right – this example successfully tests one condition (are we level 9 or up) and if that initial condition is true, we go on to test another (do we have any mana points). It does what we set out to do, but it adds a lot of structure and you have to keep track of where the code jumps to in both the true and false cases. There's also no practical limit to how deeply we can nest ifs. Our example only nests two conditions, but we can definitely add more logic if we have more conditions to check – maybe we need to be a level 9 magician, have enough mana points, be wearing orange robes, have a dragon tooth wand, and it needs to be a Tuesday to cast the lightning spell. Of course, this means even more structure and logic branches to keep track of.

We could do more nested-if examples here, but there are few cases where nested ifs are the best solution to a multiple-condition logic problem. In fact, I recommend that you avoid them when you can. I'm showing them here for three reasons. First, you're going to come across them if you are reading other textbooks, working with other people's code, or even searching for helpful solutions on the Internet – you should know that nesting ifs is possible and does work. Second, we all approach and solve problems differently. If you have a coding challenge and you want to solve it with nested ifs, go for it! You can always come back and change your solution if all the nesting starts to get out of hand. Third, there are rare cases where nested ifs are the best or only solution to a problem. But, for all the other cases, let's take a look at how we can simplify our multi-condition if-statements using the C# boolean operators.

Strict Decisions with && (and)

Here's the situation – you, a brave programming adventurer, find yourself needing to satisfy more than one condition in your game or program. Furthermore, you want to code it elegantly and without a whole bunch of extra curly braces and logic branches to worry about. This is exactly what boolean logic operators are for! There are two important "connecting" operators that allow us to test conditions together. They are && (and) and | | (or) – which one you use depends on the problem you are trying to solve. In this section, we'll look at && (and). In the next section, we'll look at | | (or).

Let's revisit our previous magic-user example where we nested one if-statement inside of another in order to code this two-condition "event" – cast a lightning spell if our character is at level 9 or higher AND if they have some mana points to spare. Writing the logic out like this, in words I mean, might help to make it clearer that we cast our lightning spell only if both our level and mana points conditions are true. Our nested-if code works, but here is another way that we code this:

```
int level = 9;
int manaPoints = 3;
Random rng = new Random();
int lightningDamage = 0;

if(level >= 9 && manaPoints > 0)
{
    lightningDamage = rng.Next(10,21);
    manaPoints--;
    Console.WriteLine("Lightning streaks across the room for "
                            + lightningDamage + " damage!");
}
else
{
    Console.WriteLine("Sorry, no lightning. Check level and mana points.");
}
```

TABLE 17.1

Pairs of Values That Might be Used In the level and manaPoints Variables

level	manaPoints	Did we cast the lightning spell?
6	0	???
10	0	???
6	3	???
10	3	???

This new version is much more compact – there is only one if and one else. We were able to do away with the nesting by putting both conditions inside the if round brackets (parentheses). Stop here and try coding this example for yourself. Run the program a few times and try changing the values of level and manaPoints in your code as shown in Table 17.1. As you go through the table, consider each pair of values for the variables level and manaPoints – will our character successfully cast lightning, yes or no?

If you try it out, and maybe fill in the ??? parts of the table, you should end up with something like this (Table 17.2).

Were you able to successfully predict the chance of lightning given the value pairs for level and manaPoints? If not, don't worry. This kind of logical thinking takes time and practice. Some of you might be intuitively realizing that we only successfully cast our lightning spell when we are above level 9 and have more than zero mana points. This is, after all, what we set out to do in our program. But how does this actually work – how does the compound if-statement know when the overall condition is true or false when there are two (or more) conditions that need to be checked? Let's build a new table (Table 17.3).

This new table is close to what we call a "truth table" in computer science. It's meant to illustrate how compound boolean operators like && (and || in the next section) work. The takeaway from this table is that we only successfully cast our lightning spell when both conditions on either side of our && operator are true. It's worth thinking of && as being very strict – every condition that is joined with an && must be true for the whole expression to be true. When we look at || in the next section, we'll see that it is much less strict. In the meantime, let's add another condition to our lightning example:

TABLE 17.2

Solutions for the ??? in Table 17.1

level	manaPoints	Did we cast the lightning spell?
6	0	No lightning.
10	0	Zippo, not a spark.
6	3	Still nothing.
10	3	Yay! Electricity flows ...

TABLE 17.3

A "Truth Table" That Makes it Clearer When Our Two Conditions Will Cause Lightning

level >= 9	manaPoints > 0	level >= 9 && manaPoints > 0	Explanation
6 → False	0 → False	False	level not high enough AND no mana points – no way we can have lightning here
10 → True	0 → False	False	level high enough AND no mana points – it was looking good, but with no mana, no lightning
6 → False	3 → True	False	level not high enough AND we have mana points – sorry, having mana points isn't enough when our level is too low
10 → True	3 → True	True	level high enough AND mana points – we did it. BOTH conditions were true and lightning happened

```
int health = 75;
int level = 9;
int manaPoints = 3;
Random rng = new Random();
int lightningDamage = 0;

if(level >= 9 && manaPoints > 0 && health > 0)
{
    lightningDamage = rng.Next(10,21);
    manaPoints--;
    Console.WriteLine("Lightning streaks across the room for "
                            + lightningDamage + " damage!");
}
else
{
    Console.WriteLine("Sorry, no lightning. Check level and mana points.");
}
```

In this update, we've included another condition – to successfully cast lightning, our character needs to be Level 9 (or greater) AND have some mana points to spare AND be alive (health more than 0). Everything I said previously still applies – all of the conditions must be true to cast our lightning spell. If any of the conditions are false, then no zap, spark, or crackle. That's how && works. Here's an example where we award the player stars based on their score at the end of a level:

```
//Ask the user for their score.
Console.Write("What is your final score (0 to 250): ");
int playerScore = int.Parse(Console.ReadLine());

//a variable to store the number of stars the player earned
int playerStars = 0;

//If the player's score is less than 50 then it's 0 stars for them.
//If their score is between 50 and 99, 1 star. If their score is between
//100 and 199, 2 stars. If their score is 200 and above, 3 stars.
if(playerScore >= 200)
{
        playerStars = 3;
}
else if(playerScore >= 100 && playerScore <= 199)
{
        playerStars = 2;
}
else if(playerScore >= 50 && playerScore <= 99)
{
        playerStars = 1;
}
else
{
        playerStars = 0;
}

//Tell the player how many stars they earned
Console.WriteLine("Stars earned: " + playerStars);
```

The boolean && (and) operator is a great way to check if values are between a certain range – like our player's score in the example above. Remember, while we often use && (and) to check two conditions, it works with more. Take a look at this last final example that might remind you of a certain trademarked dice game where five-of-a-kind is the best roll you can get …

```
Console.WriteLine("To win this game, all your dice must show the same
value …");
Random rng = new Random();
int die1 = rng.Next(1,7);
int die2 = rng.Next(1,7);
int die3 = rng.Next(1,7);
int die4 = rng.Next(1,7);
int die5 = rng.Next(1,7);

Console.WriteLine("You rolled: " + die1 + " " + die2 + " " + die3 + " " + die4 +
" " + die5);

if(die1 == die2 && die2 == die3 && die3 == die4 && die4 == die5)
{
        Console.WriteLine("Yahooooooo!");
}
```

```
else
{
        Console.WriteLine("Better luck next time.");
}
```

What is this program doing? It's setting up five variables that each simulate a six-sided die with random values. Then, we check to see if the first variable has the same value as the second variable, the second variable has the same value as the third, and so on. In other words, our single if-statement is checking to see if all five of our variables (or dice) have the same value. If they all have the same value, we shout (or output) "Yahooooooo!" – you can shout (or output) whatever you want, but to avoid a lawsuit from the makers of this dice game, I'm sticking with "Yahooooooo!" here. Try this example out. If you get a "Yahooooooo!" please let me know. For the curious, the odds of getting a "Yahooooooo!" when running this program are approximately 1 in 1,297 or 0.08%.

Now that we know how to check multiple conditions using a single if-structure and the && (and) operator, what can we do if we want our conditions to be a bit more relaxed?

Relaxed Decisions with || (Or)

When we write compound logic statements with || (or), we are relaxing the conditions compared to logic that uses && (and). Now, instead of needing all the conditions to be true, with || (or) we need only one (or more) of them to be true.

Imagine you are designing a platformer – classic! At the end of the level, you want to give your player a score bonus if they collect more than 50 coins OR if they manage to complete the level in less than 60 seconds. You could give them the bonus only if they collect more than 50 coins AND complete the level in less than 60 seconds, but that seems a bit harsh. Here's how we do the friendlier or more relaxed || (or) version:

```
int numberOfCoins = 65;
int levelTimer = 71;
int levelScore = 89;
int scoreBonus = 0;

if(numberOfCoins > 50 || levelTimer < 60)
{
        scoreBonus = 50;
        Console.WriteLine("You earned a score bonus!");
}
```

```
int finalScore = levelScore + scoreBonus;
Console.WriteLine("Your final score is: " + finalScore);
```

I know what you're thinking – what even is a text-based console window platformer? That's fair, but the logic in this little example will be useful when you start writing gamier games. In this example, we initialize a few helpful variables and hard-code some literal values for testing. Then we check two conditions – is numberOfCoins greater than 50 and is levelTimer less than 60. Unlike our lightning spell example, this time we have || (or) between our two conditions. For what it's worth, || is an unusual symbol and most people don't use it frequently. It is made up of two vertical lines called "pipes" and on most keyboards it is shift-backslash (\).

By using || (or) instead of (&&) we are saying that we're happy to give the player a bonus if they have enough coins OR finished the level quickly enough. Our if-statement has no else because it's not needed in this example. Whether the player earned the score bonus or not, we calculate the final score and output it to the console.

Try running this program a few times with different values for numberOfCoins and levelTimer. Use the values in Table 17.4 to help guide your testing.

Again, if you fill out the ??? part of the table, it should look something like Table 17.5.

This logic might seem intuitive to some people – we have two conditions, and we're looking for either of them to be true by saying this condition OR that condition. But let's formalize it a bit more to make sure we're all on the same "page" (get it, it's a book … with pages) when it comes to checking multiple conditions connected with || (or) (Table 17.6).

Remember when our player tried to cast lightning and the only way they could do it is if they were level 9 (or higher) AND had some mana points left? Compare that to our bonus score example, where the player gets a bonus in three possible cases out of four. As long as at least one of the conditions is true, an if with more than one condition connected with || (or) will be true – regardless of how many other conditions are false. Let's

TABLE 17.4

Pairs of Values That Might be Used In the numberOfCoins and levelTimer Variables.

numberOfCoins	levelTimer	Did the player get the bonus?
35	100	???
60	100	???
35	45	???
60	45	???

TABLE 17.5

Solutions for the ??? in Table 17.4.

numberOfCoins	levelTimer	Did the player get the bonus?
35	100	No bonus, keep practicing.
60	100	Bonus points ftw!!!
35	45	Bonus – let's gooooooooooo!
60	45	Yes, bonus. Thanks.

TABLE 17.6

A "Truth Table" That Makes it Clearer When Our Player Will Receive a Score Bonus

numberOfCoins > 50	levelTimer < 60	numberOfCoins > 50 || levelTimer < 60	Explanation
35 → False	100 → False	False	numberOfCoins not high enough and levelTimer too high – no bonus
60 → True	100 → False	True	numberOfCoins high enough OR levelTimer too high – bonus since we have enough coins
35 → False	45 → True	True	numberOfCoins not high enough OR levelTimer low enough – bonus since we went fast enough
60 → True	45 → True	True	numberOfCoins high enough OR levelTimer low enough – bonus since we have enough coins and we went fast enough

extend this example a bit by adding a third bonus score condition if the player captures enough enemies:

```
int numberOfCoins = 65;
int levelTimer = 71;
int levelScore = 89;
int scoreBonus = 0;
int enemiesCaptured = 15;

if (numberOfCoins > 50 || levelTimer < 60 || enemiesCaptured >= 10)
{
    scoreBonus = 50;
    Console.WriteLine("Congratulations, you earned a score bonus!!");
}
int finalScore = levelScore + scoreBonus;
Console.WriteLine("Your final score is: " + finalScore);
```

With this minor code update, we now give the player a bonus if they collect enough coins OR complete the level in under 60 seconds OR capture at least

10 enemies. As long as one of those conditions is true, the player will get the bonus, even if one or more of the other conditions are false.

With this new understanding of || (or) logic, we can revisit our hero profession example and add a few more professions:

```
//let's name the hero
Console.Write("Hero name: ");
string heroName = Console.ReadLine();

//let's figure out what the hero does
Console.Write("Hero profession (fighter/space marine/magician/professor/
bard/pirate): ");
string heroProfession = Console.ReadLine();

Console.WriteLine();

//variables for our hero's stats

int heroHealth = 0;
int specialSkillPoints = 0;

if(heroProfession == "fighter" || heroProfession == "space marine")
{
    //is this a good starting setup for a fighter or space marine?
    heroHealth = 100;
    specialSkillPoints = 5;
}
else if (heroProfession == "magician" || heroProfession == "professor")
{
    //is this a good starting setup for a magician or professor?
    heroHealth = 55;
    specialSkillPoints = 15;
}
else if (heroProfession == "bard" || heroProfession == "pirate")
{
    //is this a good starting setup for a bard or pirate?
    heroHealth = 75;
    specialSkillPoints = 10;
}
else
{
    Console.WriteLine("Sorry, that profession isn't available".);
}
string output = heroName + ", a " + heroProfession
                + ", has entered the battle with " + heroHealth
                + " health, " + specialSkillPoints
                + " skill points for the journey.";
// ... and output our string
Console.WriteLine(output);
```

With very little code, we've doubled the number of professions that our hero-building program can handle. In this case, we've said that fighters and space marines are equivalent in starting stats, as are magicians and professors, and bards and pirates. This might not seem entirely realistic, but it does show off how helpful || (or) can be – and who says games need to be realistic to be awesome, right?

We ended our && (and) section with the "Yahoooooo!" program, and I want to end this section with a similar example to remind you that we can create if-statements with more than two || (or) conditions:

```
Console.WriteLine("To win this game, you need at least one 6 …");
Random rng = new Random();
int die1 = rng.Next(1,7);
int die2 = rng.Next(1,7);
int die3 = rng.Next(1,7);
int die4 = rng.Next(1,7);
int die5 = rng.Next(1,7);

Console.WriteLine("You rolled: " + die1 + " " + die2 + " " + die3
                                 + " " + die4 + " " + die5);

if(die1 == 6 || die2 == 6 || die3 == 6 || die4 == 6 || die5 == 6)
{
        Console.WriteLine("Winner!");
}
else
{
        Console.WriteLine("Better luck next time.");
}
```

This version of our 5-dice game is quite similar in code except for the if-statement which is very different in logic. Our && (and)-based "Yahoooooo!" game needed all five variables to have the same value before we could called it a win. This version needs a six on any one (or more) of the simulated dice variables. Again, for the curious, the odds of rolling at least one 6 on five dice are approximately 59%. Compare that to the 0.08% odds of all five dice having the same value and getting a "Yahoooooo!" Which game do you think will be easier to win? Try them both – it shouldn't take too many "rolls" to figure it out.

We now know that we can use && (and) to create strict logic expressions where all of the conditions need to be true. We also know that we can use || (or) to create relaxed logic expressions where any of the conditions can be true. But can we use && (and) and || (or) together?

Multiple Decisions with && and || (Together)

Yes, we can certainly use && (and) and || (or) together in the same logic expression. However, this comes with a warning – the more you mix and match boolean operators, and the more complex your expressions become, and the more likely you are to introduce logic errors into your program if you're not careful. I'm not saying to be afraid of creating awesomely complex if-statements, I simply want to make sure you approach them with a bit of caution and realize they need to be tested thoroughly to make sure they are doing what you want them to do. Let's take a look at a modified version of our player star score example:

```
//Ask the user for their score and level time
Console.Write("What is your final score (0 to 250): ");
int playerScore = int.Parse(Console.ReadLine());

Console.Write("What is your level time in seconds (1 or more): ");
int levelTime = int.Parse(Console.ReadLine());

//a variable to store the number of stars the player earned
int playerStars = 0;

//If the player's score is less than 50 then it's 0 stars
//for them. If their score is between 50 and 99, 1 star.
//If their score is between 100 and 199, 2 stars. If
//their score is 200 and above, 3 stars.
if(playerScore >= 200 || levelTime < 30)
{
   playerStars = 3;
}
else if((playerScore >= 100 && playerScore <= 199) ||
   (levelTime >= 31 && levelTime <= 59)){
   playerStars = 2;
}
else if((playerScore >= 50 && playerScore <= 99) ||
   (levelTime >= 60 && levelTime <= 120)){
   playerStars = 1;
}
else
{
   playerStars = 0;
}

//Tell the player how many stars they earned
Console.WriteLine("Stars earned: " + playerStars);
```

In this updated version, we are awarding stars based on the players score OR the time it took them to make it through the level. Now the player earns three stars if their score is 200 (or more) OR their time is under 30 seconds. They earn two stars if their score is between 100 AND 199 OR their time is between 31 AND 59 seconds ... and so on. There's no limit to how complex you can make your if-statement conditions, but it can get tricky to keep the logic straight, so make sure to use round brackets to keep your logic organized and to test your expressions thoroughly.

The Not Operator (!)

There is one other boolean logic operator, and it's the ! (not) operator. I don't like it. I don't like it at all. In my experience, it only makes logic expressions harder to read, write, and debug. The ! (not) operator inverts or flips logic expressions – what was true becomes false, and what was false becomes true. Compare these two partial if-statements:

```
if(x > 10) //if x is greater than 10
if(!(x > 10)) //if x is not greater than 10
```

This is a fairly simple expression and it might seem like no big deal to go from "if x is greater than 10" to "if not x is greater than 10". The first expression is true for numbers from 11 and higher, and the second one is true for numbers 10 and lower. But I would like to make the case that the following expression says the same thing as the "not" expression above and is easier to understand:

```
if(x <= 10) //or if x is less than or equal to 10
```

Even in our regular non-programming lives, we don't do well with negatives – we are quickly overwhelmed when people say things like "well, I don't not want to get dinner". I like to make this point ultra-clear to my students by saying "I don't not want you to pass this class by not doing the things that I don't recommend you don't not do" ... or something like that. Can you tell what I'm saying there? Honestly, I have no idea myself. The same thing happens when we add! (not) to our logic:

```
else if(!((playerScore < 50 || playerScore > 99)
                && (levelTime < 60 || levelTime > 120)))
```

Believe it or not (pun intended, yet again), the logic expression above should be equivalent to this one from our updated player stars example:

```
else if((playerScore >- 100 && playerScore <= 199)
                || (levelTime >= 31 && levelTime <= 59))
```

Which one is easier for you to understand? I'm so convinced that the second one is easier to grasp that you won't see the ! (not) operator anywhere else in this book (unless I come up with a really good reason to use it, and I'll do my best to let you know if it happens). It's good to know that it exists because you might see it in other people's code, but I highly recommend avoiding it whenever you can. It might seem like an easy "hack" to flip your logic when you're in a rush, but ! (not) never makes code easier to understand or maintain.

Side Quests

Want to Know More?

More examples for more knowledge: Mixing and matching && (and) and || (or) is a great way to create cool and complex logic for your games and programs. Look up more examples to see how interesting conditional logic can be written.

Switch statements: There is another conditional structure that C# supports – it's called a switch statement. They're a bit more complex than our if-statements in terms of structure, but many people like them. Read up on switch statements (including Bonus Level 4) and try them in some of the examples from this level.

Want to Do More?

Make mistakes: Are you still making mistakes in your code? If you're like me, it's a definite "yes"! Are you still making mistakes on purpose to learn even more about C#? Here are some on-purpose mistakes to try out:

- Try changing any && to || (or any || to &&) to see what happens when you test out the changed logic.
- Does this kind of expression work to say if x is less than 10 or greater than 15: if(x < 10 || > 15)

A bolt of lightning: Rewrite the lighting spell example from this level and change the player level and mana point variables from hard-coded to user input. Then, test the program with a few input combinations to make sure you can still cast lightning when appropriate.

More coding, more knowledge: Dig into this level's code reward and Code Quest 9. Remember to change the details to make them your own.

Code Reward – A Professional Choice

We've seen a number of example programs where we let the user build their own character. These programs are a great way to let a player express their own creativity. But what can we do if our player isn't feeling creative or if they don't know what kind of character traits they want? We can automate the process for them! This Code Reward is an extension of our character profession examples from this level, so if you're going to code this for yourself, you can look at the code from those programs to get you started. Here's what we're going to do:

- Prompt the user to enter the name of their hero. Store this in an appropriate variable.
- Create a Random object and generate a random integer between 1 and 6. Based on the random number that was generated, use an if-else-if and assign a variable to have one of six possible character professions. I'm going to use the professions from the examples in this level: fighter, space marine, magician, professor, bard, and pirate.
- Now, write another if-else-if that "randomly" assigns our character's health and skill points as follows:
  - If the profession is fighter OR space marine – health between 80 and 100, skill points between 5 and 7.
  - If the profession is magician OR professor – health between 55 and 70, skill points between 10 and 15.
  - If the profession is bard OR pirate – health between 75 and 90, skill points between 8 and 12.
- Let's practice our && (and) logic with a fun potential character boost. Generate and store two random integers between 1 and 4 – if both random integers are 1s, give your character an extra 10 health and an extra 2 skill points. Be sure to display a message if this happens – so your player can be extra excited.
- Finally, display your player's final character.

As always, work on one step at a time, and if you get stuck, take a look at my solution for a hint.

```
/*
This is a small program that builds a simple RPG-style character using some
randomness.

This program is the Code Reward for Level 8.

Author: Aaron Langille
*/


Random rng = new Random();        //We're going to use this a lot
string heroProfession = "";     //Here is where we'll store the profession

Console.Write("What is your Hero's name: ");
string heroName = Console.ReadLine();

//Give the user a sense of what's about to happen
Console.WriteLine("I will now auto-generate a hero for you");

//let's figure out what the hero does
int professionNumber = rng.Next(1, 7);

//I'm skipping the { } here to save some space
if (professionNumber == 1)
    heroProfession = "fighter";
else if (professionNumber == 2)
    heroProfession = "space marine";
else if (professionNumber == 3)
    heroProfession = "magician";
else if (professionNumber == 4)
    heroProfession = "professor";
else if (professionNumber == 5)
    heroProfession = "bard";
else
    heroProfession = "pirate";

//variables for our hero's stats and possessions
int heroHealth = 0;
int specialSkillPoints = 0;

//time to set our character stats
if (heroProfession == "fighter" || heroProfession == "space marine")
{
    heroHealth = rng.Next(80, 101);
    specialSkillPoints = rng.Next(5, 8);
}
else if (heroProfession == "magician" || heroProfession == "professor")
{
    heroHealth = rng.Next(55, 71);
    specialSkillPoints = rng.Next(10, 15);
}
else if (heroProfession == "bard" || heroProfession == "pirate")
{
    heroHealth = rng.Next(75, 91);
    specialSkillPoints = rng.Next(8, 12);
}
```

```
else
{
    Console.WriteLine ("Sorry, that profession isn't available (yet).");
}

//..and let's see if the character gets a lucky stats-boost!?
int lucky1 = rng.Next(1, 5);      //random int between 1 and 4
int lucky2 = rng.Next(1, 5);      //random int between 1 and 4
if (lucky1 == 1 && lucky2 == 1)
{
    Console.WriteLine ("Amazing! Your hero gets an extra 10 health and 2
skill points.");
    heroHealth += 10;
    specialSkillPoints += 2;
}
else
{
    Console.WriteLine ("It's not your lucky day - no stats boost today.");
}

//space the output out a bit.
Console.WriteLine ();

//let's build our final output string:

string output = heroName + ", a " + heroProfession
    + ", has entered the battle with " + heroHealth
    + " health, " + specialSkillsPoint
    + " skill points for the journey.";

// … and output our string
Console.WriteLine (output);
```

18

Code Quest 8: My First Loot Box (Part 1)

Before proceeding with this quest:

- review Level 8
- complete Code Quest 7 (optional)
- create a new Visual Studio Console project. If you need a refresher, detailed instructions can be found at the beginning of Code Quest 1.

With this quest, we're going to try and do something really practical. We're going to write the code to create our first loot box – or random loot drop, if you prefer. Sure, it won't have fancy visual effects, animations, or cool sound effects yet (this example is revisited with some MonoGame flair in the next book). What we're going to write here is a simplified version of what happens when you destroy a clay pot in a role-playing game, grab a mystery box in a kart racer, or open a loot crate at the end of a match. We have all the programming tools we need, including random number generators, if-else-if statements, and boolean operators like && (and). There is no user input in this program.

In this quest, you're going to write code that will dispense "loot" with different frequencies – this means that some of the loot will be very rare, some will be sort of rare, some will be mostly common, and some will be really common. Here are the approximate frequencies that I'll outline below, but you can change them (and the loot items) if you want (see the side quests):

- 10% chance – a small stick (a rare and terrible drop)
- 20% chance – a weak cardboard sword (a common and poor drop)
- 40% chance – a rusty steel sword (a very common and okay drop)
- 25% chance – a glowing crystal sword (a common and good drop)
- 5% chance – a scorching sword of pure flame (a very rare and great drop)

Ready to drop some loot?

DOI: 10.1201/9781003348481-18

Main Quest – My First Loot Box (Part 1)

The code in this quest should accomplish the following tasks:

1. The magic in this program comes from a single random number. Create a Random object, then generate and store a random integer between 1 and 100.

2. Initialize a string variable to have "no loot yet". In the end, this will store the type of loot that will be generated in the next step.

3. Use an if-else-if statement and the && (and) operator to assign your loot variable according to the following:

   a. If the random number value is less than 11, set the loot variable to "a small stick".

   b. If the random number value is between 11 and 29 (greater than or equal to 11 and less than or equal to 29), set the loot variable to "a weak cardboard sword".

   c. If the random number value is between 30 and 69, set the loot variable to "a rusty steel sword".

   d. If the random number value is between 70 and 94, set the loot variable to "a glowing crystal sword".

   e. If the random number value is 95 or greater, set the loot variable to "a scorching sword of pure flame".

   f. Include an else clause that outputs something like "Something has gone wrong with your loot drop. Please try again later".

4. At the end of your program, include an output statement that tells the player what loot they have earned.

5. If you have any issues with your if-else-if, make sure there are no gaps or overlaps between your conditions and that your random number is between 1 and 100 (use an output statement to see the value, just to be sure). If everything is working properly, you shouldn't see the "try again later" message at all. Be sure to test your program a few times – can you get all of the loot options to show up at least once?

Here is the output from running my version of this quest 10 separate times. To save some page-space I'm showing the output only instead of 10 full screen shots:

```
Some loot has dropped – at your feet you see a glowing crystal sword. Awesome.
Some loot has dropped – at your feet you see a rusty steel sword. Awesome.
Some loot has dropped – at your feet you see a weak cardboard sword. Awesome.
Some loot has dropped – at your feet you see a rusty steel sword. Awesome.
```

```
Some loot has dropped – at your feet you see a rusty steel sword. Awesome.
Some loot has dropped – at your feet you see a rusty steel sword. Awesome.
Some loot has dropped – at your feet you see a rusty steel sword. Awesome.
Some loot has dropped – at your feet you see a rusty steel sword. Awesome.
Some loot has dropped – at your feet you see a glowing crystal sword. Awesome.
Some loot has dropped – at your feet you see a weak cardboard sword. Awesome.
```

That's a lot of rusty swords – I sure hope they are useful …

Side Quests

Shake off the rust: If you're tired of getting rusty swords, try changing the conditions so that they are all roughly equal – ranges of 1–20, 21–40, 41–60, 61–80, and 81–100. You should get fewer rusty swords, but you'll get more sticks and even flame swords too. Adjust the ranges to suit your own game ideas.

More loot, or maybe less: Our simulated loot box has five possible items and a safety else clause. But there's no reason we couldn't have seven items, or maybe just three. Adjust the number of branches in your if-else-if and either add more swords (this is your time to shine!) or take some away. Don't forget to leave the safety else in place so that you can catch any logic errors in your conditions.

Make it your own: Do you find my output uninteresting or uninspiring? Do you prefer loot boxes full of candy? Do you prefer loot boxes with spaceship parts and pieces? Do you prefer loot boxes with candy spaceship parts and pieces? Change the event text and the variables to make this Quest more fun for you!!

My first loot box Part 2: Did you run the program a few times? Did you get lots of rusty swords but no sticks and no flaming swords? Are you worried that the loot frequencies aren't working properly? In Code Quest 9, we'll use a loop to generate more loot and double check that it's working the way we intend. When you're ready, work your way through Level 9 and into Code Quest 9.

19

Level 9: Here We Go Again, and Again

Level 8 Recap:

- If-else-if statements let us check for multiple separate conditions so that we have more control over how and when our code is executed.
- We can nest if-statements inside of other if-statements.
- Boolean logic operators like && (and) and | | (or) allow us to check more than one condition at once.
- && (and) is strict and all combined expressions must be true, while | | (or) is more relaxed and only one or more combined expressions needs to be true.

Video Games Do the Same Things Over and Over

Have you ever noticed that we tend to repeat the same actions over and over when we play video games?

- Every time we press the jump button, our character leaps into the air.
- Every time we press the attack button, our super-charged laser pistol fires a bolt across the screen.
- A wave of enemies appears, if we manage to defeat them, we upgrade our defenses just in time for a new wave of enemies to charge forward.
- We see a scene of colorful, shining jewels. We swap individual jewels to make rows and columns of matching triplets. Those jewels disappear, and random new ones take their place. This happens again and again until we run out of time or match enough triplets to move on to the next scene.
- We are given a quest. We complete the quest. Our experience points go up. We become stronger, and we are given a new, more difficult, quest.

DOI: 10.1201/9781003348481-19

Video games are full of repetition – repeating levels, repeating mechanics, repeating dialogue, repeating events, and much more. As game programmers, it's our job to code these repeating game elements and to do that we need loops. With loops, we can execute specific sections of code until the right conditions are met. This level is going to introduce you to while and for loops. We're going to look at loops that run a specific number of times (counting loops) and loops that run an unknown number of times (sentinel loops). We'll finish with a quick look at the two biggest problems when coding loops – infinite loops and loops that don't run at all.

Are you ready, brave adventurer, to learn about loops?

Are you ready, brave adventurer, to learn about loops?

Are you ready, brave adventurer, to learn about loops?

Let's go!

While Loops Are Ifs That Repeat

What if I told you that while loops are if-statements that repeat? Since we just covered if-statements in Levels 7 and 8, maybe this sounds too good to be true, but let's take a look at an example that might help to make my point:

```
int myInt = 1;
if (myInt <= 3)
{
    Console.WriteLine("Are you ready, brave adventurer, to learn about
loops?");
}
```

This code shows a simple if-statement with no else. All the familiar pieces are there – a variable (called myInt), an if-statement that checks the variable for a condition, and some code to run if the condition is true. When we write, compile, and run it, we should get this output:

```
Are you ready, brave adventurer, to learn about loops?
```

If that example isn't clear, head back to Levels 7 and 8 for a quick review. Now, let's set up our first loop with only a couple of small changes (in bold):

```
int myInt = 1;
while (myInt <= 3)
```

```
{
    Console.WriteLine("Are you ready, brave adventurer, to learn about
loops?");
    myInt++;
}
```

First, we changed the keyword if to while. Second, we added myInt++ inside the curly braces. That's it – everything else stays the same, and when we run this small program, the output now looks like this:

```
Are you ready, brave adventurer, to learn about loops?
Are you ready, brave adventurer, to learn about loops?
Are you ready, brave adventurer, to learn about loops?
```

Whoa – small change, big difference! The if-statement version was a one-off – we checked one time to see if myInt was less than or equal to 3, and then we moved on. The while loop, on the other hand, is like an if-statement that runs and keeps checking until the condition is no longer true. That part is important so let's repeat it – a while loop keeps checking the condition until it becomes false. If we draw a diagram of this program's flow, it will look something like this (Figure 19.1).

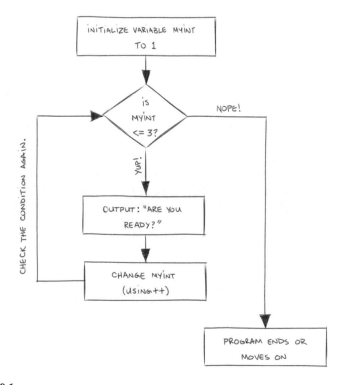

FIGURE 19.1
This is not our first flowchart, but this one shows how code can loop over-and-over again. Do you see the condition that causes this looping in the illustration?

In short, as long as the variable myInt is less than or equal to 3, we do the work in our loop body. Each time we do, myInt increases by one (thanks to myInt++). When myInt gets to 4, the while condition fails (because 4 is NOT less than or equal to 3) and the looping stops.

In general, while loops have this structure:

```
a variable with a value of interest
while(the variable meets some condition)
{
     do some cool things in here
     change the variable so that "some condition" will eventually be false
}
```

In most cases, "some condition" is related to a variable that we want to keep an eye on. When the variable changes so that the condition eventually becomes false, that's when we know to stop repeating our while loop. In our example above, the variable was myInt and the condition was myInt <= 3.

Now that we know something about while loop structure, let's look at some of the ways they can be used to repeat code in our games and programs.

Some While Loops Count

Sometimes, we want a block of code to run a specific number of times. To do this, we write what is called a counting loop. The example from the previous section is a counting loop. We initialized a variable called myInt to have a starting value of 1 and set our loop condition to myInt <= 3. By incrementing myInt by 1 each time the loop runs, we are creating a loop that runs exactly three times. Let's make a small change to the code so that we can better see how the value stored in myInt is in charge of counting our loop iterations (an iteration is what we call each run of a loop):

```
int myInt = 1,
while(myInt <= 3)
{
     Console.WriteLine(myInt + ": Are you ready, brave adventurer, to learn
about loops?");
     myInt++;
}
```

With this small update to our code, the value of myInt will be displayed along with the text of our message. This changes our output to:

```
1: Are you ready, brave adventurer, to learn about loops?
2: Are you ready, brave adventurer, to learn about loops?
3: Are you ready, brave adventurer, to learn about loops?
```

The important thing to take note of here is that thanks to myInt++, the variable is changing – incrementing in this case – until eventually the condition of our loop is false. This happens when myInt is no longer less than or equal to 3. If we change our condition, then we change the number of times our loop will run:

```
int myInt = 1;
while(myInt <= 5)
{
    Console.WriteLine(myInt + ": Are you ready, brave adventurer, to learn
about loops?");
    myInt++;
}
```

This new version will print our message five times – try it out for yourself. Another important thing to notice is that the structure of our loops is always (more or less) the same, even if we are doing different things in the loop body. Here's another example with similar structure, but performing a very different task:

```
Random rng = new Random();
int currentDieValue = 0;
int rollCount = 1;
while(rollCount <= 10)
{
    currentDieValue = rng.Next(1,21);
    Console.WriteLine("You rolled: " + currentDieValue);
    rollCount++;
}
```

In this example, I've bolded the parts of the code that make up our loop – a variable called rollCount that starts with a value of 1, a condition that tells our loop to run as long as rollCount <= 10, and a variable update statement inside the loop body so that eventually rollCount will be more than 10 to stop the loop. The parts are almost identical to our previous example – different variable names and a different stopping condition, but otherwise the same purpose or flow. The difference is that we are now simulating a twenty-sided die roll inside of our loop body instead of simply outputting a text message. In my experience, it's easier to learn about loops when you can separate the looping structure from what is happening inside the loop. Writing a loop to output a message, roll a die, battle a bunch of enemies, or read user input values always starts out the same way – with a variable, a condition, and a change that will eventually make the condition false.

Let's make another small change to our repeated die roll:

```
Random rng = new Random();
int currentDieValue = 0;
int rollTimes = 10;
int rollCount = 1;
while(rollCount <= rollTimes)
{
     currentDieValue = rng.Next(1,21);
     Console.WriteLine("You rolled: " + currentDieValue);
     rollCount++;
}
```

This is a very small change that simply moves our stop value into a variable. On its own, this change doesn't do much – the program runs exactly the same way. But it does help us to see how we can extend our example to include user input:

```
Random rng = new Random();
int currentDieValue = 0;
Console.Write("How many rolls of a d20 would you like?: ");
int rollTimes = int.Parse(Console.ReadLine());
int rollCount = 1;
while(rollCount <= rollTimes)
{
     currentDieValue = rng.Next(1,21);
     Console.WriteLine("You rolled: " + currentDieValue);
     rollCount++;
}
```

Now, this program is getting cooler. In this update, our player gets to enter how many die rolls they want to see. They might enter 1, or 10, or 1,000 – as long as they enter a positive integer, our code should give them as many dice rolls as they request. We're talking about counting loops here and even though we don't know what value the user will enter, our rollCount variable will start at 1 and count up until it reaches rollTimes. We *don't know* what the value of rollTimes will be and we *don't care* either – our program will take care of the counting for us. Code this program for yourself and run it for a few different input integers. Make sure you really test it out with some small integers, some large integers, and even some negative integers. If you test it out with a really big integer, and you get tired of watching the dice rolls scroll by, click the red stop square in Visual Studio to interrupt the program.

Now, let's take a look at some while loops that don't count iterations – instead, they just keep going until they're told to stop.

Some While Loops Don't Count

Sometimes we know exactly how many times we want a while loop to run – whether it's 1, 10, 10,000, or "user input" times. But other times we want a while loop to continue running until a condition that has nothing to do with counting is met. Think of it this way – you're playing a card game, and something happens in the game where you have to pick up three new cards and add them to your hand. You pick up your first card. You pick up your second card. You pick up your third card and you're done. If this was a loop, it would have run three times – once for each card you picked up. Now, what if something happens in your game that tells you to pick up cards until you pick up a blue card. The first card you pick up is red. The second card you pick up is green. The third card is another red card. The fourth card is yellow. This is a disaster! How many cards are you going to pick up? When will this madness end?

There is a special kind of while structure called a sentinel loop (instead of a counting loop), and its job is to run as many times as it takes to meet a certain condition. The condition for this kind of loop is different from our previous examples – it's not a matter of increasing (or decreasing) until we reach a specific value. Let's assume we want to ask the user how many health potions their hero is currently carrying. It seems reasonable to assume that this should be a number that is 0 or greater, so if we get a negative number as input, we'll loop until we get a positive value. The code might look something like this:

```
int healthPotions = 0;
Console.Write("How many health potions does your hero have (0 or more): ");
healthPotions = int.Parse(Console.ReadLine());
while(healthPotions < 0)
{
    Console.WriteLine("Sorry, a negative number won't work. Please try
again: ");
    Console.Write("How many health potions does your hero have (0 or
more): ");
    healthPotions = int.Parse(Console.ReadLine());
}
Console.WriteLine("Great! Your hero has " + healthPotions + " health
potions.");
```

I've bolded the key pieces of our loop structure – they are similar to our counting loops, but also a bit different. We have a variable called healthPotions, a condition that checks the value of healthPotions, and a way for healthPotions to eventually change. The difference in this example is that healthPotions doesn't go up or down like in a counting loop; instead, it is changed through user input. Try coding and running this example with a few input values before reading the explanation of how this code works.

In our health potion example, we are asking the user to enter a positive number. If the user enters a positive number the first time we ask them, this loop is actually skipped completely – if the user enters 5 for healthPotions before the loop, the condition (healthPotions < 0) will be false. However, if the user enters –10 or anything else that is less than 0, we'll enter the loop and try to get fresh new input from the user. Here's the important part – as long as the user keeps entering negative numbers, the code keeps executing the loop! It could run forever if it never gets positive input from the user. This is what makes a sentinel loop different from a counting loop – we really don't know when they will stop. Let's take a look at how boolean variables, sometimes called flags, can help with these kinds of loops.

Boolean Flags Can Help with Some While Loops

So far, all of the examples in this level use numbers and number variables to control when our loops run and when they end – even the sentinel loop above uses number input from the user. This makes sense because we use numbers a lot in games, but they aren't the only way that we can represent game-y elements. Aside from numbers, we've got strings for text, chars for single letters, and we've also got bools (or booleans, Level 2) that we can use for true and false states. Let's see what this means with the help of a little poison.

Your hero walks into a room. They reach into a treasure chest (or loot box), but instead of finding something that will help them on their journey, they are bitten by a mysterious and venomous creature. Your hero has been poisoned – cue the dramatic music. How are you going to deal with this in your code?

You could declare an int or float variable with the amount of poison that your hero is inflicted with. You could also have a string variable that is assigned the word "poisoned". These are perfectly reasonable ideas, and if you code things properly, they could work well. I would like to suggest storing your player's poisoned state in a bool variable instead. Here's what this might look like in code:

```
int heroHealth = 75;
bool isPoisoned = true;

Console.WriteLine("Hero starting health: " + heroHealth);
if(isPoisoned)
{
    Console.WriteLine("Oh no! Your hero has been poisoned!");
    heroHealth -= 15;
}
Console.WriteLine("Hero final health: " + heroHealth);
```

I've hard-coded this example to simplify it a bit. Most of the code should seem familiar, but the new part (in bold) sets a bool variable to true and plugs that variable directly into our if-statement. It's very important to remember (from Level 7) that if-statements use true and false conditions when deciding whether or not to run the attached code. Here, we're simply saving it the trouble of comparing anything and saying "our hero is truly poisoned". Try changing the value of isPoisoned variable to false and see what happens (hint: our hero won't take extra damage, and you won't see the poisoned output).

This kind of boolean variable is called a flag, and its job is to keep track of some true or false fact in our program. Even though the above example uses an if-statement, we can extend this idea to our sentinel (non-counting or open-ended) while loops like this:

```
Random rng = new Random();
int randomNumber = 0;
int heroHealth = 75;
bool isPoisoned = true;

Console.WriteLine("Hero starting health: " + heroHealth);
while(isPoisoned)
{
    Console.WriteLine("Oh no! Your hero has been poisoned!");
    heroHealth -= 15;
    randomNumber = rng.Next(1,101);
    if(randomNumber < 50)
    {
        Console.WriteLine("Your hero is no longer poisoned.");
        isPoisoned = false;
    }
}
Console.WriteLine("Hero final health: " + heroHealth);
```

This program is very similar in structure to the if-version above, but now instead of taking damage one time and moving on, our hero is going to keep taking damage as long as they are poisoned. How will the loop end? In this case, our hero has a 50/50 chance of self-curing each time the loop runs. Inside our loop body, we are generating a random number between 1 and 100. If that number is less than 50 (about 50% chance), we will change our poisoned flag from true to false, and when the code returns to check the loop condition, the loop will stop.

If you're going to use flags in your games and programs, be sure to name them descriptively. I use variable names that read like questions – isPoisoned, isMovingLeft, isDead – to help make it clearer that they are addressing a true or false condition. Also, use comments to make sure that you, or anyone else reading your code, can follow the logic of your flags.

Speaking of logic, let's see how we can put conditions that are more complex into our while loops. Take a deep breath and battle-on brave adventurer!

&& (and) and || (or) Work for Loops

At the start of this level, I said that while loops are simply if-statements that repeat. We know from Level 7 that we can code complex logic in our if-statements using && (and) and || (or), so it might not surprise you that we can do the same with our while loops – we can check for more than one stop condition at a time. Let's revisit our health potion example, where we asked the user how many health potions they were carrying. But this time, we're also going to limit them to a maximum of 5 potions:

```
int healthPotions = 0;
Console.Write("How many health potions does your hero have (0 to 5): ");
healthPotions = int.Parse(Console.ReadLine());
while(healthPotions < 0 || healthPotions > 5)
{
    Console.WriteLine("Sorry, a that's not a valid number of potions.
Please try again: ");
    Console.Write("How many health potions does your hero have (0 to 5): ");
    healthPotions = int.Parse(Console.ReadLine());
}

Console.WriteLine("Great! Your hero has " + healthPotions + "health
potions.");
```

Very little has changed in the program. The original version required our user to enter a number greater than zero, and this update adds an || (or) condition that says we aren't going to allow any input greater than 5. Be sure to read the while logic out loud to yourself – you should be saying something like "while the value in healthPotions is less than 0 OR the value in healthPotions is greater than 5". Our while loop is now true (and will prompt the user for fresh input) if the input value is less than 0 or greater than 5. We can make this program a bit more interesting by writing another loop to actually use the potions we've collected and introduce some && (and) logic:

```
int healthPotions = 0;
int heroHealth = 75;
Console.Write("How many health potions does your hero have (0 or 5): ");
healthPotions = int.Parse(Console.ReadLine());
while(healthPotions < 0 || healthPotions > 5)
{
```

```
      Console.WriteLine("Sorry, a that's not a valid number of potions.
Please try again: ");
      Console.Write("How many health potions does your hero have (0 or
more): ");
      healthPotions = int.Parse(Console.ReadLine());
}
Console.WriteLine("Great! Your hero has " + healthPotions + "health
potions.");

while(healthPotions > 0 && heroHealth < 100)
{
      Console.WriteLine("Your hero drinks a health potion and feels
refreshed".);
      heroHealth += 10;
      healthPotions--;
}
Console.WriteLine("In the end, your hero has " + heroHealth + " health.");
```

Our code is getting longer, and more complex, but here are some things to notice from this extended example:

- There's more than one loop – programs can have many loops!
- The second loop we've added has two conditions connected with && (and). This means as long as both conditions are true, the loop will keep running. It also means that we need to update both condition variables inside the loop body to make sure that, at some point, the loop will stop.
- One condition increments, one condition decrements. It's very common to increment loop variables using ++. After all, it's an easy way to go up by one. But it's not the only way that we can change a variable. Our second loop decrements healthPotions using −− (to show that we've used up one health potion), and heroHealth goes up by 10. You can be as creative as you like with your changing variables – just make sure that however they change, they will eventually cause the loop to stop.

We're going to see more examples of while loops that use && (and) and || (or) in the coming levels. In the meantime, let's take a look at how to restructure our counting loops in a more compact way.

For Loops Are Compact Counting Loops

Hopefully, it's becoming clear from the examples in this level that all while loops need three things to work properly:

- A variable that stores a value that will change
- A boolean (true/false) condition that involves the variable and controls when the loop body runs and when it stops
- A change in the variable that causes an eventual stop condition

It can be hard to track all three of these important elements when you're first learning about loops. Luckily, there's a more compact way of writing our counting loops using a for-loop structure. In general, it looks something like this:

```
for (initialize some variable; some condition to check; change the variable
value)
{
    do some cool things in here
}
```

Can you see all three of our loop elements in that brief and wordy description? Let's go back to our first while-loop example:

```
int myInt = 1;
while (myInt <= 3)
{
    Console.WriteLine ("Are you ready, brave adventurer, to learn about
loops?");
    myInt++;
}
```

But now we'll write it as a for-loop instead:

```
for (int myInt = 1; myInt <= 3; myInt++)
{
    Console.WriteLine ("Are you ready, brave adventurer, to learn about
loops?");
}
```

Before we do any more examples, let's use this simple one to clarify some important points about for-loops:

- The variable initialization, conditional check, and variable change all appear in the first line of the loop, called the loop header.
- We do not change the variable in the loop body – notice that myInt++ isn't in the loop body this time. The myInt++ in the loop header is all we need.
- The variable, condition, and change are all separated by semicolons (;) in the loop header.
- For-loops work the same way as counting while loops – they are simply more compact in structure by putting all the loop elements in the first line.

- Try to avoid for-loops for non-counting or sentinel operations – they're not well-suited for such tasks.

With those points in mind, here is our die-rolling example reworked to have a for-loop (go back and take a look at the while loop version for comparison):

```
Random rng = new Random();
int currentDieValue = 0;
int rollTimes = 10;
for(int rollCount = 1; rollCount <= rollTimes; rollCount++)
{
    currentDieValue = rng.Next(1,21);
    Console.WriteLine("You rolled: " + currentDieValue);
}
```

Again, notice that we aren't updating rollCount inside the loop body, just in the loop header. Here's a version with user input for the value of rollTimes:

```
Random rng = new Random();
int currentDieValue = 0;
Console.Write("How many rolls of a d20 would you like?: ");
int rollTimes = int.Parse(Console.ReadLine());
for(int rollCount = 1; rollCount <= rollTimes; rollCount++)
{
    currentDieValue = rng.Next(1,21);
    Console.WriteLine("You rolled: " + currentDieValue);
}
```

And finally, here's a brand-new example – can you tell what this code is doing:

```
int heroHealth = 100;
int numberOfGoblins = 10;
Random rng = new Random();

Console.WriteLine("You hero enters a room with " + numberOfGoblins +
" goblins.");
int goblinDamage = 0;
for(int i = numberOfGoblins; i > 0; i--)
{
    goblinDamage = rng.Next(4, 12);
    Console.WriteLine("A goblin attacks for " + goblinDamage + " damage.");
    heroHealth -= goblinDamage;
}

if(heroHealth <= 0)
    Console.WriteLine("I'm sorry to say, your hero has perished.");
else
    Console.WriteLine("After the battle, your hero has " + heroHealth + "
health remaining.");
```

If you're not sure from reading the code, try writing, compiling, and running it for yourself – that might help to clarify how this little goblin battle simulator works. Pay close attention to the for-loop that simulates our many attacking goblins. It might be a bit more fun and game-like, but it has the same elements as all the other examples in this level – a variable to watch, a condition to check, and a change that eventually stops the loop. All the loop (both counting while, sentinel while, and for) examples have something else in common – they all have a before, during, and after phase. Let's take a quick look at what that means and why it's important when writing looping logic.

Before, During, and After Loops

In Level 7, I pointed out that if-statements have a before, during, and after stage. It might seem silly to point this out again for loops, but it is important to recognize that each stage really does have an important job and that putting our code in the wrong place can cause frustrations, headaches, and errors. Here are some brief descriptions of each stage:

- *Before*: Our loop hasn't started yet – initialize any variables that we will need in our header and loop body, display any pre-loop information that is relevant to our user, and collect any input that might affect how our loop functions.

- *During*: This is our loop body – any code that needs to repeat goes in here. Don't put any output (or input) statements in here that aren't necessary. The exceptions are if you are debugging a loop problem (Cutscene 3), or if you need to collect input in order to stop the loop from running (a sentinel condition). Try to avoid declaring any new variables inside the loop body – they will not be accessible after the loop ends.

- *After*: Our loop is complete – typically this is where we show off (output) the results of our loop's work or simply continue with our program using our loop-updated variables.

Let's revisit and extend our tiny tournament stats program from Code Quest 6. Using loops, we can collect as many scores as we want and make the program even more useful. We have to do a bit more work to calculate the maximum tournament score, but it's an example that demonstrates what needs to happen before, during, and after the loop.

```
//BEFORE the loop. Initialize variables, collect input.
int currentScore = 0;        //current score being input
int maxScore = 0;            //player's max score
int scoreSum = 0;            //we need this for the average
```

```
int scoreCount = 0;            //we need this for the average
float averageScore = 0.0f;     //this is the average

//Collect input - assume good ints from the user
Console.Write("Enter the first score (-1) to quit:");
currentScore = int.Parse(Console.ReadLine());

//As long as the user enters a positive score
while(currentScore >= 0)
{
    //This is DURING the loop!
    scoreSum += currentScore;       //add the current score
    scoreCount++;                   //how many scores so far

    //If the current score is bigger than the value in
    //maxScore, we have a new max score!! (no else needed)
    if(currentScore > maxScore)
        maxScore = currentScore;

    //Collect input again - assume good ints from the user
    Console.Write("Enter the another score (-1) to quit:");
    currentScore = int.Parse(Console.ReadLine());
}

//This is AFTER the loop.
averageScore = scoreSum / (float)scoreCount;   //casting
Console.WriteLine("Your total points/score: " + scoreSum);
Console.WriteLine("Your average score: " + averageScore);
Console.WriteLine("Your maximum score: " + maxScore);
```

Try coding and running this program for yourself. It's longer than some of our other examples, but it's also pretty useful (and maybe a bit cool). Pay attention to the comments, especially the bolded notes. As a mini-practice side quest, revisit some of the previous examples in this level and see if you can identify what is happening in each of the three stages – before, during, and after the loop.

Nested Loops

In another not-so-surprising similarity, we can nest loops just like we nested if-statements (Level 7). We do this any time we want to repeat something that repeats. Here's our die-rolling example from earlier, but this time it's wrapped in a loop so that we can run the whole program more than once:

```
Random rng = new Random();
int currentDieValue = 0;
string runAgain = "yes";
```

```
while(runAgain == "yes")
{
    Console.Write("How many rolls of a d20 would you like?: ");
    int rollTimes = int.Parse(Console.ReadLine());
    for(int rollCount = 1; rollCount <= rollTimes; rollCount++)
    {
        currentDieValue = rng.Next(1,21);
        Console.WriteLine("You rolled: " + currentDieValue);
    }

    Console.Write("Do you want to run this program again?: ");
    runAgain = Console.ReadLine();
}
```

In this example, we have our die-rolling code doing exactly what it was doing earlier in the level, but now we can repeat that work over-and-over again. By wrapping our old code in a "do you want to run this again"-style sentinel loop, we have successfully nested two loops. Here are some points to keep in mind when nesting one loop inside of another:

- The first loop is usually called the outer loop. The loop in the inside is called the inner loop.
- You can nest any kind of loop inside of any other kind of loop – for loops, while loops, counting loops, and sentinel loops.
- There's no practical limit to how many times you can nest loops, but it will eventually get tricky to keep track of the code and logic.
- Each loop still needs a variable to watch, a condition that will change, and a way to change the variable to stop the loop.
- Remember, the inner loop is looping, and the outer loop is also looping. This means that the inner loop is going to run often – make sure that's the logic you're looking for. Don't nest loops when what you actually want is one loop that runs after another.

We'll see more examples of nested loops as we work our way through the upcoming levels. Here's a little spoiler of what's coming should you continue your journey with MonoGame in the next book – every loop you write in MonoGame is technically a nested loop because MonoGame is itself a loop. Game engines and frameworks have built-in loops. Strange, but true.

In the last two sections of this level, we'll look at the most common mistakes people make when writing loops – infinite loops and loops that don't run at all.

Infinite Loops

Here's some code that doesn't work properly – there's a logic error. Even with this issue, try running this example to see what happens:

```
int myInt = 1;
while(myInt <= 3)
{
    Console.WriteLine("Are you ready, brave adventurer, to learn about loops?");
}
```

If all goes well, or not-so-well I guess, you're going to get a whole lot of "brave adventurer" messages. In fact, if you leave it alone, it will run infinitely – forever! Writing your first infinite loop is a sort of programmer's rite of passage. This code comes from the very first example of this level – with one small change. Can you see why this code has gone from outputting three times to infinite messages?

We have two of the loop requirements – a variable to watch and a condition to control when the loop stops, but it's missing the variable change (myInt++;). As a result, the value of myInt never changes, so the loop condition is never-ever false and the loop goes on, and on, and on … Forgetting to update or incorrectly updating the loop variable is a very common logic mistake, and it's one of the reasons that programmers use for-loops when they can. Even though it's possible to create an infinite for-loop, it's less common since we can see all three loop requirements side-by-side in the for-loop header.

How can you make sure that you don't create infinite loops in your code? Always make sure you are updating your variable in a way that it will eventually make the loop condition false. Oh, and how do you stop an infinite loop from running in Visual Studio (maybe your example is still running now)? When your program or game is running, a red stop square appears to the right of the green play triangle that you used to start it. Usually, our programs run quickly, and we don't really notice this new button, but with an infinite loop, it will stick around. Click the red stop square, and you'll be able to edit your code again.

Loops That Never Run

What's the opposite of an infinite loop? How about a loop that doesn't run at all:

```
int myInt = 5;
while(myInt <= 3)
{
    Console.WriteLine("Are you ready, brave adventurer, to learn about
loops?");
    myInt++;
}
Console.WriteLine("Program complete");
```

If you run this example for yourself, you won't need to worry about the red stop square that we discussed above – this will run very quickly. Even though all three loop requirements are present – variable, condition, and variable update – there is a small logic error that keeps this loop from ever running. Look closely at the variable initialization – it sets the value of myInt to 5. Unfortunately, the loop condition is looking for a value that is less than or equal to 3. Like infinite loops, non-running loops are common logic errors.

The best way to make sure your loops run is to carefully check that your variables are properly set before the loop is set to start running. This is a bit tricky if you're setting the variable with user input, but if this is the case, give your player or user clear instructions on what the program needs.

Side Quests

Want to Know More?

Another type of loop: Did you notice in our while-loop examples, it's possible for a while loop to not run at all if the initial condition isn't true? In fact, all while loop will run zero or more times depending on the value stored in our variable and the condition that we're checking. But what if you absolutely need the loop code to run at least once – no matter what the variable and condition are doing? That's where do-while loops come in. They are very similar to while loops but when they check the condition is a bit different and that makes sure they run at least once. Look them up to see if they might be helpful in your code.

Want to Do More?

Examples revisited, but with more excitement: Many of the examples in this level have been hard-coded with values to help keep the code more compact. Revisit a few of them (maybe your favorites) and rewrite them to have random values or user input. I recommend checking out the poison hero, the goblin attack, and the health potion examples.

Make mistakes – before, during, and after edition: The before, during, and after phases of loops (and if-statements) might make sense to you, but what happens if you start moving some of the "before" statements into the loop? Or what about moving some of the after statements into the loop? Perhaps moving some of the statements in the loop to the before or after sections.

The variable is changing, but not in a good way: For our infinite loop example, I removed the variable-changing statement (myInt++;) completely. What happens if you put that statement back but write it as myInt--; instead? Sometimes we actually do change the variable, but we change it "wrong".

Code Reward – A More Possible Guessing Game

In Level 7, we introduced an almost impossible guessing game – we hard-coded a number between 1 and 100 and asked the player to guess the secret number. Fun! Sort of. In Level 8, we made some changes and told the player if their guess was too high, too low, or just right. It didn't make the game much easier, but at least the player was left with a bit more information. Well, brave adventurer, the time has come to turn this into a fully playable guessing game. All we need to do is add a loop that keeps repeating our game logic until the player actually guesses the number correctly. We'll add a bit more fun by randomizing the secret number, and we'll count how many guesses it takes to get it right. Here is the outline if you want to try this for yourself:

- Start with the Level 8 guessing game code
- Change the hard-coded secret number to be a random value between 1 and 100
- Introduce a new variable to count how many guesses the player has taken
- Wrap the guessing logic in a loop that iterates (repeats) until the player guesses the secret number
- Remember to increment your new guess counter in the loop
- When the loop is done (the secret number has been guessed), tell the user (output) how many guesses it took
- Pay attention to the before, during, and after stages of your loop

```
/*
This is a random number guessing game!

This program is the Code Reward for Level 9.

Author: Aaron Langille
*/

//BEFORE the loop
Random rng = new Random();

//set secret number
int secretNumber = rng.Next(1, 101);

//count the player guesses
int guessCount = 0;

//set the playerGuess to a value that is
//outside the secretNumber range and
//ensures that we will get into our loop
int playerGuess = -1;

while (playerGuess != secretNumber)
{
    //DURING the loop

    //if we are in here, the player is guessing
    guessCount++;

    //prompt the user for an integer between 1 and 100
    //this is their guess

    Console.Write("I'm thinking of a number between 1 and 100, what is your
    guess: ");

    //this is how the loop with eventually stop
    playerGuess = int.Parse(Console.ReadLine());

    //if the playerGuess is equal to the secretNumber
    if (playerGuess == secretNumber)
    {
        //they did it!
        Console.WriteLine("Amazing!!! You actually guessed it!");
    }
    else if (playerGuess < secretNumber)
    {
        //they didn't do it.
        Console.WriteLine("Your guess was too low.");
    }
    else
    {
```

```
      //they didn't do it.
      Console.WriteLine("Your guess was too high.");
   }
}

//AFTER the loop
Console.WriteLine("It took you " + guessCount + " guesses.");
Console.WriteLine("Game over.");
```

20

Code Quest 9: My First Loot Box (Part 2)

Before proceeding with this quest:

- review Level 9
- complete Code Quest 8 (required)
- create a new Visual Studio Console project. If you need a refresher, detailed instructions can be found at the beginning of Code Quest 1.

So, you completed Code Quest 8, and looking down at the pile of rusty steel swords at your feet, you're wondering if your loot box is working correctly or malfunctioning. It's a fair thing to wonder, and it highlights the importance of testing our games and programs. It's not always enough to simply write the code and run some quick tests – sometimes we need to really dig in and make sure that the code we've written works exactly the way we want it to. In this quest, we're going to use loops to really test our Code Quest 8 loot box. If you haven't completed Code Quest 8, go back and get it done – you're going to need it.

The main task here is to make sure that our loot box is working the way we want it to. It can be hard to tell if random elements are working properly without testing many, many times. We're going to use a while loop or a for loop – your choice – to pull many loot items from our loot box. The user or player will decide exactly how many times. Then, we're going to use variables to keep track of how many of each different type of item we've received. If we do this enough times, we should either find out that the loot box isn't working properly or find out that our code is working perfectly.

This quest should work whether you completed Code Quest 8 as I described or if you changed it up a bit. You'll simply need to keep track of the items and frequencies in your own code instead of comparing them to mine.

Ready to empty our "infinite" loot box and count all the items? Head to the Main Quest below.

DOI: 10.1201/9781003348481-20

Main Quest – My First Loot Box (Part 2)

This is our most complicated program so far, so it will be important, when you code it, to make small changes and test often. Try to complete each step before moving on to the next.

The code in this quest should accomplish the following tasks:

1. Start with your code from Code Quest 8 – I recommend copying and pasting all of the code from your previous Code Quest 8's Main(). Test this to make sure it works before moving on to the next step.

2. At the top of your program, create some int variables to store the counts of your different loot items. You'll need a variable for each possible loot item you might pull out. My version will need five variables: one for the sticks, the cardboard swords, the steel swords, the crystal swords, and the flame swords. If you added or removed loot items from your version, adjust your number of variables accordingly.

3. Next, prompt the user to enter the number of loot items they want to pull from the loot box. Parse and store the user's input. This is the variable that will tell our loop when to stop.

4. Below your user input statements, wrap the rest of the code in a while or a for loop (your choice) that runs the number of times input by the user. You'll need to declare and initialize another variable that counts how many times the loop has already run so that your loop will know when to stop - in other words, you need a counter variable to compare to the stopping number. What is in the loop body should be all the code needed to create a random integer between 1 and 100, the variable that stores the loot item text, and the if-else-if that assigns the loot item text according to the random number value – in short, all of the code from the Code Quest 8. If you're using a while loop, be sure to adjust your counting variable before the end of the loop body or you will write an infinite loop.

5. In your if-else-if statement – the one from Code Quest 8 that picks a specific loot item – update your loot count variables each time you pull a particular type of loot. In my example, if I pull a stick out of the loot box, my new stick count variable is incremented by 1. If I pull a cardboard sword, that variable gets incremented, and so on. Make sure you are specific variable that counts each of the loot types.

6. Finally, remove the old quest output from the program – we no longer want to know each individual item that is pulled from the loot box. Instead, after your loop body, output the value of your five loot counting variables so that you (or your user) can see how many items of each loot type were produced. With a bit of math (divide

the number of loot items of a specific type by the total number of loot pulls), you should be able to tell if the items are appearing at roughly the frequencies that we asked for.

Here is the output from my version, run three separate times (Figures 20.1, 20.2, and 20.3).

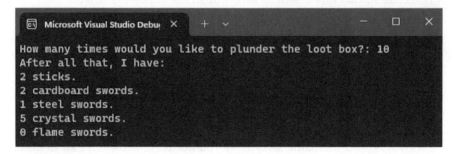

```
How many times would you like to plunder the loot box?: 10
After all that, I have:
2 sticks.
2 cardboard swords.
1 steel swords.
5 crystal swords.
0 flame swords.
```

FIGURE 20.1
Let's open ten loot boxes to see what we find ...

```
How many times would you like to plunder the loot box?: 1000
After all that, I have:
129 sticks.
193 cardboard swords.
381 steel swords.
250 crystal swords.
47 flame swords.
```

FIGURE 20.2
How about 1,000 loot boxes?

```
How many times would you like to plunder the loot box?: 1000000
After all that, I have:
100593 sticks.
191343 cardboard swords.
404721 steel swords.
252573 crystal swords.
50770 flame swords.
```

FIGURE 20.3
How about one million loot boxes?

You might notice that the more loot we pull from the boxes, the closer we get to the expected loot frequencies that we set up in Code Quest 8 (or that you set up in your changes to Code Quest 8). This kind of testing is one way that we can make sure our random number generation and logic structures are working the way we want them to.

Side Quests

Show me all the loot: If you're really curious about each individual piece of loot, print them out as they are created. There will be a lot of output, but sometimes it's cool to see everything that's happening instead of just the summary values.

Percentages are easier to see: It can be hard to tell from one million loot box pulls if we have 40% steel swords and 5% flame swords. To make it a bit easier, do a bit of math using the number you collected from the user to convert your raw counts into percentages before outputting them to the console. This will give you rough percentages that should be easier to digest.

Make it your own (again): Do you find my output uninteresting or uninspiring? Do you prefer loot boxes full of jewels? Do you prefer loot boxes with armor and trinkets? Do you prefer loot boxes with bejewelled armor and trinkets? Change the event text and the variables to make this quest more fun for you!!

21

Cutscene 3: Yikes, Gremlins!

Video Games Have Errors

Have you ever played a game that crashed halfway through a boss battle? Have you ever found a glitch that allowed you to walk through walls, fly instead of jump, or accidentally collect multiple power-ups? Have you ever suffered a fatal blow when your opponent was clearly out of attack range? Have you ever had a game that was utterly unenjoyable or unplayable until the developers released a patch or fix?

Most modern video games are very complex – they have many (many!) software pieces that work together to make your experience fun and engaging. When everything is working properly, we, as players, can easily get lost in a new world and spend hours happily collecting XP (experience points) to level up our characters. But when things aren't working properly all the fun and joy are replaced by frustration and disappointment.

As programmers, we try to write code with minimal glitches and malfunctions – preferably zero. But, as our game code gets more complex, our job can switch from programmer to bug hunter! In fact, video game software is often complex enough that big studios hire playtesters specifically to find the glitches, and many programmers get their start "squashing bugs" – fixing errors in the code – before moving on to more advanced coding tasks.

In this cutscene, I'll describe some of the reasons that different types of errors sneak into our programs. Then we'll take a look at some of the ways that we can seek out and exterminate them.

Are you ready to battle the gremlins that lurk in the shadows of our code? I hope so – because here we go!

Bugs, Glitches, and Gremlins. Oh My!

Why are there so many ways to describe the things that go wrong with our game programs? I suppose it's a matter of context and who is describing the

DOI: 10.1201/9781003348481-21

FIGURE 21.1
Gremlins may be cute, but they can cause lots of tricky errors in our code. Silly gremlins.

problem. As a programmer, I use the term "bug" when there's something not working. Gamers often say that a game "glitched-out" when something bad or unexpected happens. During World War II, pilots would use "gremlins" to describe mysterious issues with the machinery of their planes. I know, gremlins isn't a common software or programming term, but I think it's a fun and game-y way to describe weird problems (Figure 21.1).

Whatever you want to call them, errors in our programs or games are (almost[1]) never a good thing. At best they cause unexpected and erratic behavior, at worst they can cause crashes (the program stops working completely) and even corrupt our data (like game saves that can't be loaded any more).

Before we look at ways to avoid, seek out, and eliminate problems in our code, let's be clear on what we're actually looking for.

Kinds of Errors

Programming errors come in three common varieties – two we are familiar with and one that is being introduced for the first time:

- *Syntax errors*: We have no choice but to deal with these errors because they stop our programs from compiling and running at all. Visual Studio is very happy to point out these errors to us and to give us tips on how to correct them. When we're new to programming, they are our most common errors but are also the "easiest" to find and solve, in most cases.

- *Logic errors*: These are non-syntax problems in our code that cause the program to run incorrectly. They are not caught by the compiler and can only be found through testing – sometimes lots of testing. These are the errors that we are most concerned with in this cutscene.

- *Runtime errors:* These are errors that we haven't looked at yet – well, not directly, at least. They only happen when the program is running – hence, the name "runtime" errors. It's easy to confuse them with logic errors, but where logic errors can cause small problems – like subtracting from a score when we meant to add to it, runtime errors typically cause the program to crash. A common cause of runtime errors is bad input (Level 4, Bonus Level 3), but there are other ways that runtime errors cause grief. Runtime errors aren't a big concern for the examples we'll cover in our adventure together, but they do exist and can be troublesome at times. I'll leave some ideas in the side quests on what to look up if you're interested in learning more about finding and preventing them.

Let's take a look at some of the ways to avoid, find, and remove errors from our code and we'll start by removing some of the code itself!

Reduce Code

There's an old programming joke that I heard when I was (much) younger and it goes something like this:

How do you write a program with no bugs in it?
Don't write the program at all.

Okay, maybe you're not doubled over in a fit of laughter, but there are some nuggets of truth hidden between the setup and the punchline – all programs potentially have errors, and the more code we write, the more likely it is that errors will pop up. This is why many experienced programmers tell beginners to write only the statements that are needed – and no more.

What does this mean? Let's revisit some code from Level 7:

```
//start with a player score of 100.
int playerScore = 100;

//create a random object named rng
Random rng = new Random();

//generate a random bonus between 1 and 20
int bonus = rng.Next(1, 21);

//if the player bonus was 10 or more
if (bonus >= 10)
{
   //add the bonus to the score
   playerScore += bonus;
   Console.WriteLine("Final score: " + playerScore);
}
else
{
   //the bonus was 9 or less
   //subtract the bonus (like a penalty)
   playerScore -= bonus;
   Console.WriteLine("Final score: " + playerScore);
}
```

In this example, we used an if-statement to either add a bonus or subtract a penalty from the player's final score, but we put an identical output statement in both the if and the else parts. To be clear, this isn't an "error" – whether we add to or subtract from it, we want to see the final score. It is however, two lines of code where one is enough to do the job. Let's make a small change:

```
//start with a player score of 100.
int playerScore = 100;

//create a random object named rng
Random rng = new Random();

//generate a random bonus between 1 and 20
int bonus = rng.Next(1, 21);

//if the player bonus was 10 or more
if (bonus >= 10)
{
   //add the bonus to the score
   playerScore += bonus;
}
else
{
```

```
//the bonus was 9 or less

//subtract the bonus (like a penalty)
playerScore -= bonus;
}
Console.WriteLine("Final score: " + playerScore);
```

If we have the same statement in both the if and else parts, we should really move it outside the if-statement. Why is this such a big deal? After all, we saved only one line of code in an example that is about 10 statements long. The big deal is that every extra statement we write in our code is:

- more to write
- more to review when we're debugging or looking for problems
- an opportunity for more errors to creep into our program

It's easy to dismiss this example as trivial or silly, but in reality, every statement we are able to remove is a statement that future-us doesn't have to worry about. Beginners often write "extra" code because it helps to make the logic clearer to them (at least at first). I strongly agree with this approach – you should start out writing code you understand, even if it is longer than it needs to be. With practice, you'll learn to avoid some of the unnecessary lines of code. Until then, try reviewing your code from time to time and ask, "could any of these statements be removed without affecting how the program works"? If the answer is yes, get rid of them!

There are other ways that we reduce the amount of code in our games and programs. We use loops (Level 9) to repeat the same task(s) over and over. Methods (Level 10) are another way for us to write a set of related statements once and call or execute them repeatedly. Even objects (Levels 10 and 11) can help us reduce and reuse the code we write.

We're not here to write programs and games that have so few statements that they aren't fun or interesting. Instead, try to accept the idea that bug hunting and extermination are easier when we reduce the amount of not-so-useful code.

Now, what do we do after we've chopped a few useless statements from our program but it's still not working the way we want it to? Begin the testing phase!

Test, Then Test Again

The goal of testing is to ensure that our programs run smoothly and the way we want them to. If we test thoroughly and properly and everything is

A-OK, we can be confident that our players and users will have an enjoyable experience. If we test and things go a bit (or a lot) sideways, then we should really find the problem in the code and fix it. Testing our programs for errors is something that becomes more important and also more difficult as our games and programs get more complicated. Entire textbooks have been written on how to test complex software. In part, this is because complexity increases the chance of introducing errors, but it's also because there are more "things" to test. Think about our very first example – Hello, World! This program has a single output line that uses a string literal. As long as there are no syntax errors and we are able to compile and run it, if we see the correct output, then we've officially and thoroughly tested the code. In fact, many of our beginning examples are like this – if they successfully compile and run, they've also been tested. But, as we've journeyed through the levels together, our coding skills have improved, our programs have grown in complexity, and so has our need for more testing.

We can't always guarantee an error-free experience, but there are some common testing strategies that will help you to find and squash some of them – and that's a lot better than finding and squashing none of them. Here are some testing tips to consider as your programs get more complex:

- *Test often*: Sometimes we get "in the zone" and write lots of code before taking a break to compile and run what we've written. The more code we write, the more we have to work through if an error appears - especially if it's a tricky logic error. Try to write only a few lines (or whatever you think is reasonable) between test runs. If an error shows up, it's likely because of the few lines you just added – that should be easier to solve, right?

- *Comment out some code and test again*: One of the easiest ways to remove misbehaving code is to simply comment it out. If you're worried that a particular statement or set of statements are causing you problems, use line comments (//) or a block comment (/* */) to remove that suspicious code temporarily. If the error still shows up – it's not in the commented-out code, and you can uncomment it to bring it back. If the error is gone, you've found the troublesome statements, and you can zero-in on that pesky bug. Many beginners delete code (instead of commenting it out) only to find that the deleted code wasn't actually the problem. Commenting is often a much easier and safer way to isolate errors.

- *Test more than the minimum*: Don't be "lazy" with your testing. Sometimes errors will show up in very obvious and immediate ways, other times they hide in the obscure shadows of what our players and users will try to do. How much you need to test and what kinds of input or data you need to test with will very much depend on the complexity of what you're testing and how confident you want to be that it's error-free. In general, test more than the minimum of cases, input, or operations.

- *Don't overdo it*: If you spend all your time testing, you won't spend much time working on your programming project. Yes, testing is important, but so is pushing forward and getting your awesome game or program completed. Find the happy place where you have tested enough that you feel confident things are likely to work most of the time (if not all of the time) and move on. You can always come back and do more testing later if new issues come up or when you need a break from coding.

- *Ask for help*: I have a sure-fire way of making my students grumpy. When they are quietly staring at their code in frustration, I'll wander over and ask them "what seems to be the problem"? They'll quickly explain the issue and – usually in no time at all – I'll show them exactly where the problem is. It seems like I've got super-debugging powers, but in truth, it's a combination of two things: 1) I have more than 30 years of experience solving errors in my code and in my students' code and 2) fresh eyes can often see a problem where tired (and frustrated) eyes can't. It's good to practice finding and squashing your own bugs, but when you've been at it for a while and the frustration is starting to build, try asking someone else to take a look for you. Whether you ask them to run the program a few times to help find the bugs or ask them to help review the code to squash them, a fresh perspective can often be really helpful.

Let's say you've decided to buy into what I've recommended so far in this cutscene. You've written a small console game of moderate complexity. You found a few lines of code that weren't doing anything useful, and you've set them free (deleted them or commented them out). You and your game design teammates have tested the game and found 10 bugs – nine of which you were able to find and exterminate. But no matter how many times you test and no matter how long you all stare at the code, no one can seem to track down the final gremlin in the game.

It's time to put on your cap of +1 initiative and learn how to track down the trickiest errors with the help of tracer code.

Tracer (or Debug) Code

Tracer code, sometimes called debug code, is made up of output statements that tell us what our program is doing at specific times. We call these statements tracer code because, unlike our program's normal output statements, we use them to "trace" the execution of our program, and we remove them before we release our game or program to the public. Tracer code has a very specific task – to help us find logic errors in our code – and to a player our user it would be unhelpful and just look like nonsense. Let's take a look at an uncommented version of our guessing game code (Level 9: Code Reward):

```
Random rng = new Random();
int secretNumber = rng.Next(1,101);
int guessCount = 0;

int playerGuess = -1;

while (playerGuess!= secretNumber)
{
     guessCount++;
     Console.Write("I'm thinking of a number between 1 and 100, your guess
is: ");
     playerGuess = int.Parse(Console.ReadLine());

     if (playerGuess == secretNumber)
     {
              Console.WriteLine("Amazing!!! You actually guessed it!");
     }
     else if (playerGuess < secretNumber)
     {
              Console.WriteLine("Your guess was too low.");
     }
     else
     {
              Console.WriteLine("Your guess was too high.");
     }
}

Console.WriteLine("It took you " + guessCount + " guesses.");
Console.WriteLine("Game over.");
```

What I really like about this example is that it has almost every topic we've covered so far, it's a complete game (even if it's a simple one), and it's complex enough that if there's an error in the code, it might be tricky to find. If you haven't already coded and run this game a few times, I strongly recommend doing that before moving on. What I'm going to show you next is going to make the output much more "messy" but also much more helpful in finding any errors that might come up. Take a good look at the bolded output statements in the updated version:

```
Random rng = new Random();
int secretNumber = rng.Next(1,101);
Console.WriteLine("The secret number is: " + secretNumber);
```

```
int guessCount = 0;
int playerGuess = -1;
Console.WriteLine("Starting value of guessCount: " + guessCount);
Console.WriteLine("Starting value of playerGuess: " + playerGuess);
while (playerGuess != secretNumber)
{
    Console.WriteLine("At the start of the while loop.");
    guessCount++;
    Console.WriteLine("Value of guessCount: " + guessCount);
    Console.Write("I'm thinking of a number between 1 and 100, your guess
is: ");
    playerGuess = int.Parse(Console.ReadLine());
    Console.WriteLine("Current value of secretNumber: " + secretNumber);
    Console.WriteLine("Current value of guessCount: " + guessCount);
    Console.WriteLine("Current value of playerGuess: " + playerGuess);
    if (playerGuess == secretNumber)
    {
        Console.WriteLine("Amazing!!! You actually guessed it!");
    }
    else if (playerGuess < secretNumber)
    {
        Console.WriteLine("Your guess was too low.");
    }
    else
    {
        Console.WriteLine("Your guess was too high.");
    }
    Console.WriteLine("End of the while loop.");
}

Console.WriteLine("It took you " + guessCount + " guesses.");
Console.WriteLine("Game over.");
Console.WriteLine("End of the game.");
```

I know what you're thinking – what a mess! But the point of all these output statements is to give us more information about the game while it runs. Running this version of the game produces output like this:

```
The secret number is: 32
Starting value of guessCount: 0
Starting value of playerGuess: -1
At the start of the while loop.
Value of guessCount: 1
I'm thinking of a number between 1 and 100, your guess is: 50
Current value of secretNumber: 32
Current value of guessCount: 1
Current value of playerGuess: 50
Your guess was too high.
End of the while loop.
At the start of the while loop.
Value of guessCount: 2
I'm thinking of a number between 1 and 100, your guess is: 10
```

```
Current value of secretNumber: 32
Current value of guessCount: 2
Current value of playerGuess: 10
Your guess was too low.
End of the while loop.
At the start of the while loop.
Value of guessCount: 3
I'm thinking of a number between 1 and 100, your guess is: 32
Current value of secretNumber: 32
Current value of guessCount: 3
Current value of playerGuess: 32
Amazing!!! You actually guessed it!
End of the while loop.
It took you 3 guesses.
Game over.
End of the game.
```

It's likely that I've got too much tracer code in this example since I would normally only add statements where I think there might be errors in my program. But, despite the messier code and messier output, it does show the places that we often want to get a bit more clarity on how our program is running – variable values, double-checking user input, loop starting and ending conditions, and so on. Normally I'd put some tracer code in my if-statement logic, but this example only has output statements in the if, so they are acting like tracer code already. Don't forget, when you find your mysterious logic or runtime error, be sure to comment out (or delete) your trace code output statements – your player isn't going to want to see that messy output.

There is no right or wrong way to use tracer code in your programs, though some companies or teams might have standards that you'll need to follow. It's simply another programming tool that helps us to write fun, engaging, and bug-reduced games and programs.

A Bit of Style Goes a Long Way

It's easy to think that code-is-code, and that if it compiles, we're good-to-go! That's true to a point, but code that is hard to read is also hard to understand and debug. We rarely sit and write an entire game (or program) in a single coding session. It can take weeks, months, or even years, depending on the scale of the project. If the code is "sloppy" and lacking in style conventions (style elements that are common among all programs of a particular language), are you going to be able to remember where you left off, what needed to be fixed, or even what you were thinking when you wrote a particular section? Will your teammates be able to understand,

update, and use your code if it looks unorganized and confusing? Maybe …
but maybe not.

Following the style guidelines below will help your code look organized,
clear, and even professional – the kind of code that is either bug-free or
where bugs can more easily be found and squashed:

- Always use descriptive variable names that describe the value being
  stored – score, health, and numberOfGoblins are better variable
  names than s, h, and gobs.

- Use proper camel case (Level 3) for your variable names –
  numberOfGoblins is easier to read than numberofgoblins.

- Code inside curly braces (for if-statements, loops, or methods) should
  be indented. Visual Studio will help you with this one.

- Blank spaces can be used to break up chunks of code as-needed.

- Try to avoid excessively long statements – break them into multiple
  statements when you can.

- There should only be one statement per line (wherever possible).

- Line comments and block comments should be used to describe any
  statements or blocks of code that need some description.

For examples of proper style, take a look at any of the code rewards at the
end of the levels. I've tried to set a good example for you to follow with
each one.

All this talk about avoiding, finding, and fixing problematic code can
feel rather discouraging. Let's finish this cutscene with a bit of positive
reinforcement and shed some light on where these errors come from.

Stay Calm, Errors Happen

I wanted to end this level on a reassuring note – if you're finding a lot of
syntax, logic, and even runtime errors in your programs, you're not alone.
Coding errors are an inevitable part of programming and we all make
mistakes! The number and kind of mistakes we make changes as we
practice and learn, when we choose to focus more or less on what we're
working on, and even depending on the type of project we're working on.
Below are some of the common reasons that bugs, glitches, and gremlins
happen to all of us.

- *Learning*: When we first learn to program, most of our attention
  goes to the basic tasks – what is the syntax for this if-statement,

how many variables do I need for this program, why is line 14 underlined in Visual Studio, etc.? That doesn't leave us with a lot of attention for problems like – should I be using < or <= here, is there any integer division in my program that might cause math errors, or what should I do if the user enters "I like video games" when I ask them for a number. It's the same story for experienced developers when we're learning new features of our programming language, game engine, or framework – when things are new, we often make more mistakes. With time, practice, and a bit of reading and research, you'll be better able to divide your attention to both the basics of writing your games and keeping an eye out for potential problems.

- *More code, more errors*: I've said this before, but it's worth repeating – every line of code you write has a chance of introducing an error. Our examples have been, and will remain relatively short, and that means there aren't many places for errors to creep in. But our examples are also not complete, releasable, video games. Even the simplest indie titles can have thousands of lines of code, and AAA titles can have millions. With so much code, it's almost inevitable that some parts won't work perfectly all the time.

- *Rushing*: Sometimes we are in a rush to get a new part of our game written, and instead of doing things the "right way", we do them the "fast way" – hard-coding values instead of using variables or user input, skipping user input checking and assuming they will enter good values, and using short-cut algorithms instead of taking the time to write our code properly. Usually when we rush our programming, it's with the best intentions to come back to the code and fix things up, but often we forget and the "hacked" code shows up as a bug, glitch, or gremlin during playtesting. At the very least, if you're in a rush, leave yourself (or your teammate) a comment as a reminder that the code should be reviewed at a later time.

- *Lack of testing*: You write a bit of code that asks the user to enter an integer between 1 and 100. You write some input validation checks to make sure the values are entered properly (wise decision). Then, you test your code with −1, 10, and 105. Everything *seems* to work fine. How confident are you that your program will work with any integer the user might enter? Should you test inputs of 1 and 100 – the boundary cases? Should you test a few more numbers in the middle? Is there any code later on in your game that will cause problems if the user enters 81? Testing our code is essential to making sure that it works properly, but testing takes time and we often do just enough to say we "checked it". Many bugs are found in games that are "under tested" before they are released. Players love to test the limits of what they can and can't do for input (keyboard, mouse, controllers, you name it), where they can and can't go in your levels, and what they can and can't do with mechanics – if there are glitches left behind by the developers, the players will (unfortunately) find them.

- *Poor style*: Despite my mom's insistence that I clean up my room as a kid, I never did. To me, it was a "waste of time". Even though everything was scattered everywhere, I knew that I didn't want to spend my time tidying – it made more sense to me to spend the time looking for things when I needed them. Turns out, I probably wasted way more time looking for things than the time it would have taken me to tidy up my chaotic room. If you're scratching your head wondering what this has to do with programming, here it comes – messy code is like a messy room. It's easy to write code "fast and messy" today, but when it comes to fixing issues tomorrow, you're going to spend way more time working through the mess you left for yourself. Do yourself a favor and follow the C# style conventions from the last section. They may take you a bit more time and effort in the moment, but future-you will be so grateful that past-you wrote clean, easy-to-read code.

In case you're wondering, I now keep my room and code very clean. Present and future-me are both very grateful that past-me eventually learned this lesson.

Side Quests

Want to Know More?

Is this everything there is to know about bugs and testing? No, it's not! There are lots of ways to test and remove errors from your code. Do a bit of digging and see what other cool tips, tools, and techniques you can find.

But you didn't actually tell us how to deal with runtime errors: This is true, I skipped that one. Runtime errors are most common when dealing with user input on the console, when accessing array elements, and when trying to use an object that hasn't been properly initialized. It's important to deal with these errors when we are writing software that will be used by more people than us, our classmates, and our friends, but it's not really important in the context of our adventure together. There are examples of dealing with runtime errors caused by bad user input in Bonus Level 3, and I encourage you to look up try and catch blocks, the TryParse() method, and other ways of handling runtime errors.

Note

1. There are cases where an accidental logic error actually turns into a new game (or program) feature. A mistake in writing the jump mechanic might lead to a flying mechanic that ends up in the final game. But these kinds of bug-becomes-feature events are rare.

22

Level 10: Crafting Custom Objects

Level 9 Recap:

- Loops let us repeat sections of code.
- All loops keep repeating until a condition changes that tells them to stop.
- While loops can be set up to stop after a certain number of iterations (repetitions) or to keep going until some event (like specific user input) happens.
- For loops are a more compact version of counting while loops.
- Watch out for infinite loops and loops that don't run at all – these are common mistakes.

Games Are Made of Objects (Part 1)

Close your eyes for just a moment. Think about the last game you played, or even the game you are playing right now. Picture just one level, area, or scene. Now, picture everything that is in that level, area, or scene. Think about the things that are moving and the things that are still. Think about the different things you can interact with and even the things that you can't. Think about the characters, obstacles, platforms, crops, crafting ingredients, loot boxes, pickups, jewels, coins, cards, dice, information items, animations, images, and even the music and sound. Now – here's the challenging part – think about how you might write code that makes all those level, area, or scene elements work together.

Ok, maybe that last part isn't fair. After all, the goal for this level and this series of books is to start thinking about how we can represent all those cool game-y things in code. To do this, we're going to introduce the ideas of objects and object-oriented programming. Almost all modern games are made up of objects – special bundles of code that are designed to more accurately represent "real world" or maybe "real game world" things and their interactions. This object-oriented way of thinking and coding may seem a bit tricky at first, but what we're going to learn in this level and in

DOI: 10.1201/9781003348481-22

Level 11 will make our games and programs much more interesting and (eventually) easier to code.

In this level, we're going to learn how to write object classes or "blueprints" that will define what potential objects can do. Don't worry if you're not sure what that means yet, that's what we're here to figure out together. We're also going to introduce the idea of methods (sometimes called functions). In the next level, you'll learn how (and where) to use these blueprints to create objects that we can use and control in our programs and games.

If you want, you can skip this level (and Level 11) and jump to some of the early MonoGame content and examples in the next book. You have lots of awesome programming knowledge now about data types, variables, math operations, random numbers, if-statements, and loops. This is all you need to get started with MonoGame. However, to make things more interesting, fun, and like real game design, the later MonoGame examples use objects – so come back here and go through this level (and Level 11) when you need them.

Either way, we've saved the most challenging – and rewarding – levels for the end of our console journey. In true video game fashion, you're going to use everything you've learned so far. So, put on your best armor, recharge your energy, and rev the engine of your kart to maximum, because our adventure is about to become objectively (pun intended, yet again) cooler.

Why Object-Oriented Programming?

Before looking at the "how" of object-oriented programming (OOP), let's take a quick moment to try and understand why this book is using OOP as a way of writing more advanced code. If you've been programming for a while now, or if you happen to hang around with programmers (a really awesome bunch of people, I'm sure), maybe you've already heard of OOP, data-oriented programming, functional programming, composite architectures, or any number of other ways of writing complex software and games.

Each of these software-writing models (or paradigms) is designed to help us coders write great software as efficiently and effectively as possible. They all have their strengths and weaknesses that make them appropriate for some projects and a poor choice for other projects. Some focus on speed and performance, while others focus on ease of programming. Some of them are newer and seem more exciting, and others have been around for some time and are more established with a larger community to support us.

I've chosen to introduce you to OOP in this series of books for a few reasons:

- It is well-established with lots of resources to help you learn and practice.
- OOP is still taught in most college and university coding courses.

- Understanding the principles of OOP will help you in your quest to learn other programming paradigms.
- Most modern game engines, including Unreal Engine, Unity, GameMaker, Godot, and more, support multiple programming paradigms including OOP.
- MonoGame, the subject of the next book in this series, is well-suited for OOP.

It would be great if this series of books could introduce you to all of the major programming paradigms that are commonly used today. Who knows, maybe more "Welcome Brave Adventurer" books will do just that. But, for now, let's focus on the popular, robust, and effective OOP!

A Change in Thinking – Object-Oriented Programming

This level is going to ask you to do something that can seem pretty challenging – write code that is meant to represent "real" or at least "game-real" objects (Figure 22.1).

FIGURE 22.1
Object-oriented programming means thinking of our game elements as having attributes and behaviors. It really helps if you can visualize your objects like this courageous hero and sturdy die.

Before now, we wrote code that calculated, looped, and logiced, but in this level, we are going to simulate. To better understand what this means, let's revisit the code for our die and our simple hero (from previous levels). The die is just a few statements like this:

```
Random rng = new Random();
int numSides = 6;
int myRoll = rng.Next(1,numSides);
Console.WriteLine("You rolled: " + myRoll);
```

This works, but it doesn't seem very natural. In real life, we would pick up our pre-configured die and then roll it. When the die stops rolling (across the counter top, the table, the floor, or down the stairs), we would then take a look at what number was facing up. Our code – while functional – is missing those real-world "behaviors". What about our simple hero:

```
string heroName = "Chell";
int heroProfession = "Test Subject";
int heroHealth = 100;
int damageTaken = 15;
heroHealth -= damageTaken;
```

Again, we have the same issue as our die – this code works, but it doesn't feel very heroic. Instead of a loose collection of variables and statements, our hero should feel more whole with behaviors like taking damage, dealing damage, and even perishing (oh no!). If we're going to put this hero in a game, we might also want them to have coordinates (where they are on the screen), inventory (what they are carrying), and even animations.

Surely, there has to be a better way to represent these cool game-y things than just a bunch of loosey-goosey C# statements, right? What we're going to start doing in this level is bundle our game object statements into a new structure called an object class. Using object classes, we'll be able to create attributes (properties) and behaviors (actions) that more easily and realistically simulate the things we find in games (Figure 22.2).

Don't worry! The code we've learned so far isn't going away – many of the statements we write will seem very familiar it's the structure and how we interact with that structure that's going to be new.

It is very natural to find the idea and the structure of OOP to be confusing and even frustrating at first. In the case of simple objects, like dice, we're actually going to create way more code than we need to – just so we can treat them like objects instead of simple variables. But, as our programs and games get more complex and as you become more comfortable with writing and using objects, you'll find that it really is the most effective, efficient, and natural way to represent our game elements. Give it time, and more importantly, give it practice, and your games will spring to life with OOP-y goodness!!

My goal with this level (and Level 11) is to introduce you to the fundamentals of OOP so that you can make more interesting console (and MonoGame) programs. You can certainly do cool things without learning to write your own objects, but with them, your games and programs will really shine. It's also worth repeating that most modern game engines and app frameworks take an object-oriented approach. It is definitely an important topic, and while we're only going to touch on the essentials here, I encourage you to keep learning about OOP after you're done with these books.

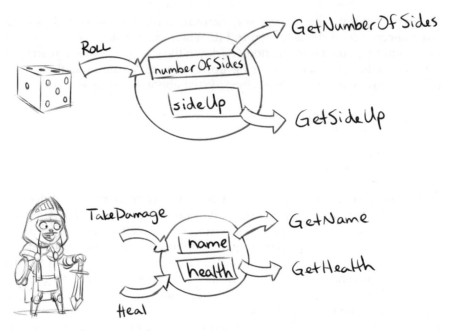

FIGURE 22.2
Sometimes it's helpful to simplify our idea of what objects are. Here we are using circles to show what attributes each of our object types has, as well as the behaviors that allow us to inspect and alter them.

My Approach to Teaching and Learning OOP

It's easy to think that programming is a one-way-only type of exercise – as if there is only one right way to complete a task. This might be true when our programs are very simple, or it might be true for very specific and technical elements, but outside of those cases, there are many ways to do almost everything. Yes, programming is largely a technical exercise, but there are lots of places where you can let your personal creativity and experience guide you. OOP is a great example of a technical structure driven by creative ideas.

What I'm going to show you in this level is a classic approach to writing object classes. We are going to securely encapsulate our object attributes. We are going to write full methods to set and access our object attributes. We are going to write our own constructors and ToString() methods. If none of that makes sense to you yet, don't worry because we're going to discuss all of those ideas. The point I'm trying to make here is that I'm going to show you how to write object classes based on my own experiences as an instructor and programmer – it's a way that I hope will make all of the important object-oriented features both clear and interesting.

But my way isn't the only way. There are lots of useful shortcuts and creative efficiencies that are built into C# (and Visual Studio) that can help you write awesome objects in the future. As your programming adventure extends beyond these books, you might find yourself on a team that has its own "best practices" for writing object classes. Even if you decide to code-solo, you'll develop your own way of doing things over time.

This level is where we're going to learn the first part of OOP – writing object classes, sometimes called object blueprints. There will be lots of code examples for you to follow along with, and while you'll be able to compile the code to make sure the syntax is accurate, you won't really be able to run and test the objects until our journey reaches the next level. In Level 11, we're going to look at how to use the object blueprints to create and interact with objects. We'll use die and hero object examples through both levels, and there will be a bonus object waiting for you in the code reward.

Alright adventurer, we've set up the quest, we've given it some background, and we know what's waiting for us when it's complete. Are you ready to leave the inn (or space dock, or cozy farm, or start screen) and get started?

Creating a New Object Class for Our Project

In all of the previous levels, we have created our projects in Visual Studio and written our program's code in the Main() method of the file Program.cs. Now, we're going to create new files to store our object classes or blueprints. We do this so that the code for each of the objects we write is kept separate. After all, we might write many different objects for a single program or game, and it is much simpler to keep track of them all if they are in different files.

Assuming you have created a new Visual Studio console project or have opened an existing project that you want to add an object class to, there are two ways to start creating new class files:

1. Use the Project drop-down menu to select Add Class.
2. Right-click your project name in the Solution Explorer tab and select Add, and then select Class.

Either way, you should see a window that looks something like this (Figure 22.3).

Make sure you highlight the option that says Class and has the small C# icon beside it. Now, and this part is very important, at the bottom you're going to specify the name of your class. By default, it says Class1.cs, but

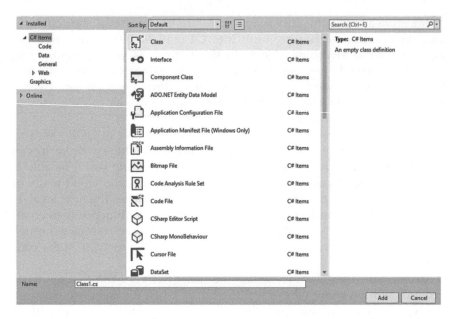

FIGURE 22.3
Creating a new class file in our Visual Studio project means opening a new window like this one. Be sure to name your class file in a way that properly reflects the type of object you are going to describe with code.

when we write object classes, we need to name the file with the same name as the type of object we're creating. What does this mean? If I'm creating a die class, then I want my file to be named Die.cs. If I'm creating a hero class, then I want my file to be called Hero.cs.

If you're following along with this level's examples, create a new Visual Studio project and add a new Die.cs and Hero.cs file. When you're done, you should see the files in your solution explorer like this (Figure 22.4).

If you want to see the code that Visual Studio creates by default, click each of the files in the solution explorer. They should open in the main editor window, and, aside from a different project or namespace, the Hero class should look like this:

```
namespace MyFirstObjectClasses
{

    internal class Hero
    {
    }
}
```

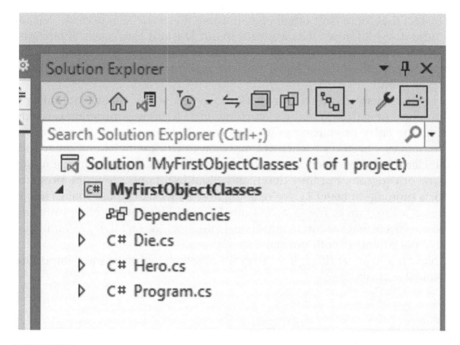

FIGURE 22.4
The Solution Explorer pane will help you keep track of all your object class files.

And, the Die class should look like this:

```
namespace MyFirstObjectClasses
{

    internal class Die
    {
    }
}
```

I know, neither file has much to look at yet, but let's consider what code is (and isn't) there:

- In terms of structure and syntax, the two object classes are similar to the code we've seen and written before.
- There is a namespace, just like all our previous C# files – mine is MyFirstObjectClasses because that is the name of my Visual Studio project.
- Previously, we would have worked in a class called Program (internal class Program), and we will again in Level 11. Here our example classes are called Hero and Die.
- There is no Main().

The fact that there isn't much code in these files is to be expected – Visual Studio doesn't know what we want in our Die and Hero class blueprints. It's our job to write that code, and we'll learn how to do that in the coming sections of this level. But the lack of Main() deserves a bit of explanation.

Try to remember, all the way back to Level 3, where I said that Main() is the "entry or starting point for our program". A game or program can only have one entry or starting point, and for all of our projects, it belongs in Program.cs – even if or when we move on to work with MonoGame. Both the Hero and Die object classes will describe objects that we can use in our game or program, but they don't, and shouldn't, impact how the program starts running. In Level 11, we're going to see how we can use Main() in our project's Program.cs file to access our Die and Hero object blueprints and create objects that we can manipulate. Until then, the fact that Die and Hero have not Main() is both normal and appropriate.

Now brave adventurer, let's give our object classes their most important element – attributes.

Attributes – The Heart of Our Objects

What are a hero's most important attributes or qualities – bravery, strength, honor, and the ability to get along well with others? These are very heroic attributes, but when it comes to video games, especially when we first learn to program, we can probably get away with a name and a number of health points to get us started. What about dice? What properties matter most? If you're like me, you value coolness – awesome colors that glow in the dark, or maybe weird shapes and patterns that make them look ancient or futuristic. But, for practical reasons, the most important attributes of a die are the number of sides it has and which side is currently up (that's the side that matters the most).

When we write object classes for our games and programs, we need to decide on the attributes – or properties – that define the current state of the objects that we'll (eventually, in Level 11) create or use. It's easy to get carried away and to try to add all sorts of wild and wonderful details, but it's always a good idea to include only those attributes that are most important for the functioning of your object. You can always come back and add more attributes to your object class (blueprint) later if you find that something is missing. A good starting place is to ask yourself:

1. What attributes are most essential for my object to function properly?
2. What data type should the attributes be?
3. What are good names for the attributes?

TABLE 22.1

An Example of Determining Which Attributes Are Most Appropriate, What Data Types They'll Be, and What Names They Will Have

	Die	Hero
Essential attributes	1. Number of sides 2. Which side is face-up	1. Hero name 2. Health value
Data type	1. int (we can't have a decimal number of sides) 2. int (we can't have a decimal side up)	1. String (because text) 2. int (but a float could work if that's better for you)
Attribute name	1. numberOfSides 2. sideUp	1. heroName 2. heroHealth

For each of our objects, it's good to write down the attributes we'll need to code in the object classes. It's also good form to write down the data type and variable names that we'll use for these attributes. In Table 22.1, you can see how I would approch the three attribute questions for our upcoming Die and Hero objects.

With answers to these questions, we start adding some code to our object class. The code for our object attributes goes inside the class curly braces, like this for the Hero:

```
namespace MyFirstObjectClasses
{

    internal class Hero
    {
        //Hero attributes to store the state of a Hero object
        private string heroName;
        private int heroHealth;
    }
}
```

The attributes for the Die also go inside the class curly braces, like this:

```
namespace MyFirstObjectClasses
{

    internal class Die
    {
        //Die attributes to store the state of a Die object
        private int numberOfSides;
        private int sideUp;
    }
}
```

You might notice that in both cases we are simply declaring variables with two minor differences from examples in previous levels. The first difference is that they are inside object classes, and we're calling them something new – attributes – because they now have a special job. Remember, we are writing blueprints that will define how future objects are created and used. For now, we're simply saying that all our heroes will have string names and int health values, and that all our dice will have integers for the number of sides and side-ups. We might imagine them to look like this for now (Figure 22.5).

Some of these values will be set once, like the hero's name and the die's number of sides, and some will change throughout the game, like the hero's

FIGURE 22.5
This is a simplified view of our objects and their attributes. We'll add more complexity to our image as our object classes get more code.

health and the die's side up. The specifics of how those values are set and changed will be revealed in the coming sections. The specifics of when those values are set and changed will be revealed in Level 11.

The second difference from previous variable declarations is the keyword *private*. We haven't seen that keyword before, mostly because we haven't needed it for anything. However, privacy and protection are very important ideas in OOP. By setting our object attributes to private, we are encapsulating (or protecting) them from direct access from any other object or code that is, or might be, interacting with our objects. I know, from lots of experience and conversations with new coders, that what I just said doesn't make a lot of sense right now. Privacy? Protection? Encapsulation? Direct access?

Think of it this way, in the real world, objects have built-in mechanisms that prevent you from doing undesirable or silly things to them. When dice are manufactured, the number of sides is firmly set, and they arrive in our hands or pockets in a non-changeable state – usually in the form of hardened plastic, metal, or unbreakable glass. Also, the only fair way to change the side up is to roll them properly – we can't (or shouldn't) manually flip them to whatever "side up" that we want.

Similarly, once a real-world hero's name is set, it usually sticks (though a heroic name change could certainly be possible), and their health is usually protected by bones and muscle and skin and armor (and maybe some cool magic). The only acceptable way to affect a hero's health is for them to engage in battle, have a run-in with the environment, drink a health potion, or spend a restful night in a friendly inn – we can't simply force them to have an arbitrary health increase or decrease.

In code, we represent these kinds of protections by labeling our object attributes as private. When they are private, attributes can only be directly modified by code inside the object class or blueprint. We allow our game to safely change and manipulate our objects through special methods called mutators and accessors (or setters and getters), which we'll write later in this level and we'll learn to use in Level 11. This way, we can say "hey, a die object must be rolled properly to get a new side up" or "hey, a hero's health can only be changed through damage they suffer, or through proper healing".

There are alternatives to private but they should only be used in special cases, and for now, I strongly recommend that you leave your attributes private until you feel more comfortable writing and using object classes. Making your attributes public allows other objects and parts of your game (or program) code to modify and access them without any safeguards – like setting the side up on your die to any integer (even negative ones) or changing your heroes' health in a way that might not make any sense at all (Figure 22.6).

You can also make them protected, which allows them to be directly accessed and manipulated by "related" classes or objects but protected from others. This is a feature of object inheritance that we won't cover in these

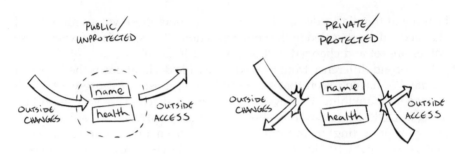

FIGURE 22.6
When we use the private keyword on our attributes, we are protecting them from accidental
changes that might happen in other files or programs in our project. The idea of protection, or
encapsulation, is a bit tricky at first, but it's still worth putting private in front of your attributes.

books. For now, it's enough to know that setting your object attributes to
private is a good and safe object-oriented coding practice. With that in
mind, let's learn how to set our attributes' default values.

Constructors – Setting the Default Attribute Values

In the previous section, we said that both our Die and Hero objects would
have two attributes each – numberOfSides and sideUp for the Die,
heroName and heroHealth for the Hero. What we didn't do is say what
values those variables would be set to. This is where constructor methods
come in handy. Methods, which we're seeing for the first time here, are
small bundles of code that perform a specific task. When writing object
classes, methods are the behaviors, or actions that our objects can perform
and constructors are special methods that are designed to set the starting or
default values for the objects that we'll create and use in our game.

For the Hero class, a first constructor might look something like this:

```
namespace MyFirstObjectClasses
{

    internal class Hero
    {
        //Hero attributes to store the state of a Hero object
        private string heroName;
        private int heroHealth;

        //Unparameterized constructor (no parameters)
        public Hero()
        {
```

```
            heroName = "Unknown Hero";
            heroHealth = 100;
        }
    }
}
```

A first constructor for the Die class might look something like this:

```
namespace MyFirstObjectClasses
{
    internal class Die
    {
        //Die attributes to store the state of a Die object
        private int numberOfSides;
        private int sideUp;

        //Unparameterized constructor (no parameters)
        public Die()
        {
            numberOfSides = 6;
            sideUp = 1;
        }
    }
}
```

There are a few things to pay attention to in this new code:

- The first line, called the header, starts with the word public (yes, this one needs to be public so that it can be used to create objects later), followed by the type of the object (Hero or Die), and round brackets.
- The constructor has its own set of curly braces { }.
- Inside the curly braces is the code we need to give all our attributes a value.
- The constructor including the header (first line), its curly braces and the code inside all sit within the class curly braces.

What we've done with these few lines of code, is define the values that our attributes will have when we eventually create objects using these blueprints. When we create a Hero object, it will have the name "Unknown Hero", and it will have 100 health points. When we create a Die object, it will have six sides and the one will be the side that is up. The constructor's job is to set the objects' default values, and the way we've written these constructors, all objects of the same type will have the same starting attribute values. If we create a thousand Hero objects, they will each have the name "Unknown Hero", and they will each have 100 health points.

Similarly, if we create a million Die objects they will each have six sides and they will all be showing one as their side up.

To make our objects more interesting, we can write constructors that are more flexible using parameters. For our Hero class, it would mean writing something like this:

```
namespace MyFirstObjectClasses
{
    internal class Hero
    {
        //Hero attributes to store the state of a Hero object
        private string heroName;
        private int heroHealth;

        //Unparameterized constructor (no parameters)
        public Hero()
        {
                heroName = "Unknown Hero";
                heroHealth = 100;
        }

        //Parameterized constructor (two parameters)
        public Hero(string nameIn, int healthIn)
        {
                heroName = nameIn;
                heroHealth = healthIn;
        }
    }
}
```

In this updated version, we've added a second constructor. Notice that the header is very similar to the one we had before, but now there are variables inside the round brackets. These variables are called parameters, and when the time comes to create our Hero objects (look out for Level 11), these parameters will let us specify custom name and health values. The parameter types match the types of our attributes, but the names are different from our attribute names – this helps us to keep track of which variable is the object attribute and which is the constructor parameter. In Level 11, we'll take a closer and more illustrated look at how this works and how we can use these parameters to pass interesting values to our constructors and create objects that have unique attribute values. For our Die example, we might set up a second constructor, including a parameter like this:

```
namespace MyFirstObjectClasses
{
    internal class Die
    {
        //Die attributes to store the state of a Die object
        private int numberOfSides;
        private int sideUp
```

```
        //Unparameterized constructor (no parameters)
        public Die()

        {
                numberOfSides = 6;
                sideUp = 1;
        }

        //Unparameterized constructor (one parameter)
        public Die(int sidesIn)

        {
                numberOfSides = sidesIn;
                sideUp = 1;
        }
    }
}
```

Notice that for the Die constructor, we only have one parameter to set the number of sides. The number of parameters in your constructor header is a matter of how many variables you think you might need to pass in when an object is created. For the Hero, it might make sense to pass in a value for both the name and the health attributes. But for our Die, it doesn't make much sense to set a starting value for the sideUp variable. Don't get me wrong – you certainly could add a parameter for sideUp if that's what you need for your program or game, but in this example, I'm going to allow different dice objects to have a different number of sides, but they'll all start with a sideUp value of 1 (for now!).

At this time, both our Hero and Die object classes have two constructors each. They both have a zero-parameter constructor that hard-codes default values for the attributes, and they both have a parameterized constructor that allows us to specify different starting attribute values during object construction. This is a common thing to do in OOP. Sometimes you might want to create objects and pass no information in, and other times you might want your objects to be created with specific starting values. By writing different constructors in our object classes (blueprints), we give ourselves (or our coding teammates) options. We'll see how to take advantage of those options in Level 11.

Before we leave constructors behind, let's take a moment to consider our two parameterized constructors from our two examples. The constructor parameters allow us to specify the starting values of heroName and heroHealth for our Hero and the value of numberOfSides for our Die. If we use meaningful values like "Heroic Hannah" and 100 for our Hero, and 6, 12, or 20 for Die, we have nothing to worry about – these values make perfect sense. But if we were to use −501 for our healthIn parameter or 248371615 for our sidesIn parameter we're likely to run into problems later in our game(s). A negative heroHealth value means our hero is starting out with some major health issues and a die with 248-million sides is rather unusual indeed. With a bit of extra, but familiar, code in our parameterized constructors, we can make sure that our objects start with reasonable default values. Here's a modified version of the Hero's constructor:

```
public Hero(string nameIn, int healthIn)
{
    if(nameIn == "")
        heroName = "Unnamed Hero";
    else
        heroName = nameIn;

    if(healthIn < 1 || healthIn > 100)
        heroHealth = 100;
    else
        heroHealth = healthIn;
}
```

In this updated code, we have added some if-statements to make sure that the nameIn and healthIn parameters make sense for our hero. If the nameIn parameter value is empty when we try to create a Hero object ("") then we'll set the heroName to "Unnamed Hero" – an empty name attribute might cause us problems when we try to display our output the hero's name in our game. If the nameIn parameter value is not empty, then we'll use that value for our hero's name. Similarly, if the incoming healthIn parameter value is 0 or less, or if it's greater than 100, we'll set the hero health to 100 – we don't want our hero to start with a health deficit or with too much health. If the healthIn parameter value is between 1 and 100, we'll set the heroHealth attribute to that perfectly reasonable value. Here's an updated Die constructor:

```
public Die(int sidesIn)
{
    if(sidesIn == 6 || sidesIn == 12 || sidesIn == 20 || sidesIn == 100)
        numberOfSides = sidesIn;
    else
        numberOfSides = 6;
    sideUp = 1;
}
```

Like our Hero example, this updated constructor has a bit of extra code to make sure that the numberOfSides for our Die object isn't set to something silly or unreasonable. In fact, this code makes sure that our Die has only 6, 12, 20, or 100 sides – any other number for the sideIn parameter results in the Die defaulting back to a safe and familiar six sides.

Writing code like this in our constructors helps to make sure that our object attributes are always set to safe and useful starting values – this is another important part of OOP. You can write any code that you need or want in a constructor, and what I've written in the examples above is just one way to handle potentially "bad" parameter values. As you journey beyond this book and learn more about OOP, writing object classes, and writing methods like constructors, you'll also discover many ways of making sure that your objects start and stay in a usable state.

If you're following along with the examples in this level, take a moment to update your constructors with the new parameter-checking if-statements. When you're ready, we'll take a look at how we can access and update our object attributes after they have been constructed.

Getter/Accessor Methods – Retrieving Attribute Values

At the risk of repeating myself – object constructor methods only run when the object is first created, and their job is to set the default or starting values for the attributes. Once the objects have been created and their starting values set, we need different methods to access and change the attribute values. These methods are often called getters and setters because they let us get and set the values stored in our object attributes. More formally, methods that let us access attributes are called accessors, and methods that allow us to change, alter, or mutate attribute values are called mutators. Together, constructors, accessors, and mutators are the "behaviors" of our object – they define what our object is capable of doing.

Let's say you're writing a small hero game. You construct your hero by calling the constructor method, and you set some default values for the heroName and heroHealth values by using the constructor parameters (this will be more clear in Level 11). You want to make sure that your hero received their name and health values properly. Or, maybe your game has been running for a while and you want to double check your hero's name and see how much health they have left after some epic battle and healing sessions. Since our attributes are private (on purpose), we need to code a way to peek inside our hero object. This is exactly what getter or accessor methods are for. For our Hero object class, we could write a pair of methods like this:

```
public string GetName()
{
     return heroName;
}


public int GetHealth()
{
     return heroHealth;
}
```

Let's break these methods down a bit:

- Like the constructor, these methods have a header (the first line of each method) that starts with the word public (so that we can call these methods later on).
- Unlike the constructor, there is a data type next in the header. This data type (string in the first method, int in the second) tells the method that we are allowing something to exit the method.
- The next part of the header is the name of the method (it can be anything, but I recommend naming it so that it's clear what it does), followed by round brackets. Neither GetName nor GetHealth need any parameters so the round brackets are empty.
- Both methods have curly braces to contain their statements.
- Both methods return a value – GetName returns heroName, and GetHealth returns heroHealth. "return" is a C# keyword that says "let this value exit the method".
- Like the constructor, getter/accessor methods sit between the curly braces of the class definition. Be careful not to accidentally put your accessors inside of your constructor.

For very little code, that's a lot to process. The purpose of both the GetName and GetHealth methods is to give us a copy of the attribute values so that we can see (but not change) the current values stored in our object attributes. Here are the accessors for the Die class. They are very similar to the Hero class accessors, except that they both have int return types since both Die attributes are ints:

```
public int GetNumberOfSides()
{
      return numberOfSides;
}

public int GetSideUp()
{
      return sideUp;
}
```

Even though I've written two accessor (or getter) methods for each of our object class examples, you're not required to write one for every attribute in your object classes. If you have a complicated object with many attributes, you can start by writing accessors for the attributes that you are most likely to access at some point in your program. You can always return to your object class and write more accessors when you need them. Here's where our objects stand now (Figure 22.7).

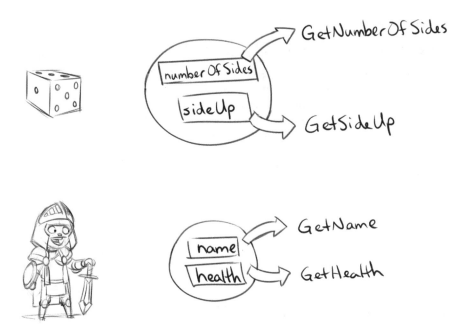

FIGURE 22.7
With our accessor methods in place, we now have a way to inspect or access our object attributes, and our illustration looks like this.

It's worth noting that the accessors in our object classes return the attribute values instead of outputting them using Console.WriteLine() – a very common thing for beginners to do. There's nothing stopping us from outputting the values, and occasionally it makes sense to do so, but in general, I don't recommend it. When we output (or display) an attribute value in an accessor method, we temporarily see the value, and then it is gone. By returning values instead of outputting them, we leave ourselves with options on how we might use the values – we might print what side of the Die object is up, store a Hero object's health value for use in a calculation (how much health do all the heroes in your game have), or even use it in an if-statement condition that says to stop the game if one of the Hero object's health values is less than or equal to zero. By returning values in our accessors (and sometimes mutators), we provide a way to get the value, but we decide somewhere else (Level 11) what to do with the values when we get them.

Accessing or getting our object attributes is really important. But it's setting or mutating the attributes that makes our objects seem dynamic and alive. Let's take a look at how we code "changeability" into our objects.

Setter/Mutator Methods – Changing Attribute Values

Setter or mutator methods let us change attribute values. They are kind of like constructors (they also set our attribute values), but mutators are called or used on objects after they have been constructed.

Let's assume that our heroes need a way to both take damage and heal, and dive right into some mutator code for our Hero object class:

```
public void TakeDamage(int damageAmount)
{
     heroHealth -= damageAmount;
}

public void Heal(int healAmount)
{
     heroHealth += healAmount;
}
```

Again, let's breakdown what is happening:

- We see the public keyword to start the method header. This is needed so that we can call our methods later.
- Both setter/mutator methods have void next – this tells C# that nothing is exiting or returning from these methods. The goal of our mutators is to change an attribute, not to view or otherwise access it. You can return a value from a setter/mutator method, but in my example, there's really no need.
- The names of these methods – TakeDamage and Heal – are up to you. As always, I recommend using names that make it clear what task the methods accomplish.
- Both of these methods have a parameter in the round brackets. TakeDamage has a value that will be the amount of damage our hero will take, while Heal has the amount of health that we'll recover.
- Both of these methods change (or mutate) the health attribute.
- Both of these methods go inside the class curly braces – be careful not to accidentally put them inside any other methods or constructors by mistake.

Here's how I imagine our objects with the mutators in place (Figure 22.8).

While the point of accessors is a bit simpler – get the values stored in the attributes – mutators can feel a bit more complex. For example, I have written two "setter" methods for the heroHealth attribute and none for

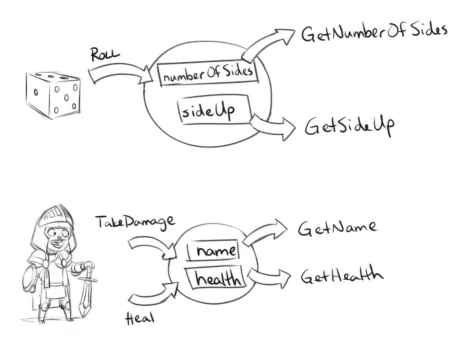

FIGURE 22.8
With our mutator methods in place, we now have a way to mutate or modify our object attributes, and our illustration looks like this.

the heroName attribute. When we write mutators, we ask ourselves "which attributes are going to need to change during the game or program"? In this example, I am assuming that once the hero name is set, we won't want to change it. So, there's no mutator for heroName. Could you add a hero name mutator? Absolutely! But in this case, I'll leave it out to keep the code a bit shorter.

It's more important for this example that we are able to change the hero's health – both up and down. You could write a single method that would accept an integer – if the integer is negative, the hero's health goes down; if it's positive, the hero's health goes up. This would work, but would be trickier (in my humble opinion) to use later (again, looking at Level 11). Writing two methods is more code, but it will make it very clear when the hero's health is going up and when it's going down. Naming the methods TakeDamage and Heal helps to reinforce what they are actually doing and makes our hero feel more heroic than methods called SetHealthDown and SetHealthUp.

You might also notice that I haven't included any extra code in the setters or mutators to deal with the hero's health going below zero (too much damage) or going above 100 (too much healing). I'll leave that for you to try out as a side quest at the end of this level.

What about a mutator for our Die class? Since the number of sides on a die is set when it's constructed, we don't want to add a mutator that allows us to change the numberOfSides attribute. In the real world, we can't turn a d6 into a d20, so let's not allow our game to do that either. What we need is a mutator that changes our sideUp attribute. This is one of my favorite mutator examples – the infamous Roll method:

```
public void Roll()
{
        Random rng = new Random();
        sideUp = rng.Next(1, numberOfSides + 1);
}
```

The Die class' Roll method is pretty cool. It has the same structure as the Hero mutators (a header with public and void, followed by the method name), but this time there are no parameters. We don't want someone saying "I want a 5" and then allowing them to pass that value in. Our players can wish for a 5, but we're going to let randomness determine their fate. Inside our Roll mutator we create a Random object (yes, we can do this). We then generate a random number between 1 and numberOfSides + 1, and this is the value we use to update our sideUp attribute. Pretty neat, eh? Our sideUp attribute is dependent on the number of sides that our Die has (remember to use + 1 because of the way Random's Next method works), and the result is randomly generated. We can even call this method (more on method calls in Level 11) in our Die's two constructors like this:

```
//Unparameterized constructor (no parameters)
public Die()
{
        numberOfSides = 6;
        Roll();

}
//Parameterized constructor (one parameter)
public Die(int sidesIn)

{
        numberOfSides = sidesIn;
        Roll();
}
```

With this small change, our Die objects seem more realistic – when a Die is created, it will have a random sideUp value. This isn't something you have to do – you can have all your dice start with the same value if you want. I just think it's a small, fun change for this class.

Object Helper Methods

Sometimes we write methods that don't access or change our object attributes – instead they just support the object in some other way. These are sometimes called helper methods. Not every object has helper methods, but in some cases, they can be quite … helpful. Let's take our Hero, for example. We have accessor methods to retrieve the name and health attributes. We have mutators so that our hero can take damage and heal. But what else does a simple game hero do – they deal damage to their foes. Dealing damage doesn't usually depend on or affect a hero's health (though in some games, super-attacks might cause some health depletion), and it's even rarer that it would depend on or affect a hero's name. This means that a damage-dealing method has nothing to do with our attributes and might look like this:

```
public int DealDamage()
{
        return 10;
}
```

This is a really simple method that has an int return type and returns 10 every time it's called. While it does show that the hero's health and name have nothing to do with dealing damage, this method is a bit boring. A more interesting version might look like this:

```
public int DealDamage()
{
        Random rng = new Random();
        int damageAmount = rng.Next(8, 21);
        return damageAmount;
}
```

This version uses a Random object to deal damage between 8 and 20 every time this method is used. You can modify it anyway you want – as long as there is a return statement with an int value, this method will work fine. You can even change it to have parameters for the minimum and maximum damage amounts (seems like a good idea for a side quest).

As I mentioned before, not all objects need helper methods. Our Die example doesn't do much other than roll, so there's no helper method for that object class. But if there's something your object class needs to do, and to do this thing it doesn't need to access or change the attributes, a helper method is the way to go!

If you want more examples of object classes, including attributes, constructors, accessors, mutators, and even helper methods, be sure to check the online resources for this book. Also, consider extending your journey into the next book, where we'll see the examples from this level and other object classes put to work in MonoGame.

Full-Object Classes from This Level

Just in case you want to see the whole Hero and Die classes from this level, here they are. Remember, if you're going to copy them for yourself, they need to be stored in separate files that are named Hero.cs and Die.cs. I've left the namespace that I introduced at the start of this level, but you can change it if your project uses a different name:

```
namespace MyFirstObjectClasses
{
    internal class Hero
    {
        //Hero attributes to store the state of a Hero object
        private string heroName;
        private int heroHealth;

        //Unparameterized constructor (no parameters)
        public Hero()
        {
            heroName = "Unknown Hero";
            heroHealth = 100;
        }

        //Parameterized constructor (two parameters)
        public Hero(string nameIn, int healthIn)
        {
            if (nameIn == "")
                heroName = "Unnamed Hero";
            else
                heroName = nameIn;

            if (healthIn < 1 || healthIn > 100)
                heroHealth = 100;
            else
                heroHealth = healthIn;
        }

        //This is an accessor that returns the hero's name
        public string GetName()
        {
            return heroName;
        }

        //This is an accessor that returns the hero's health
        public int GetHealth()
        {
            return heroHealth;
        }
```

```
            //This is a mutator to reduce the hero's health
            public void TakeDamage(int damageAmount)
            {
                    heroHealth -= damageAmount;
            }

            //This is a mutator to add to the hero's health
            public void Heal(int healAmount)
            {
                    heroHealth += healAmount;
            }

            //Helper method to deal damage to foes
            public int DealDamage()
            {
                    Random rng = new Random();
                    int damageAmount = rng.Next(8, 21);
                    return damageAmount;
            }
      }
}


namespace MyFirstObjectClasses
{
    internal class Die
    {
        //Die attributes to store the state of a Die object
        private int numberOfSides;
        private int sideUp;

        //Unparameterized constructor (no parameters)
        public Die()
        {
                numberOfSides = 6;
                Roll();
        }

        //Parameterized constructor (one parameter)
        public Die(int sidesIn)
        {
                if (sidesIn == 6 || sidesIn == 12 || sidesIn == 20 || sidesIn
== 100)
                    numberOfSides = sidesIn;
                else
                    numberOfSides = 6;
                Roll();
        }

        //This is an accessor that returns the die's number of sides
        public int GetNumberOfSides()
        {
```

```
            return numberOfSides;
    }

    //This is an accessor that returns the die's current side up
    public int GetSideUp()
    {
            return sideUp;
    }

    //This mutator allows us to change to a random side (like
    //rolling a die), based on the number of sides
    public void Roll()
    {
            Random rng = new Random();
            sideUp = rng.Next(1, numberOfSides + 1);
    }
  }
}
```

Side Quests

Want to Know More?

Oops, I want more OOP: We have only scratched the surface of OOP in this level. If you want to know more about OOP and ways to use it in your games and programs, look up some more OOP tutorials and resources online.

OOP, but make it faster: Since this book is about learning the fundamentals of programming, I've taken a very deliberate approach with our object examples. What I didn't show you is that there are some shortcuts for creating set/get methods in C#. These shortcuts aren't applicable in all cases, but they're a cool thing to know. Look up C# {get; set;} to learn more.

OOP, but make it even more awesome: Learning how to write and use object classes is just the start of your OOP journey. The next step is using those object classes to create related classes using inheritance. This opens the door to object polymorphism! Once you feel like you have a handle on objects, look up C# object inheritance and polymorphism to create even more powerful objects.

OOP, but make it more debuggable: Game objects are sometimes simple, like the examples in this level, but they can also be very complex with many attributes. Sometimes we want to see an object's state, and we don't want to call every accessor one at a time. Luckily, there's an "easier" way to get your object's state. Look up the C# object ToString methods to see how you can write a special accessor that is very useful for debugging your objects.

OOP, but with shared attributes: In this level's examples, we defined instance attributes – this means that each object we create will have its own copy of the attribute. In other words, each Hero object has their own heroName and heroHealth – changing the health of one Hero object has no impact on the others. The same idea holds true for the Die objects and their numberOfSides and sideUp attributes. However, sometimes it's helpful to have attributes that are shared between all objects of a specific type. Look up static attributes in C# objects to learn more.

Want to Do More?

This Hero is out of control: In our Hero class, we wrote overly simple TakeDamage and Heal mutators. When we're learning new concepts, we often start simple and work our way to more complex code. The issue with the TakeDamage and Heal methods is that they will allow the Hero's health to go below zero and above 100. Let's assume that our game won't work well with negative health or extreme health above 100. Write an if-statement in TakeDamage that says if the updated health is below 0, set it to 0. Write an if-statement in Heal that says if the updated health is above 100, set it to 100.

This Hero is too simple: In our Hero class, we wrote a simple but cool DealDamage helper method. Modify the method header to take two int parameters – one for the minimum amount of damage and one for the maximum amount of damage. Update the method code to use the minimum and maximum parameters instead of hard-coding the damage to be between 8 and 20.

Code Reward – An Objectively Better Loot Box

For this code reward, we're revisiting loot boxes from Code Quests 8 and 9. This time, we're going to create a loot box object class, or blueprint. It's going to work roughly the same way, but it will be object-oriented, which makes it more appropriate for a game that we might write in MonoGame or some other engine. Here's the outline if you want to try it for yourself. If you get stuck or simply want to see the solution, you'll find it on the next page:

- The loot box object will have two attributes – a string to store the loot item and a boolean to keep track of whether the loot box is full (true) or empty (false). Make your attributes private to encapsulate and protect them from any accidental shenanigans.
- The loot box has one constructor that takes no parameters. The constructor sets the full boolean to true and uses an if-statement

structure to set the loot item attribute according to the following algorithm:

- The loot box has one accessor that returns the value of the full attribute (true or false). This way we can tell if the loot box has loot in it or if it's been emptied already. Why don't we have an accessor for the loot attribute? Well, most loot boxes don't let you peek at what's inside before you open it.
- The loot box has one mutator that dispenses loot. This is an unusual mutator because it does two jobs – it sets the full attribute to false and also returns the value of loot (so that it can be used later in our game).
- There should be no output statements in your loot box object class methods.

If you try this code for yourself, remember to create a new file to store your loot box object class. I used a project called Level10CodeReward, which you'll see reflected in the namespace.

```
/*
If you're going to copy and paste all of this code (from the online version),
remember to store this in a file called LootBox, in a project called
MyLootBoxObject.

This is a simple loot box object class! Even though it looks a bit more
complex, especially the constructor, it has the same properties as the Hero
and Die from Level 10.

This program is the Code Reward for Level 10.
Author: Aaron Langille
*/

namespace Level10CodeReward
{
    internal class LootBox
    {

        //LootBox object attributes
        private string loot;
        private bool isFull;

        //LootBox constructor - each LootBox object will be created
        //the same way. No parameters for this constructor. The magic
        //for this object happens here.
        public LootBox()
        {
            isFull = true; //the LootBox starts full

            Random rng = new Random();
            //here is our random value between 1 and 100
            int lootValue = rng.Next(1, 101);

            //this is just a safety value, in case there's a problem with
            //the logic below.
            loot = "no loot yet";

            if (lootValue < 11)
            {
                loot = "a small stick";
            }
            else if (lootValue >= 11 && lootValue <= 29)
            {
                loot = "a weak cardboard sword";
            }
            else if (lootValue >= 30 && lootValue <= 69)
            {
                loot = "a rusty steel sword";
            }
            else if (lootValue >= 70 && lootValue <= 94)
            {
                loot = "a glowing crystal sword";
```

```
        }
        else if (lootValue >= 95)
        {
            loot = "a scorching sword of pure flame";
        }
    }

    //here is our accessor - it simply returns the
    //value of isFull, in a game this would let us
    //ask the LootBox if it's full (true) or empty (false).
    //We'll try this in Level 11.
    public bool GetIsFull()
    {
        return isFull;
    }

    //here is our mutator - this is like opening the LootBox
    //and removing the awesome loot (which we'll return
    //so the player can have it. This method is a mutator
    //because we're going to set IsFull to false and we'll set
    //the loot string too.
    public string DispenseLoot()
    {
        //if the box is full, dispense (return) the loot.
        if(isFull == true)
        {
            isFull = false;
            return loot;
        }
        else //the box is empty, let the player know!!!
        {
            return "Sorry, no loot in here.";
        }
    }
}
}
}
```

23

Code Quest 10: A Companion for Our Hero (Part 1)

Before proceeding with this quest:

- review Level 10
- complete Code Quest 9 (optional)
- create a new Visual Studio Console project. If you need a refresher, detailed instructions can be found at the beginning of Code Quest 1.

Exploring, adventuring, and jumping from platform to platform can get pretty lonely without someone to talk to. In game design, the quick dialogue and quips that NPCs (non-player characters) deliver are called barks, and in this code quest, we're going to write a very simple NPC object class. This blueprint will be the foundation for an in-game character that will "talk to us", and we'll revisit it in Code Quest 11.

Our basic NPC class will have all the features that we explored in Level 10, including attributes and behaviors (in the form of methods). I recommend keeping the Die and Hero classes handy for reference and as a reminder of object class structure.

When you're ready to design a companion that will keep us company (sort of) on our journey, head to the Main Quest below!

Main Quest – A Companion for Our Hero (Part 1)

In this quest, we're going to design and code a basic NPC blueprint or object class. We won't be able to test it out until Code Quest 11, but as long as the code shows no errors, you can be reasonably sure that your class is on the right track. If you get stuck, there's an outline of the class structure below to help you out.

Your NPC object class should have the following features:

1. After creating your Visual Studio project, create a new class file called SimpleNPC.cs. All of your code will go in this file.

DOI: 10.1201/9781003348481-23

2. Create three private string attributes for your NPC – one for their name and two separate variables for different barks (things the NPC says).

3. Write a non-parameterized constructor that sets the name attribute to "Monty", the first bark to "I'm glad to be on this adventure with you." and the second bark to "I really hope this adventure is over before dinner".

4. Write a parameterized constructor with parameters for the NPC name and both bark strings. In the body of the constructor, set the attributes to the parameter values.

5. Write an accessor method called GetName that returns our companion's name.

6. Write an accessor method called TalkToMe that returns one of the two bark attributes. One way to do this is to create a Random object in the body of this method and use it to create a random number between 1 and 100. If the random number you create is less than 50, return the first bark. If the random number is 50 or greater, return the second bark. This method header takes no parameters but does return a string.

7. Write two mutator methods – one to change the first bark to a new string, and another to change the second bark to a new string. Both of these method headers return nothing (void) but do need to take in a single parameter each.

Since there's no output until we create some NPC objects using our blueprint (Code Quest 11), here is an outline of my NPC object class to help you with this Quest (Figure 23.1).

Side Quests

Clean up the parameters: In both the Hero and Die classes, we added some code to check that our incoming parameters would be appropriate for our objects. We could do some of that here too. Consider adding some checks in the parameterized constructor and mutators – if the incoming string is empty (""), set the NPC name or barks to something more appropriate.

Make it your own: Do you find my NPC uninteresting or uninspiring? Do you prefer adventure companions that are more complex? Do you prefer adventure companions that are less complex? Do you prefer adventure companions that are entirely different? Change the attributes and behavior methods to make this quest more fun for you!!

Really make it your own: Do you always refuse requests for NPCs to join your party because you prefer to adventure in quiet and comfortable solitude? If so, write an object (preferably a game-y one) that is more fun and interesting for you. Decide on some important attributes, then add a parameterized and non-parameterized constructor that will set the default values. Finally, add some accessors (getters) and mutators (setters) to give your object class some meaningful behaviors.

```
 9    internal class SimpleNPC
10    {
11        //non-paremeterized constructor
12        public SimpleNPC()
13        {
14            //constructor code here
15        }
16
17        //paremeterized constructor
18        public SimpleNPC(string nameIn, string bark1In, string bark2In)
19        {
20            //constructor code here
21        }
22
23        //accessors
24        public string GetName()
25        {
26            //accessor code goes here
27        }
28
29        public string TalkToMe()
30        {
31            //accessor code goes here
32        }
33
34        //first mutator
35        public void ChangeBark1(string bark1In)
36        {
37            //first mutator code goes here
38        }
39
40        //second mutator
41        public void ChangeBark2(string bark2In)
42        {
43            //second mutator code goes here
44        }
45    }
```

FIGURE 23.1

This quest is a bit different, so here's a code outline to help you on your journey.

24

Level 11: A Factory for Our Objects

Level 10 Recap:

- Object-oriented programming is used to make many modern video games, including those made with game engines.
- Object classes (blueprints) describe our game elements using attributes (variables) and behaviors (methods) in a way that makes them seem more like real things.
- Attributes define the current state of our object.
- Constructors are special methods that we use to set the starting values of our object attributes.
- Accessor or getter methods let us see or retrieve our attribute values.
- Mutator or setter methods let us change our attribute values.

Games Are Made of Objects (Part 2)

So you've thought about how you might code some of your game elements – your hero, trees, buildings, pickups, NPCs, potions, vehicles, and coins – as C# object classes or blueprints. You've created some new files in your Visual Studio game project and written some attributes, constructors, accessors, and mutators – now what?

Object classes are great for describing the potential objects for your game. But to realize that potential, you need to create actual and specific instances of those objects – your hero, trees, buildings, pickups, NPCs, potions, vehicles, and coins. Think of it this way, a house blueprint gives us an idea of what's possible, but the actual house that we create from that blueprint is where the real excitement is!

Games are made up of objects that run, jump, collide, speak, take damage, deal damage, heal, cast spells, level up, rotate, bounce, disappear, drift, blink, drop loot, interact with other objects, and so much more. In Level 10, we learned how to describe the possible attributes and behaviors of our objects, and in this level, we're going to learn how to manufacture and manipulate specific instances of those objects. But first, let's make sure we're really clear on the difference between an object class and an object.

DOI: 10.1201/9781003348481-24

An Object Class Isn't an Object

If I said to you, "an object class isn't an object", would you know what I mean? Or would you tilt your head to one side, narrow your eyes slightly, and say back to me "what do you mean"? If you're in that second group, fear not, because there's a simple analogy to help you understand the difference – a blueprint isn't a house. In Level 10, we looked at how to describe objects in much the same way that a blueprint describes a future house. In most cases, the blueprint tells you everything that's important – the shape and size of the house, the dimensions and layout of the individual rooms, how the plumbing and wiring should be installed, and even some of the materials that could be used during construction.

There are also some things that a house blueprint doesn't tell you – what color the walls should be painted, what kind of flooring to buy, and whether that small room in the back will be someone's bedroom or an off-the-hook dedicated gaming room complete with LED lighting and immersive sound experience. By leaving these details out, we can make many structurally similar houses from the same blueprint, while leaving the specifics of wall color, type of flooring, and room use up to each of the future home-owners. This idea applies to many things beyond houses – we create a blueprint, schematic, or specification that describes the common attributes and behaviors for almost any product, but some details aren't set until the product is created, and some can even be changed afterward during everyday use.

Let's say you and I both want to buy the newest gaming console from the Super Duper Gaming Company. They offer three models – lite, regular, and pro. Each of the models is offered in power-up blue, mega-combo green, super-charged red, and into-the-void black. Also, you can get a copy of the newest Super Duper Gaming Company Game installed for an extra charge or skip it to save a few bucks. You can bet that the Super Duper Gaming Company has a blueprint for this great new console. You can also bet that the blueprint allows for the different models, colors, and game installation options. This way, when you place your order, you can customize your console the way you want (pro, power-up blue, game included), and I can do the same (lite, mega-combo green, no game).

This brings us back to the original point above – an object class (a C# object blueprint) is not an object. An object class describes the common attributes and behaviors for a type of object, and an object is a specific thing that we make according to the description in the object class – the same way that a house (or console) is made according to the description in a blueprint. When we create an object, we say it is an instance of the object class, and that object is created through an action called instantiation – it's an unusual word, but you're likely to come across it when you're working with object-oriented languages like C#.

Once we have written an object class (or blueprint), we can instantiate (or create) many objects – each with common attributes and behaviors, but also with unique values or states. For example, with a Hero object class, we can create several heroes, each with their own specific name and health values. Regardless of their name and health values, all of our heroes can take and deal damage because the Hero class defines those behaviors. With a Die object class, we can create dice with different numbers of sides and different sides that are facing up – but they all roll in a similar way. Thinking beyond our Level 10 examples, we can write a platform object class and then create many platform objects that support our players and enemies – they can all have different positions in the level, and some might move while others stay-put. We can write a gem object class and then create gems of different colors, sizes, and values that can all be collected by our player. In other words, object classes define the objects that our game can potentially have or use, and the instantiated objects actually are the game.

The Lifecycle of Objects

I like to think of an object having three phases – blueprint (object class or pre-production), construction (instantiation or production), and regular use (or post-production). I imagine an object's lifecycle looking something like this (Figure 24.1).

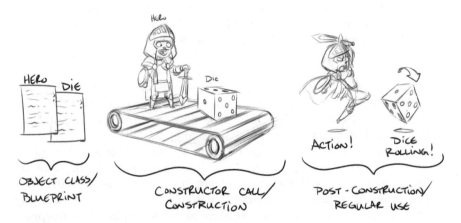

FIGURE 24.1
All objects in our games and programs have three phases in their life cycle – a blueprint phase where the objects are described, a construction phase where they are manufactured with starting values, and a regular use phase where they are accessed and changed as needed.

Let's take a closer look at each phase.

- *Object Class (blueprint):* In this phase, we define our future objects. We define theattributes that will store the state of individual objects, and we write behaviors (in the form of methods) that will determine what the object can do. Even though we don't really have objects in this phase, it is the first step in making sure that we can create useful objects for the next two phases.

- *Construction (instantiation):* In this phase, we bring our objects into existence according to what was written in the object class. In other words, each object in our game (or program) will appear only after an appropriate constructor call. Think of this step like manufacturing or production – this is where all the parts get assembled and the default settings are applied. This is the only time where we call the constructor – that special method from the object class that is used to set the starting values for our object. If our object class has more than one constructor, then we have options for which one to use. If there are parameters in the constructor header, we can even set custom starting values. We'll take a closer look at how to call constructors later in this level.

- *Regular use:* Once our objects have been constructed, they move into a "regular use" mode. We no longer call the constructor (that would replace the current object with a new one); instead, we use the accessors (getters) to get the value in the attributes, and we call the mutators (setters) to change the state of the object. This is why we have accessors and mutators in our object class – for the regular use phase. We'll take a closer look at how to call these methods later in this level.

Technically, there is a fourth phase in an object's lifecycle – destruction. Why isn't destruction in our illustration and explanation? First, object destruction is typically an automated process. Deep inside the machinery of C#, there are ways for your game (or program) to determine if an object is no longer being used. When this happens, the object is removed from memory and can't be accessed any more. Second, by the time you're needing to remove or destroy objects manually, you'll be well beyond the brief introduction to object-oriented programming in this book.

Don't Panic – You've Done This Before

If all of this object-talk seems a bit confusing – instantiation, constructors, accessors, mutators, and lifecycles – don't panic, brave adventurer!! You've seen and even coded some of these ideas before. Here's a reminder:

```
//instantiate a new Random object called rng by
//calling the non-parameterized constructor
Random rng = new Random();

//call Random's Next() method to get a random
//integer between 1 and 100
int myRandomNumber = rng.Next(1,101);
```

In these two lines of code, you've seen the construction and regular use phases of the Random object class (even though you probably haven't looked at the object class code). You've also instantiated an object by calling a constructor from the Random object class, and called a behavior method too (.Next()). We'll clarify all of this (and more!) in the next few sections by revisiting our Hero and Die object classes from Level 10.

Back to Our Regular Program.cs

When we write object classes (or blueprints), we store the code in separate files that have the same name as the classes themselves. This is an important part of keeping our objects, games, and programs organized. Now, in what might seem like a strange twist, we're going to return to our trusty Program.cs to instantiate (or create) our actual objects. It's not too strange of a twist if you remember that Program.cs, or more specifically, Main() in Program.cs is the entry point of our program – this is where C# starts executing our code. This means that Main() is going to be our object factory. If you're following along with the examples in this level, all of the new code will go in the Main() method of your Program.cs file.

Luckily, all of our Visual Studio projects have a Program.cs which contains a Main(), so we don't need to worry about adding anything new to our projects. I'm going to keep using the MyFirstObjects project that we started and used in Level 10. It has a Program.cs file as well as completed Hero and Die object classes. All of the examples in this level will assume all three of these files are present and accounted for (Figure 24.2).

Now that we know the difference between object classes and objects, a bit about the life cycle of objects, that creating and using objects isn't completely new to us, and that we're going to return to Program.cs to create our own objects, we can *finally* get to work. Are you ready to embark on the last leg of our console-based adventure?

Alright, let's instantiate some fun!

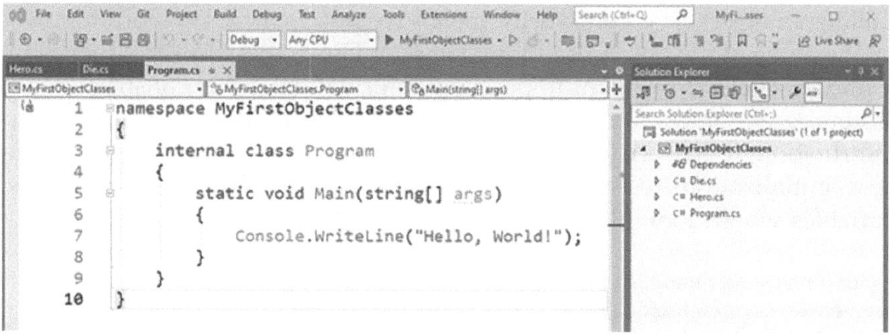

FIGURE 24.2
Although we write our object blueprint code in the specific object class files, we create and use
our instances of our objects in the Program.cs file. Remember, Program.cs is where we wrote all
of our code before we started our object-oriented journey.

Creating Objects with Constructors

Creating, or instantiating, a new object is similar to creating a new variable
using our built-in types. For example, built-in type variable declarations
look like this:

```
string playerName;
int playerScore;
float playerScoreMultiplier;
```

While object declarations look like this:

```
Random rng;
Hero myHero;
Die d20;
```

In either case, built-in types or object types, a declaration specifies the type
and the name of the variable. No real difference there. Where things change
is during assignment. For our built-in types, we might write:

```
playerName = "Arthur";
playerScore = 112;
playerScoreMultiplier = 1.25f;
```

But, for our object types, we need to use the new keyword and call one of
the object class constructors:

```
rng = new Random();
myHero = new Hero();
d20 = new Die(20);
```

Calling an object class constructor means we put the new keyword followed by the name of the object (Random, Hero, or Die in this case) and then some round brackets. If we want to pass any information to our constructor, and assuming we have a constructor in our object class that can accept information, it goes inside of the round brackets. For the sake of completeness, initializations (combined declarations and assignments) for our object variables would look like this:

```
Random rng = new Random();
Hero myHero = new Hero();
Die d20 = new Die(20);
```

Let's try to answer some of the questions that might come up at this point:

- *What is up with new?* "new" is a special keyword that is used when we're instantiating objects. It tells C# to set aside some memory for the object and that our variable will be assigned a new instance of that object type.
- *Where do I put my object-type declarations or initializations?* In the case of simple programs, your object declarations and initializations will go in the Main() method of your Program.cs class (though we do change this up a bit in MonoGame and other game engines).
- *I can re-assign built-in type variables, can I do the same with object variables?* Technically, yes you can, but when you do this, you are replacing your current object with a new one. In most cases, we use the object's accessor and mutator methods to manipulate the object rather than re-assigning its variables.
- *How do I know what constructors are available for me to call and whether or not they take any parameters?* If you are the author of the object classes or have access to the object class code, you can look inside those files to see what constructors are available to you, and what, if any parameters they might take. If you aren't the author, you'll need access to some documentation that shows you what constructors (as well as accessors and mutators) are available. Remember, constructors have the same name as the object class itself so they are pretty easy to find if you have the documentation.

Let's take a closer look at what it means to call constructors that have no parameters. In our Hero and Die object classes, we have constructors that look like this:

```
public Hero()
{
    heroName = "Unknown Hero";
    heroHealth = 100;
}


public Die()
{
    numberOfSides = 6;
    Roll();
}
```

Since there is nothing in the round brackets of these constructor headers (remember, the header is the first line of a method), these constructors are expecting no values, and we can instantiate objects like this (inside of Main() in our Program.cs):

```
Hero myFirstHero = new Hero();
Hero mySecondHero = new Hero();
Die myFirstD6 = new Die();
Die mySecondD6 = new Die();
```

In the case of the objects above, both myFirstHero and mySecondHero will have "Unknown Hero" and 100 for their heroName and heroHealth values, while both Die objects will have numberOfSides set to 6 and sideUp set to a random value because of the roll() method call. I imagine our objects looking something like this (Figure 24.3).

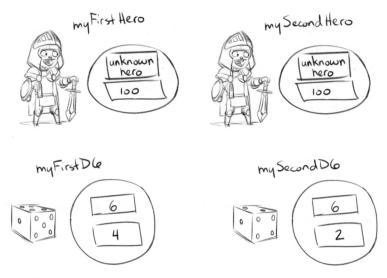

FIGURE 24.3
Is this how you imagined our objects as well?

How do we know that our objects will look like this? Well, that's what we defined as our starting values in the unparameterized constructors of our two object classes – look back at the code above. When we learn how to call our accessor (getter) methods in the next section, we'll verify the starting values of these four objects.

In the meantime, both our Hero and Die classes have parameterized constructors as well.

```
public Hero(string nameIn, int healthIn)
{
    if (nameIn == "")
       heroName = "Unnamed Hero";
    else
       heroName = nameIn;

    if (healthIn < 1 || healthIn > 100)
       heroHealth = 100;
    else
       heroHealth = healthIn;
}


public Die(int sidesIn)
{
    if (sidesIn == 6 || sidesIn == 12 || sidesIn == 20 || sidesIn == 100)
            numberOfSides = sidesIn;
    else
            numberOfSides = 6;
    Roll();
}
```

When we call a parameterized constructor, we need to provide an appropriate literal or variable inside of our constructor's round brackets, like this:

```
Hero myThirdHero = new Hero("Raven", 100);
string fourthHeroName = "Robin";
int fourthHeroStartingHealth = 75;
Hero myFourthHero = new
     Hero(fourthHeroName, fourthHeroStartingHealth);
Die myThirdD6 = new Die(6);
Die myFirstD20 = new Die(20);
```

If were we to try calling our constructors like this, we would get syntax errors in Visual Studio:

```
Hero myThirdHero = new Hero(100, "Raven");
Die myThirdD6 = new Die(6.5f);
```

FIGURE 24.4
If we change the attribute values in our objects, we need to change our illustration of them too.

In the case of our Hero constructor, the parameters need to be the right type and they need to be supplied in the right order. Try these statements for yourself to see the complaints that you get from Visual Studio.

When we successfully supply the right parameters, in the right order, our four new objects might look like this (Figure 24.4).

One thing that new programmers find confusing is how the values (literals or variables) we put inside the round brackets of our constructors become the values for our object attributes. When we define parameters in our object classes, we are saying "by putting a value here when you call this method, it will be passed to the method". Here's a diagram with partial classes to help illustrate this idea (Figure 24.5).

When we call a parameterized constructor, the values we put inside the round brackets are passed to the variables that were defined in our object class – in this case, "Sam" and 100 are passed to the parameters nameIn and healthIn (dotted arrows). These are special variables, defined in our constructor header, that can then be used inside the body of our constructor. Here we are simply using them to set the values for our object attributes – heroName and heroHealth, respectively (solid arrows). Using parameters like this is the safest and most common way of sending values from the Main() method in Program.cs to our objects during construction. We'll see

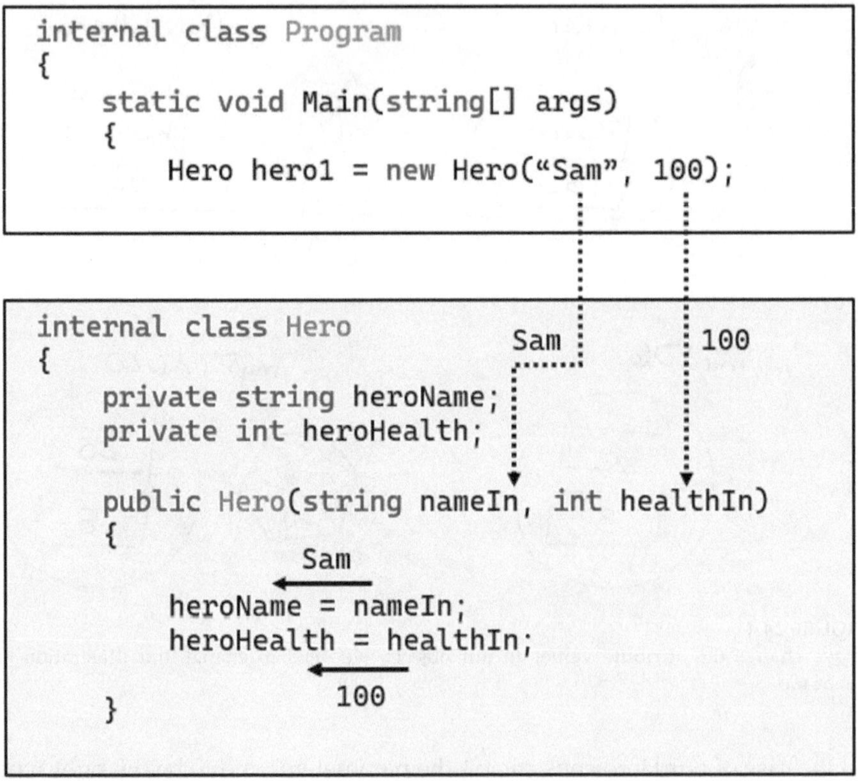

```
internal class Program
{
    static void Main(string[] args)
    {
        Hero hero1 = new Hero("Sam", 100);
```

```
internal class Hero                    Sam        100
{
    private string heroName;
    private int heroHealth;

    public Hero(string nameIn, int healthIn)
    {
                        Sam
        heroName = nameIn;
        heroHealth = healthIn;
                        100
}
```

FIGURE 24.5
Sometimes, it's hard to imagine the flow of values in our code, especially when we're calling methods and passing values through arguments. This is how the data flows when we call our Hero constructor with argument values.

in the next section that return statements are the safest and most common way of passing values from our objects back to Main().

Knowing when to call one constructor or another (or many others) is a matter of what you want to do in your game or program. For example, if I want a six-sided Die, I can simply call the unparameterized constructor of my Die class – it creates a Die object with six sides, and I don't have to go through the extra work of passing anything when I call the constructor. However, if I want a 20-sided Die, I have no choice but to call the parameterized constructor – that's the only way I can say that I want 20 sides. It's the same idea for the Hero class – if I want to specify my hero name and starting health value, I have no choice but to call the parameterized constructor. In the unlikely event that I want anonymous heroes with a guaranteed 100 starting health, I can use the non-parameterized constructor. If an object class has multiple constructors, choose the one that best suits your object-constructing needs.

In this section, we've taken a look at how to instantiate (or create) objects by calling the object class constructors – both unparameterized and parameterized. But this only brings our objects into existence. To peek inside our objects, or to change their state, we need to call our accessors and mutator methods. Let's start with our accessors.

Accessing or Getting Object Properties by Calling

For this section (and the next), I'm going to start by instantiating the following Hero and Die objects in the Main() of my Program.cs file:

```
Hero myFirstHero = new Hero();
Hero mySecondHero = new Hero("Raven", 100);
Hero myThirdHero = new Hero("Robin", 75);
Die myD6 = new Die();
Die myD20 = new Die(20);
```

To call any of an object's accessors (see Level 10 for object class definitions of our Hero and Die accessor methods), you use the object name, followed by a period (or dot), then the method name, and then round brackets. Like this:

```
myFirstHero.GetName();
myFirstHero.GetHealth();
myD6.GetSideUp();
myD6.GetNumberOfSides();
```

If you put these accessor calls in Main() below the object initialization statements, your program should compile and run without any errors (assuming you have the complete Die and Hero classes in your Visual Studio project). However, there's no output, so how can we be sure that everything is working properly?

It's important to remember that accessor methods return values – like Random's Next() method, something comes out of the method call. We could rewrite the above accessor calls like this:

```
Console.WriteLine("First Hero's name: " + myFirstHero.GetName());
Console.WriteLine("First Hero's health: " + myFirstHero.GetHealth());
Console.WriteLine("D6 number of sides: " + myD6.GetNumberOfSides());
Console.WriteLine("D6 side up: " + myD6.GetSideUp());
```

When we do this, the values that are returned from the accessor methods are passed to the Console.WriteLine() statements and we are able to peek at some of our object attributes. The above statements should produce output like:

```
First Hero's name: Unknown Hero
First Hero's health: 100
D6 number of sides: 6
D6 side up: 3
```

Of course that last value will be a random value between 1 and 6, thanks to the Roll() method call in our Die object's constructor. These statements are an easy way for us to see what our object's attribute values are at any point when our program is running. But what if we wanted to do something more with the values in our objects? For example, let's compute the total health of all our Hero objects by adding the following statements:

```
int firstHeroHealth = myFirstHero.GetHealth();
int secondHeroHealth = mySecondHero.GetHealth();
int thirdHeroHealth = myThirdHero.GetHealth();

int totalPartyHealth = firstHeroHealth + secondHeroHealth + thirdHeroHealth;
Console.WriteLine("Our party has a combined " + totalPartyHealth + " health
points.");
```

Let's also add some code that will roll our 20-sided die and tell us how lucky we are:

```
myD20.Roll();
int myD20Roll = myD20.GetSideUp();
Console.WriteLine("You rolled: " + myD20Roll);
if(myD20Roll == 20)
    Console.WriteLine("Amazing!! That's an amazing roll!");
else if(myD20Roll == 1)
    Console.WriteLine("Ouch, that's tough.");
else
    Console.WriteLine("Not bad, not bad at all.");
```

In this code, we've jumped ahead a bit and called our Roll() mutator – spoiler alert, it's very similar to calling an accessor. But we've also called our GetSideUp() accessor to see what value is stored in our sideUp attribute after the Roll(). We've stored this value in a variable called myD6Roll so that we can tell the player how good, bad, or mediocre their roll was.

In both of these examples, we've called our object accessor (getter) methods to retrieve the value of the object attributes. When we call an object method that has a return value, the value is "returned" to the code where the method call was made. Then we can decide what to do with the value that has been returned to us – usually output it or store it for later use. Here's a diagram with partial classes to help illustrate how return statements in our object classes send values back to our accessor method calls in Main() (Figure 24.6).

```
internal class Program
{
    static void Main(string[] args)
    {
        Die myD20 = new Die(20);
        int myD2Roll = myD20.GetSideUp();  ←⋯
        ─────────→
        Value in myD20's sideUp attribute
    }
}

internal class Die
{
    private int numberOfSides;
    private int sideUp;

    public Die()
    {
        numberOfSides = 6;
        Roll();
    }

    public int GetSideUp()
    {
        return sideUp; ⋯⋯⋯⋯⋯⋯⋯⋯⋯⋯⋯⋯⋯⋯⋯⋯
    }
```

FIGURE 24.6
Sometimes it's hard to imagine the flow of values in our code, especially when we're calling methods and returning values to be stored in variables. This is how the data flows when we call our Die's GetSideUp accessor method.

In the end, with accessor methods, we get the state, or values, stored in our object attributes. Now, let's take a look at how to manipulate and change our object attributes by calling the mutator methods.

Mutating or Setting Object Properties

To call any of an object's mutators, you use the object name, followed by a period (or dot), then the method name, and then round brackets. If the mutator needs a parameter, you must supply it (the same way we did for our parameterized constructors). Assuming we have our Hero and Die objects still initialized from the previous section, we should be able to call the mutator methods like this:

```
myFirstHero.TakeDamage(10);
myFirstHero.Heal(5);
mySecondHero.TakeDamage(15);
mySecondHero.Heal(5);
myThirdHero.TakeDamage(3);
myThirdHero.Heal(4);
myD6.Roll();
myD20.Roll();
myD100.Roll();
```

There are a few things worth mentioning about these mutator calls:

- It's common for mutators to use parameters to get values that will modify the object attributes. For our Hero object class, TakeDamage takes an integer parameter that is the amount of health the hero loses. It's the same idea for the Hero's Heal method, except we add the parameter amount instead of subtracting it. Parameters can be passed to methods as literals (as in the example above) or as variables.

- Not all mutators use parameters. For example, the Die object's Roll method needs no information or value to do its job.

- Most mutators don't return anything, so there's no need to put them in an assignment statement – like we do when we call accessors. Most mutators have void in their header, which means no value is returned. Sometimes mutators return a value, but this is somewhat unusual.

- Mutating one object does not change the attributes of another object. Each object is a separate entity with its own copy of the attributes. If one Hero object takes 10 damage, the others are not affected. Similarly, if I use the Roll() method on one Die object, it has no effect on the others.

In most programs, we move back and forth between accessors to see the state of the object and mutators to change the state of the object. If there are any helper methods in our object class, they usually get called as well (the same way as accessors and mutators). Here is a short example using the Hero class:

```
Hero firstHero = new Hero();                         //constructor call
string firstHeroName = firstHero.GetName();    //accessor call
Console.WriteLine(firstHeroName + " has entered the battle.");
```

```
Hero secondHero = new Hero("Aaron", 100);          //constructor call
string secondHeroName = secondHero.GetName(); //accessor call
Console.WriteLine(secondHeroName + " has entered the battle.");

int firstHeroDamage = firstHero.DealDamage();   //helper method call
Console.WriteLine(firstHeroName + " deals " + firstHeroDamage + " damage.");

secondHero.TakeDamage(firstHeroDamage);            //mutator call
int secondHeroHealth = secondHero.GetHealth(); //accessor call
Console.WriteLine(secondHeroName + " has " + secondHeroHealth + " health
left.");
```

And, here's a short example using the Die class:

```
//constructor call
Die firstDie = new Die();
//constructor call
Die secondDie = new Die(20);

//accessor call
Console.WriteLine("First die is showing: " + firstDie.GetSideUp());
//accessor call
Console.WriteLine("Second die is showing: " + secondDie.GetSideUp());

//accessor calls
int sumOfDice = firstDie.GetSideUp() + secondDie.GetSideUp();
Console.WriteLine("Sum of the Dice is: " + sumOfDice);

Console.WriteLine("Rolling both dice.");

//mutator call
firstDie.Roll();
//mutator call
secondDie.Roll();

//accessor call
Console.WriteLine("First die is now showing: " + firstDie.GetSideUp());
//accessor call
Console.WriteLine("Second die is now showing: " + secondDie.GetSideUp());

//accessor calls
sumOfDice = firstDie.GetSideUp() + secondDie.GetSideUp();
Console.WriteLine("Sum of the Dice is now: " + sumOfDice);
```

In the Code Reward for this level, we'll extend these last examples by
creating two Hero objects that will wage an epic life-and-death battle using
two Die objects to determine battle damage and healing amounts. This
battle will use almost every tool, technique, and trick we've learned, so take
some time to review how the objects are created, how their accessors and
mutators are used, and how they seem to interact in this dynamic example.

Side Quests

Want to Know More?

Please, I want some more: one of the most effective ways to understand object classes and object instances is to look at examples. Seeing how other coders set up their attributes, constructors, accessors, mutators, and even helper methods is a great way to understand what is possible with object-oriented programming. Take some time to look up object classes in C# and explore different examples, different styles, and different ideas.

Want to Do More?

What's in that loot box: in Level 10's Code Reward, you'll find a full object class for a loot box. Write some Main() statements to create a LootBox object by calling the constructor, check to see if your LootBox object is full by calling the only accessor method, and call the mutator to dispense the precious loot! Be sure to store your loot in an appropriate variable when you call the mutator.

What's in those loot boxes: repeat the work from *What's in that loot box*, but this time create five separate loot box objects and dispense the loot from each one. Be sure to show off all the awesome loot that was dispensed.

Objects of your very own: did you create your own object classes after Level 10? If you did, head to your project's Program.cs and Main() to bring your objects to life – instantiate your objects. Be sure to test out any constructors, accessors, and mutators that you defined in your object classes.

Code Reward – An Epic Battle

As promised, this level's code reward is an epic life-and-death battle between two Hero objects. We're going to ignore the DealDamage() helper method in the Hero class – instead, we're going to use a Die object to determine how much damage each Hero object does to the other. This Code Reward has elements of everything we've talked about in this book – literals, variables, input, math, random numbers, if-statements, loops, object classes, and object instances. It is also a pretty close approximation of how we might code a battle in a real game – all that's really missing are the graphics, sounds, and maybe some different input devices. We'll revisit this example in the next book (if you choose to continue your journey!).

Before you continue, you should know that the way that I have coded this reward, the battle isn't "perfect". For example, the first hero always attacks first, the second hero might attack even if their health is less than zero, and it's possible that both heroes perish in the end. When we code complex programs, we often start with a program that is close to what we want, even if the details aren't perfect. Sometimes, it takes a lot of energy and code to get everything just right, and while I encourage you to modify this program to make it as perfect as you want it to be, I've left it a bit imperfect to keep the code a bit simpler.

If you want to try coding this on your own, here's how my solution works:

- Be sure to include the Hero and Die object classes in your project.
- Prompt the user and collect string input for your two hero names.
- Create two Hero objects but call the parameterized constructor. Each hero has 100 starting health (you can use a literal here) and a name from the input you collected.
- Create a 20-sided Die object by calling the parameterized Die constructor.
- Here is the action part of the program:
  - Roll the Die object by calling the Roll() mutator method.
  - Store the Die object's side up value by calling the SideUp() accessor method and storing the result in an integer variable. This is the first hero's attack value.
  - Display the attack value to the user so they can see the strength of the first hero's attack.
  - Subtract the first hero's attack strength from the second hero's health value by calling their TakeDamage() method and passing the attack value.
  - Display the second hero's remaining health to the user.
  - Duplicate these action steps for the second hero – roll the Die object, store and display the attack value, subtract the attack value from the first hero's health, and display the first hero's remaining health to the user.
- Now, to automate the battle, write the action part of the program in a while loop that runs as long as both heroes have health that is greater than 0. If either hero has health less than or equal to zero, the battle will end. Don't worry about the change portion of your loop – if you've coded the action parts properly, eventually one of your heroes will have zero or fewer health points.

- Finally, tell your user which hero perished using an if-else-if statement – if both heroes have health that is zero or less, they have both perished; else, if the first hero's health is zero or less, they have perished; else, the second hero has expired.
- Bonus: add the LootBox object class from the Level 10 Code Reward to your project. Create a LootBox object and reward the winner of your battle by dispensing some awesome loot!

I used a project called Level11CodeReward, which you'll see reflected in the namespace.

As always, if you get stuck or simply want to see the solution, feel free to take a look! This kind of coding takes some practice. So, be patient with yourself and keep trying with simpler examples. Very soon, you'll be ready to tackle programs like this one.

```
/*
Remember, this code goes in Program.cs in your project. You'll need to make
sure the Hero and Die classes are also in your project.

This is a program that uses the Hero and Die object classes to simulate an epic
battle between two heroes.

This program is the Code Reward for Level 11.
Author: Aaron Langille
*/

namespace Level1CodeReward
{
    internal class Program
    {
      static void Main(string[] args)
      {
          //Giving our heroes names will make the battle more fun.
          Console.Write("Hero 1, what is your name: ");
          string hero1Name = Console.ReadLine();

          Console.Write("Hero 2, what is your name: ");
          string hero2Name = Console.ReadLine();

          //Create two Hero objects with user-input names and 100 health
          Hero hero1 = new Hero(hero1Name, 100);
          Hero hero2 = new Hero(hero2Name, 100);

          //int variable for our attack damage
          int attackDamage = 0;

          //A Die object to determine attack amounts
          Die d20 = new Die(20);

          //Some output for spacing and a battle notice
          Console.WriteLine();
          Console.WriteLine("The battle begins …");

          //I used this variable to count the battle rounds (optional)
          int roundCount = 1;

          //Eventually, one of our Hero objects will have health <= 0 and
          //this loop will start.
          while (hero1.GetHealth() > 0 && hero2.GetHealth() > 0)
          {

              //Let's get a fresh roll on our Die object.
              d20.Roll();
```

```
//What side is up - this is our attack strength
attackDamage = d20.GetSideUp();

//Output the first Hero's attack strength
Console.WriteLine(hero1.GetName() + " attacks for "
                        + attackDamage + " damage.");

//Second Hero takes damage
hero2.TakeDamage(attackDamage);

//Output the second Hero's remaining health
Console.WriteLine(hero2.GetName() + " is wounded and has "
        + hero2.GetHealth() + " health remaining.");

//The next few lines repeat the action
//but for the second Hero's attack.
d20.Roll();
attackDamage = d20.GetSideUp();

Console.WriteLine(hero2.GetName() + " attacks for "
                        + attackDamage + " damage.");
hero1.TakeDamage(attackDamage);
Console.WriteLine(hero1.GetName() + " is wounded and has "
        + hero1.GetHealth() + " health remaining.");

//At this point, both Hero objects have taken damage
//and eventually one will have health >= 0.
//Display that a battle round has ended, and
//increase the round counter variable.
Console.WriteLine("--------End of round " +
roundCount + " -------");
roundCount++;
}


//LootBox for the winner
LootBox winnerLootBox = new LootBox();
string winnerLoot = winnerLootBox.DispenseLoot();

//Who perished?
if(hero1.GetHealth() <= 0 && hero2.GetHealth() <= 0)
{

Console.WriteLine("Both heroes have perished!! No loot for
anyone.");
}
```

```
        else if(hero1.GetHealth() <= 0)
        {
            Console.WriteLine(hero1.GetName() + " has perished.");
            Console.WriteLine(hero2.GetName()   +   "   earns   -   "   +
winnerLoot);
        }
        else
        {
            Console.WriteLine(hero2.GetName() + " has perished.");
            Console.WriteLine(hero1.GetName() + " earns - " +
winnerLoot);
        }
            //That's the end of this program.


        }
    }
}
```

25

Code Quest 11: A Companion for Our Hero (Part 2)

Before proceeding with this quest:

- review Level 11
- complete Code Quest 10 (required)
- for this Code Quest, you can actually use the project you created for Code Quest 10. All the code for this Code Quest will go in the Program.cs file, in the Main() method.

In many games, particularly real-time strategy (RTS) games, we spend a lot of our time constructing buildings or units. Usually, there is a little image and description that tells us what the unit or building is, how much it costs, and what it's going to do to help us win the battle. When we click on the little image, the building or unit is constructed and now we can use it in whatever way we need. Instantiating objects from an object class works in a very similar, but less flashy, way.

In Code Quest 10, we created a blueprint for a simple NPC character that might join our hero on their journey. Now we're going to "click the little image and construct" our hero's companion. Of course, we don't have an actual button to click in this case. Instead, we're going to use code to instantiate, access, and mutate our simple companion.

When you're ready to bring our companion to life (sort of), head to the Main Quest below!

Main Quest – A Companion for Our Hero (Part 2)

In this quest, we're going to instantiate (or create) an object from the SimpleNPC class that we designed in Code Quest 10. We're also going to test our accessor and mutator methods to make sure that everything works properly.

All of the code for this Code Quest should be in the Main() method or your project's Program.cs file. It's probably most convenient to use the Program.cs of your Code Quest 10 project. If you prefer to create a new project, that's ok too, but you'll need to copy your SimpleNPC class/code to the new project.

DOI: 10.1201/9781003348481-25

To create and test your SimpleNPC objects, complete the following tasks:

1. Create two SimpleNPC objects, one using the un-parameterized constructor, and one using the parameterized constructor. For the constructor parameters, pass in string literals (or variables if you prefer) for our companion's name and the two barks.
2. Write a for loop that calls your first SimpleNPC object's accessor method – TalkToMe() – five times. Output the result of calling the method.
3. Repeat step 2 for your second SimpleNPC object.
4. Prompt the user and collect two different strings. Use these two strings and the appropriate mutator methods – ChangeBark1() and ChangeBark2() – to change the bark attributes of your second SimpleNPC object.
5. Repeat step 2 to show off the mutated (changed) barks of your second SimpleNPC object.
6. Add any narrative or story text you want to make your program more interesting.

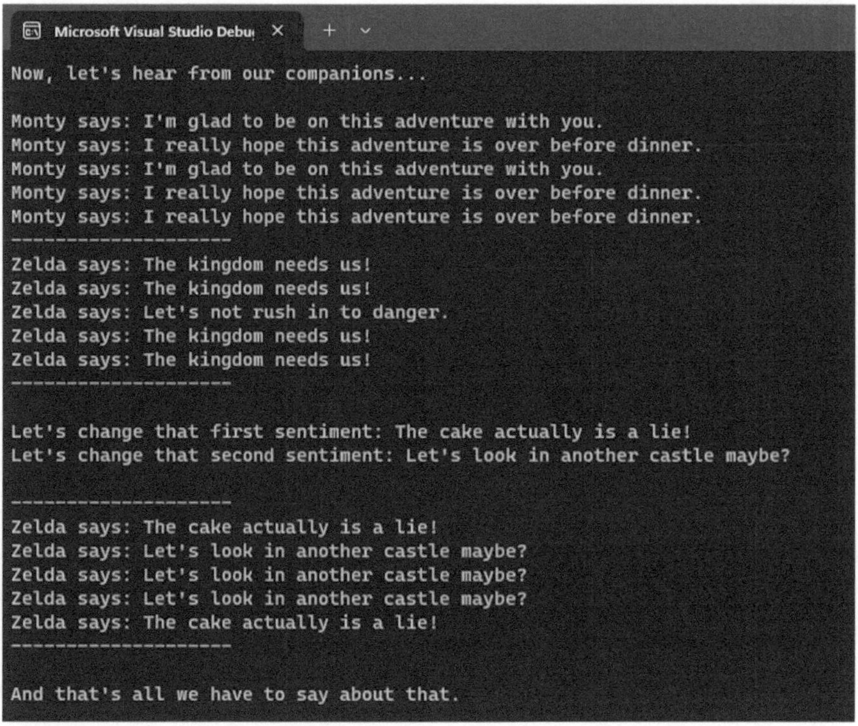

```
Microsoft Visual Studio Debu   ×     +   ∨

Now, let's hear from our companions...

Monty says: I'm glad to be on this adventure with you.
Monty says: I really hope this adventure is over before dinner.
Monty says: I'm glad to be on this adventure with you.
Monty says: I really hope this adventure is over before dinner.
Monty says: I really hope this adventure is over before dinner.
--------------------
Zelda says: The kingdom needs us!
Zelda says: The kingdom needs us!
Zelda says: Let's not rush in to danger.
Zelda says: The kingdom needs us!
Zelda says: The kingdom needs us!
--------------------

Let's change that first sentiment: The cake actually is a lie!
Let's change that second sentiment: Let's look in another castle maybe?

--------------------
Zelda says: The cake actually is a lie!
Zelda says: Let's look in another castle maybe?
Zelda says: Let's look in another castle maybe?
Zelda says: Let's look in another castle maybe?
Zelda says: The cake actually is a lie!
--------------------

And that's all we have to say about that.
```

FIGURE 25.1
One more time, here is some output to help guide you through this quest.

In the end, this program is going to create a lot of text. In most games, we don't ask our NPCs or companions to talk (or bark) constantly like this, but this is a good way to test that everything is working the way it should. Figure 25.1 is the output from my solution to this Code Quest.

Side Quests

Make it your own: Did you write a somewhat or completely modified object in Code Quest 10? If you did, try to test your objects using the steps that are outlined above. Try creating more than one object using each of your constructors, call all your accessor methods (be sure to output the results), and change your objects by calling your mutators.

26

Cutscene 4: The Adventure Ends ... Or Does It?

Game Over!

There is a very special feeling of accomplishment that comes from finishing a video game. You know that feeling, right? It happens when you've explored every corner of a strange land and found every piece of rare and valuable loot. It happens when you've leveled up a thousand times, memorized every attack and defense combination, and sent every minion, mini-boss, and mega-boss back into the darkest depths. It happens when you've finally sorted all the jewels and crushed all the candies. It happens when you've watched every cutscene, read every line of dialog, and revealed every piece of lore. It happens when there are no more platforms to run or jump across. It takes practice, patience, and, most of all, perseverance – but it's worth it in the end because great games change us forever by teaching us something about ourselves.

I hope that when you look back on the adventure that you started in this book, you'll feel a similar sense of accomplishment through the practice, patience, and perseverance that you put into learning how to code. Afterall, you've battled your way through variables, literals, built-in data types, and collecting input. You've leveled up your knowledge of powerful math operations and the chaos that is random number generation. You explored all the twists and turns of if-statements, and in true gamer fashion, you chose to grind your way through loop logic like a pro. You even managed to make new objects out of nothing but a handful of C# statements. However you started this journey, hopefully you have learned something about yourself and a bit about programming too.

Congratulations, brave adventurer. Your adventure is over ...

DOI: 10.1201/9781003348481-26

Actually, the Adventure Is Just Beginning?

... for now. Where you go next is up to you. If you picked up this book to learn what all this programming fuss was about, perhaps your adventure really is over. But maybe there's a new spark inside of you that grows with every line of code that successfully compiles. Maybe these are just the first steps in a lifelong journey to code games, apps, and other awesome software. How can you feed this new interest?

There are lots of coding resources out there and picking the right ones depends a lot on your personal goals. If you enjoyed this journey and want it to continue, there is a second book in this series that takes everything we've learned here and applies it to coding small games using the MonoGame framework. This is a great place to start if you're not yet ready to jump into game-specific engines like Unity or Unreal Engine, or if you simply want to work in a code-first game environment (which is exactly what MonoGame is). If that sounds like your next adventure, look for *A Gamer's Introduction To Programming In MonoGame: Welcome, Brave Adventurer 2!* (coming soon, or recently published – depending on when you're reading this).

It's also possible that your programming path veers off in a different direction. The skills you've learned here are transferable to other languages, other development environments, and other kinds of projects. Even if things look a bit different, don't forget the essentials – literals are data we can see in the code, variables are named storage containers, math operators calculate, random numbers are awesome, if-statements are like decisions, loops repeat, and objects are powerful. These are features of all modern programming.

What's Left in This Book?

Finally, you might be wondering why there are still some pages left, even though we're talking about the end (or the end for now) of our adventure together. What follows are a few bonus topics that aren't part of our main quest, but that you can explore now (if you haven't already). In the final pages, you'll find a Bonus Code Quest that gives you a sneak peek into what a MonoGame program looks like. You'll also find bonus levels that give you a bit more insight into binary, weird C# math behaviors, how to collect input from the user more robustly, a bit more information about conditional checking (for if-statements and loops), some information on variable scope, and some tips on finding and using the online resources that accompany these books.

FIGURE 26.1
In true video game fashion, you've unlocked an achievement! Congratulations, you definitely earned this.

A Fond Farewell

Wherever your journey takes you next, thank you for joining me through this part of it. Until we meet again, brave adventurer, happy gaming, and happy coding (Figure 26.1).

27

Bonus Code Quest: Cornflower Blue! (MonoGame Sneak Peek)

Before proceeding with this quest:

- install Visual Studio
- install the MonoGame framework libraries (see Level 1)

Main Quest: Cornflower Blue! (MonoGame Sneak Peek)

Have you ever played a video game where you see a preview of a level or area before you start? This is the game designers' way of giving you a quick overview of where you're going without giving away all the fun (and perilous) details. They do this to set expectations, build excitement, and give you a sense of what skills you're going to need to succeed. Like Code Quest 1 (way back at the start of your adventure), this quest is low on actual coding but it will tell us if the MonoGame libraries are installed and working properly, and it's a great excitement-building preview of where we're headed in the next book.

Creating a New MonoGame Project in Visual Studio

Creating a MonoGame project in Visual Studio starts with the usual first step – creating a new project. But, in the next step, instead of creating a console program like we did in Code Quest 1, we're going to scroll or search for "MonoGame Cross-Platform Desktop Application". Be a bit careful here, as there might be more than one MonoGame project template. If you don't have any MonoGame project templates, you'll need to install (or re-install) the MonoGame libraries (see Level 1) (Figure 27.1).

Then, as usual, we give our project a name – I'll use BonusCodeQuest – and we tell Visual Studio where to store the project on the hard drive. Once we click the final "Create" button, we have the start of our first MonoGame project. If there is nothing in the editor window of Visual Studio, click on "Game1.cs" in the Solution Explorer panel (see the right-most box in Figure 27.2). If you don't see the Solution Explorer panel, you can bring it up using the View menu and select Solution Explorer.

DOI: 10.1201/9781003348481-27

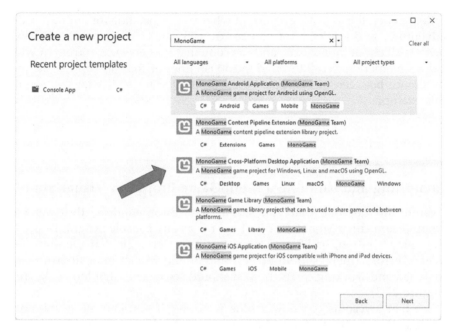

FIGURE 27.1
For the first time, we're not selecting a console application for our project. For this bonus quest, we're going to use the MonoGame Cross-Platform Desktop Application option. Woohoo!

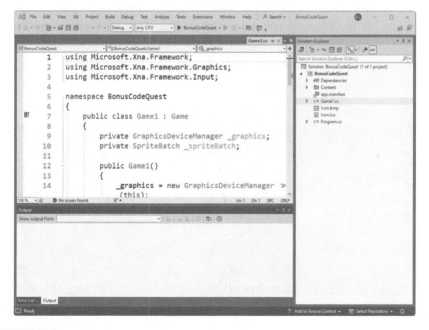

FIGURE 27.2
If this is your first MonoGame project, be sure to spend a bit of time to look at the different files in the Solution Explorer and the different code that is given to us in the editor pane.

Remember, this is just a preview of where we're heading for our next code adventure, so don't let what you see overwhelm or worry you – the next book is all about MonoGame and the code that you now see in front of you. Take a moment to scroll through the 50-ish lines of code and appreciate the difference between our console-based Code Quest 1 and what you see in this example.

Compiling and Running a MonoGame Project in Visual Studio

Despite all the code that you see in the editor window, the way we compile and run a MonoGame is the same as any console program – press the "play" button, or F5, or Debug → Start Debugging! If there are no syntax errors (there shouldn't be), and if the MonoGame libraries are installed and working correctly, you should see a result that looks like this (Figure 27.3).

See that awesome cornflower blue window? If you join me in the next book, that's where our future MonoGame examples are going to appear.

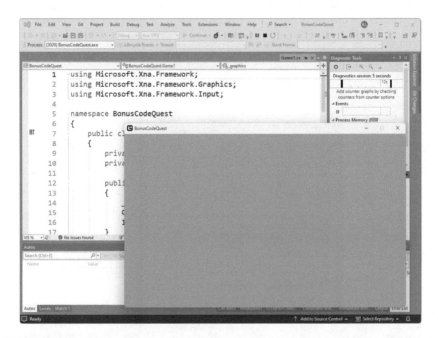

FIGURE 27.3

If all goes well, you'll see a lovely blue window when you compile and run the default code. This window, believe it or not, is the basis of all the examples in the next book in this series.

A More Fiery Start

We can't make text or images appear in our cornflower blue window just yet, but we can make a small change to the initial BonusCodeQuest code. This way, we'll see that the write-compile-run cycle is the same whether we're learning to code in a console project or writing our own video games in a MonoGame project.

If it's still open, close the blue MonoGame window so that you can see the Visual Studio editor. Make sure that you are looking at the Game1.cs code (click on that file in the Solution Explorer if needed) and scroll down to line 45 (or thereabouts). It should say:

```
GraphicsDevice.Clear(Color.CornflowerBlue);
```

Change this to:

```
GraphicsDevice.Clear(Color.Firebrick);
```

Then, re-compile and re-run your program. Did the color change to a fiery brick red? If you make any mistakes – or syntax errors – the program won't re-compile or re-run until you fix them. When you do see your "fire brick" window, take a moment to appreciate completing this quest – you made this happen, and it could be just the start of our next awesome adventure together.

Side Quests

Keep practicing (MonoGame): If you completed A More Fiery Start, you might have noticed that Visual Studio gave you a list of color options when you edited GraphicsDevice.Clear(Color.CornflowerBlue). Follow the steps from A More Fiery Start again, but try some of the other color options. It's not a big change, but it is fun to see the window change colors with very little coding effort.

Make mistakes (MonoGame): Even though the MonoGame code is more complex and creates a cooler output window, the idea of coding errors is exactly the same. Try making a few on-purpose syntax errors like these:

- add or remove a curly brace ({ or })
- add or remove a semicolon (;)
- change the case of a letter or word
- add a random word in a random place

28

Bonus Level 1: A Bit about Binary

As programmers of modern games, apps, and other software, we don't often have to worry about the technical details of how data is stored in memory – it's usually enough to know that ints are whole numbers, floats are decimal numbers, and strings are text. As long as we use the right variable types for the data we want to store, we don't need to worry about what is going on behind the scenes. However, with a bit more explanation about how binary data works, we can better understand a few things that we glossed (or skipped) over in earlier levels:

- What does it mean to say ints and floats are 32 bits, but doubles are 64 bits?
- Why do built-in data types have maximum and minimum values like the roughly −2 billion to +2 billion for ints?
- Why can't we put double values in int variables (more on this in Bonus Level 2)?
- Why do ints (and other data types) overflow when we try to go past their minimum and maximum values (more on this in Bonus Level 2)?

Storing Data in Bits

To answer some of the questions above, we need to understand what a bit is. Put simply, a bit is the smallest piece of digital information. A bit is usually a single transistor that has an off and on state, and all of our digital devices are full of transistors that turn off and on very, very quickly (billions of times per second). This two-state nature of our digital bits is why we say that our data is stored in a binary way – binary means two possible states. The CPU, RAM, hard drive, and other components respond to the specific configuration of transistors – which ones are off and which ones are on – and this determines what calculations are done, what values are inside our variables, what is stored on the hard drive, what appears on our screens, what sounds come out of our speakers, and so on.

But, since most of us aren't familiar with transistors, let's talk about light bulbs instead. Imagine you have one light bulb nearby. How many different

DOI: 10.1201/9781003348481-28

states can the bulb be in? Assuming we keep it simple and forget about dimming bulbs and different colors (modern light bulbs are so cool), one light bulb can have two states – off and on. This is kind of like a single transistor or bit inside our computers, consoles, and other digital devices.

With one bulb, we can have two states (Figure 28.1). Normally we would say those states are off and on, but there's nothing stopping us from calling them stop and go, no and yes, false and true, zero and one. We could even say that off means stand still and on means jump around. That might sound odd, but stay with me on this.

Now, what happens if we add a light bulb – now we have two bulbs. How many different states can we have? Take a moment to think this through before reading on.

If you take the time to sketch this out, we can have four different states with two bulbs – or two bits (Figure 28.2). Now we can represent four different pieces of information instead of two. Maybe it's the numbers zero to three, or the colors red, blue, green, and yellow. Whatever it is that we want to assign to each pattern of off and on bulbs (or bits), we get four options with two bulbs. What happens with three bulbs?

That's right, we're up to eight possible states with only three bulbs (Figure 28.3). Without illustrating it (too much page space), 4 bulbs mean 16 states, and 5 bulbs mean 32. If you haven't noticed the pattern yet, every bulb (or bit) we add to our scenario doubles the number of states we can represent. If I'm teaching in a room that has 10 light bulbs (they can even be those annoying fluorescent ones), and if each bulb has a dedicated switch, I

FIGURE 28.1
Computer transistors (or bits) are like light bulbs that can be off or on.

FIGURE 28.2
Two light bulbs, four distinct patterns.

FIGURE 28.3
Three bulbs, eight distinct patterns.

can make 2^{10} or 1,024 different configurations with those 10 bulbs. If you don't like the notation 2^{10}, start with 1 bulb and 2 states (off and on) and keep doubling 10 times – 2, 4, 8, 16, 32, 64, 128, 256, 512, and 1,024!

So, what does this have to do with ints and other built-in data types? In order to make C# operate efficiently, each built-in data type is given a certain number of bits (or bulbs) to work with. In the case of ints, C# sets aside 32 bits. If you do some quick math (or a lot of doubling), you'll see that 32 bits gives us 4,294,967,296 different combinations of off and on. That's 4 billion (and change). But I said that an int stores numbers between –2 billion and +2 billion – and if you remembered that fact, good for you! To make this happen, C# takes one of the 32 bits and uses it to note whether the number is positive or negative, and the other 31 bits are for the number part. The 31 bits is 2,147,483,648 different combinations of off and on. In other words, with 32 bits, an int variable or literal can be positive or negative and have a number part of roughly 0 to 2 billion.

Different Bits for Different Data Types

Whenever I talk about light bulbs in my classes or with groups of new programmers, I relate them to the 32 bits of an int variable or literal. I do this because ints are one of the first data types that we use and they are fairly simple because they don't have any pesky decimals to worry about. But our other built-in data types are also stored with bits including floats with 32 bits (just like ints) and doubles with 64 bits.

When you declare an int variable (or use an int literal in your code), C# sets aside 32 bits of memory space. The fact that it's declared as an int tells C# that it won't need to store a decimal portion. When you declare a float variable (or use a float literal in your code), C# sets aside 32 bits – same as an int – but this time those 32 bits will be used to store both a whole number portion and a decimal portion for our number. Exactly how C# and other languages store decimals in binary is a bit more complex than I want to explain with light bulbs that are off and on, but if this subject interests you, I encourage you to do a bit more reading elsewhere.

We'll talk some more about the difference between ints and floats in Bonus Level 2, including why we can't store a 32-bit int value in a 32-bit float variable.

Not all data is stored using 32 bits. Doubles, for example, use 64 bits (that's why they are called doubles – double the memory of an int or float). Other built-in data types that we didn't use in this book like longs (really big whole numbers) use 64 bits, shorts (smaller whole numbers) use 16 bits, and decimal (really precise decimal numbers) use a whopping 128 bits.

Don't worry – you don't really need to memorize all of these bit-facts to be a good programmer. You can always look up the number of bits and value ranges of the built-in data types if you need to. What is important to keep in mind is that all data in your games and programs is stored using bits and the number of bits determines the properties of each data type.

Bits & Bytes (and Kilos, Megas, Gigas …)

Even though bits are the smallest units of memory that can be accessed, it's very unusual for any part of our program to reference a single one. For efficiency reasons, computers and digital devices group bits in clusters of 8 instead – and we call 8 bits a byte. This means that our 32-bit ints are 4 bytes ($4 \times 8 = 32$), floats are also 4 bytes, longs and doubles are 8 bytes ($8 \times 8 = 64$), and decimals are 16 bytes ($16 \times 8 = 128$).

I mention this here because it's very rare to see anything other than built-in data types measured in bits. You are much more likely to see bytes used when talking about the amount of memory (RAM and hard drive space) that some piece of data is using. You can always convert from bytes to bits by multiplying by 8 if you want to, but more often than not, programmers, IT-folk, and computer buffs will use bytes instead.

In fact, 8 bits or 1 byte is so small in today's digital world that you're even more likely to hear the terms kilobyte, megabyte, gigabyte, and terabyte – a kilobyte is one thousand bytes, a megabyte is one million bytes, a gigabyte is one billion bytes, and a terabyte is one trillion bytes. We don't use these terms when talking about individual variables or literals in our code, but we do use them when we talk about all the data that makes up our finished game – really small games can be a handful of megabytes while AAA titles can be hundreds of gigabytes. Having lots of games (and other software) on your computer or console might mean investing in a terabyte of storage space – that's 8,796,093,022,208 bits (in case you're curious). Now, how many ints could we store with that much space?

29

Bonus Level 2: A Slight Miscalculation

As gamers, we like to think that our consoles, PCs, and other digital devices are really, really accurate. It's most comforting to think that we lost a match because the people (or bots) we were playing against were better than us – or maybe luckier than us in some cases. But, how would you feel if I told you that you lost, or even worse won, that last game because of a math error? Now, I'm not saying this happens often, but it turns out that computers aren't always as accurate as we expect them to be. Let's take a look at a few cases where the math in our code doesn't quite add up (that's a rare math pun, in case you missed it).

Overflow

You've written an awesome new game and you've invited some people to playtest it. One of the players is having an epic run – they've collected all the collectables, cleared all the areas, earned every bonus and score multiplier imaginable. In fact, they've earned a score of 2147483647 with only one thing left to do – jump over the final flagpole. As expected, the player manages to clear the pole and earn another 100 points. On the final screen of the game, you congratulate the player on their fantastic play and their amazing score of –2147483549. Way to go player! Wait, what?

In this example, our player's score is so good that it can't be contained in an int variable. Here is some code so that you can see this issue for yourself:

```
int score = 2147483647;
Console.WriteLine("Current score: " + score);
Console.WriteLine("Adding 100 points …");
score += 100;
Console.WriteLine("New score: " + score);
```

The output from this code is:

```
Current score: 2147483647
```

DOI: 10.1201/9781003348481-29

```
Adding 100 points …
New score: -2147483549
```

If you read Bonus Level 1, you saw that integers are stored using 32 bits and that their maximum positive value is 2147483647. Yes, I cheated by setting our score variable to this value in our example, but when you try to go past this value, by adding 100, or 10, or even 1, the value exceeds what the int variable can hold and it actually wraps around to the negative values. This is called overflow – our int variable is at its maximum capacity and when more is added it overflows into the negatives. This isn't a common problem in games since we rarely deal with numbers in the billions, but it does happen from time to time. Here are some things to know about integer overflow:

- It affects all whole number data types – int, long, short, byte, etc.
- It works in reverse too – try the code above, but start at –2147483648 and subtract 100. You'll end up at 2147483548.
- Multiplication can also cause overflow – set an int variable to 1 and write a for loop that doubles it 32 times.

So, your player's score is too big to store in an int variable – what can you do? Luckily, there are some other data types that are larger to accommodate an epic run in your game. We don't use them often because they use double the memory, but long variables would work in this situation:

```
long score = 2147483647;
Console.WriteLine("Current score: " + score);
Console.WriteLine("Adding 100 points …");
score += 100;
Console.WriteLine("New score: " + score);
```

This time, your player's score is a well-earned and accurate 2147483747. If your player manages to overflow a long variable, I'd rethink your scoring algorithm.

Decimal Errors

Most new coders seem to accept the idea of integer overflow pretty easily – integer data types can only hold so much, and when you go too far in either direction (positive or negative), there are consequences. But decimal errors, that's another story. We want to think that computers are unerringly accurate, but take a look at the code below:

```
float myFloat = 0.1f;
for(int i = 1; i <= 5; i++)

{
        Console.WriteLine("Adding 0.1");
        myFloat += 0.1f;
        Console.WriteLine(myFloat);
}
```

If you've gone through all of the regular levels including Level 9 (loops), there's nothing particularly special about this code. We have a float variable called myFloat that starts with a value of 0.1. Then, using a for loop, we add 0.1 to the variable, five times, and display the results. The output from this code is:

```
Adding 0.1
0.2
Adding 0.1
0.3
Adding 0.1
0.4
Adding 0.1
0.5
Adding 0.1
0.6
```

No problem here, right? If you were to update your for loop to run 10 times instead of 5, the output would be:

```
Adding 0.1
0.2
Adding 0.1
0.3
Adding 0.1
0.4
Adding 0.1
0.5
Adding 0.1
0.6
Adding 0.1
0.70000005
Adding 0.1
0.8000001
Adding 0.1
0.9000001
Adding 0.1
1.0000001
```

Hmm, something worrisome has happened. Starting at what should be 0.7, we see a slight (very slight) error – we're over by 0.00000005. Why is this happening?

It turns out that storing decimals in a binary way comes with some inaccuracies. The example above does a really good job of illustrating that our decimal numbers aren't always perfectly precise, but there are other, less obvious ways that precision errors can creep into our calculations – like repeating decimals or truncation errors.

Whether or not any of these slight errors are actually a problem depends on your game or program. In most cases, we can simply ignore these errors – most game events aren't so accurate that an error of 0.00000005 will affect the outcome. In other cases, where someone's safety is a concern – software for self-driving cars, airplane automation systems, or similar applications that need a high level of accuracy – you might want to find ways of reducing or even eliminating these errors. There are lots of resources online and in other great books that will give you ideas on how to write highly accurate decimal calculations – but be aware that the solutions might cost you more memory, more CPU computation, or more complex code.

For the rest of us, it's enough just to know that our decimals aren't always as accurate as we think they are – but they're usually accurate enough.

Integer Division and Integer Remainder

Integer division isn't like overflow or decimal errors – it's not actually a "problem" with the way C# calculates or stores a value. Instead, it's an operation that many new programmers simply find confusing and forget to account for in their code. The confusion, as far as I can tell, comes from the fact that, outside of coding, we rarely think about division being different between integers and decimal numbers – but C# and other high-level languages treat them differently. We first saw this in Level 5, and here is another example as a reminder of what integer and non-integer division look like:

```
int totalScore1 = 100;
int numberOfMatches1 = 3;
int averageScore1 = totalScore1 / numberOfMatches1;
Console.WriteLine("Average score 1: " + averageScore1);

float totalScore2 = 100;
float numberOfMatches2 = 3;
float averageScore2 = totalScore2 / numberOfMatches2;
Console.WriteLine("Average score 2: " + averageScore2);
```

Here are two sets of statements that calculate the average score of two players that have played three matches each and have earned a total score across the matches of 100 points. The first set of statements uses integers for both the score and the number of matches, while the second set uses floats. The output from this code is:

```
Average score 1: 33
Average score 2: 33.333332
```

Now, you might want to jump up and yell "C# can't do division accurately!", but C# has done exactly what it is supposed to do. When both operands (the variables or literals in the operation) are integer types, C# does the division and simply drops (or truncates) the decimal portion! That's right, it just ignores the decimal part of the division completely. When at least one of our operands is a float, we get a more expected answer with the decimal intact.

It's very common to think that the loss of decimal is an error, but this is actually how C# is programmed to work. There are cases where this behavior is actually useful. For example, imagine that you have 4 players in your game, and as a team, they have earned 123 coins that are to be divided equally among the players. How many coins does each player get?

```
int numCoins = 123;
int numPlayers = 4;
int coinsPerPlayer = numCoins / numPlayers;
Console.WriteLine("Each player gets " + coinsPerPlayer + " coins.");
```

If you take the time to write and run this code, you'll see that each player gets 30 coins. You might realize that you could do this with float variables (and literals) and get the same answer by simply dropping the decimal part yourself (using floats, the players get 30.75 coins each). What, then, are the advantages to using ints when we can get a reasonable, and possibly more accurate, answer using floats? First, some data should be represented as ints. We can't have a fraction of a player or a fraction of a coin, so using float variables would be a misrepresentation of our players or coins. Second, while 30.75 is a more accurate answer, it hides one fact that might be of interest to us – how many coins are left over after the players have each taken their cut of the treasure? It turns out that there is a handy operator that pairs perfectly with our integer division operator – modulus (%). Check out this updated example:

```
int numCoins = 123;
int numPlayers = 4;
int coinsPerPlayer = numCoins / numPlayers;
int coinsLeftOver = numCoins % numPlayers;
Console.WriteLine("Each player gets " + coinsPerPlayer
    + " coins. " + coinsLeftOver
    + " coins will be donated to charity.");
```

The modulus (%) operator is the remainder from an integer division operation. When we divide two integers like 123/4, the result (called the dividend) is the whole number portion, or 30 in this case. When we use %, the result is the remainder, or 3 in this case. Think back to your long division days – 123/4 is 30 with a remainder of 3. Even though it might seem like more energy and thought-power to use integers in this example, it does represent the number of players and coins properly as non-decimal variables and has the added bonus of being able to quickly determine how many coins are left over.

Personally, I like to use modulus to have code run at regular intervals. Try coding and running this example for yourself:

```
int numberOfSteps = 100;
int interval = 3;
int score = 0;

for (int currentStep = 1; currentStep <= numberOfSteps; currentStep++)
{
    if (currentStep % interval == 0)
    {
        Console.WriteLine("Adding to your score!!");
        score++;
    }
    else
        Console.WriteLine("Skipping this step " + currentStep);
}

Console.WriteLine("Final score: " + score);
```

This code is a pretend game loop that runs for 100 steps. The player is awarded with a point every time they survive 3 time steps – of course, there's nothing happening to the player to jeopardize their survival, but let's not worry about that. The magic in this program is the if-statement that says "if the current step is evenly divisible by 3 (evenly divisible means a modulus, or remainder, of 0), the player gets a point added to their score". If it's not evenly divisible, we skip that step. We can change this code by adjusting the interval – try changing it to 1, 2, 3, 5, and 10.

In the end, both integer division and the modulus operator have a place in our code, and the missing decimal part isn't technically a calculation error. But it is something to watch out for. If you have int variables in your code or calculations and you're getting an unexpected result, check for some sneaky integer division.

Casting Revisited – Converting from One Type to Another

Most of the time, we write code with types that don't change – we put integer literals into integer variables, we use floats when we want decimals, and all of our text shows up as strings. However, there are times when we need to change from one type to another. In some cases, these type changes can happen automatically, but in other cases, we need to write code to change them manually. Let's take a quick look at both cases, starting with automatic conversions.

Throughout most of the levels in this book, I've tried to write examples that avoided any confusion with data types. One of our examples from Level 3 was the following initialization statements:

```
int playerScore = 50;
float scoreModifier = 2.5f;
string playerName = "Aaron";
bool playerHasHighScore = false;
```

In these four statements, we assign an int literal to an int variable, a float literal to a float variable, a string literal to a string variable, and a bool literal to a bool variable. Nothing confusing there (I hope). What I didn't tell you is that we can bend the rules a little bit and assign compatible data types. What does this mean? Take a look at this one statement:

```
float scoreModifier = 10;
```

This code will compile without any issues because int values (literals or variables) are compatible with float variables. Afterall, they are both 32 bits in size, and an int value is simpler (no decimal to worry about) than a float so there is no issue automatically converting our integer literal 10 into a float so that it can be stored in our scoreModifier variable. In general, smaller and simpler data types can be stored in bigger and more complex variables, but I leave it to you, brave adventurer, to try out some different combinations to see which ones work and which ones don't. These kinds of automatic conversions are often called "widening conversions" because the smaller, simpler, or narrower data type is converted into a larger, more complex, or wider type.

There is a similar automatic conversion when we use multiple types in a single expression like this:

```
float finalScore = (105 + 16) * 2.5f;
```

Since one of the operands on the right is a float, the resulting type is also a float – there are more examples of this in Level 5. This is true when we use variables as well:

```
int baseScore = 105;
int bonusScore = 16;
float scoreMultiplier = 2.5f;
float finalScore = (baseScore + bonusScore) * scoreMultiplier;
```

We also see automatic conversion when we combine strings with other types:

```
string output = "Player 1, final score: " + finalScore;
Console.WriteLine(output);
```

Non-string types are automatically converted to strings when they are concatenated like the example above. We've seen this a lot throughout the examples in this book, even if we weren't actively thinking about this conversion.

Unfortunately, things are not always this easy. Sometimes, we need to convert from one type to another in our code and it can't be done automatically. While integers are compatible with float variables, we can't say the same in reverse:

```
int scoreMultiplier = 2.5f;
```

This will result in a syntax error because C# knows that, even though they are both 32 bits in size, a float is more complex than an int and this statement isn't allowed. We can take charge of the situation and force C# to convert the float by casting like this:

```
int scoreMultiplier = (int) 2.5f;
```

By putting the type in round brackets, we are confirming that we want C# to "cram" or "squish" the float literal into the int variable – we are also confirming to C# that we understand that the decimal will be lost when we do this. That's right, casting a float to an int truncates (drops) the decimal portion. If you were to output the value of scoreMultiplier it would be 2, not 2.5. This is called a narrowing conversion because we're taking data that is large, complex, or wide, and we're altering it to fit into a smaller, simpler, or narrower container.

Of course, casting works for variables as well. Here's an example from earlier in this Bonus Level:

```
int totalScore = 100;
int numberOfMatches = 3;
float averageScore = totalScore / (float)numberOfMatches;
Console.WriteLine("Average score 1: " + averageScore);
```

In this example, we are storing totalScore and numberOfMatches as ints, because we want to represent them as whole numbers. If we try to do our average division with these two variables, we'll lose our decimal place (integer division). By casting one of the variables (either one or both) to float, we are telling C# to temporarily treat one of the operands as a float so the final result will also be of type float. This isn't a narrowing conversion like the previous example, but it does show how casting can be used to temporarily change the type of a variable to get a more accurate result.

For more examples of casting and type conversions, be sure to revisit Math Functions in Level 5 and Generating Random Numbers and Casting in Level 6.

30

Bonus Level 3: Input Made (A Little Bit) Friendlier

In this bonus level, we're going to look at two input-related issues – what happens when the user enters unparsable input on the console and how to make our string input a bit less sensitive to capitalization. We've been working around these problems by assuming the user would always enter parsable input – integers that had no decimals, numbers that were formatted properly, and so on – and string input that was perfectly accurate. In part, we did this because very few people are going to write console programs outside of the examples in this book. But, for those of you who want to practice their coding skills with more console programs and also want to know how to deal with trickier input, the explanations and examples below are for you.

TryParse() – Dealing with Unparsable Input

Before we deal with unparsable input, I'd like to remind you that input is covered in Level 4. In Levels 7 and 8, there are examples of checking input values using if-statements, and in Level 9, there are examples of validating input using loops. Let's revisit an early input example from Level 4:

```
Console.Write("Hello player! What is your first name: ");
string playerName = Console.ReadLine();
Console.Write("And, what is your age: ");
int playerAge = int.Parse(Console.ReadLine());
Console.Write("How many hours of video games do you play per week: ");
float playerGameTime = float.Parse(Console.ReadLine());
```

In this example, we are asking for three types of input from the player – string for their name, int for their age, and float for the number of hours they play per week. For what it's worth, the string input is almost impossible to break. Whatever the user enters on the console will be interpreted as a string and the program will carry on.

The problems happen when the user enters something unparsable for the integer or float values. The Parse() methods' job is to make sure that the

DOI: 10.1201/9781003348481-30

input is appropriate for converting. For example, 100, 57312, and −19 can all be parsed and converted to int while 100.65, 57,312, and "applesauce" cannot. Similarly, 51.11, −421.45, and 0 can all be parsed and converted to float while 51.1.1 and "applesauce" cannot. When the program is running and tries to parse input that can't be properly converted, the program will stop and a runtime error will pop up (see Cutscene 3 for more on runtime errors). What we need is a way to handle bad input without the program crashing.

This is where the TryParse() methods come in handy. I didn't use this code in the previous levels because the syntax is a bit unusual and I wanted to keep our examples as simple as possible. But I know that there are some of you who really want to know how to deal with this input issue, so here we go!

The TryParse() methods return a boolean (or bool) value so they are 100% usable in if-statements or loops. I'm going to jump straight to loops because, in most cases, that's how you're going to want to use these methods − you're going to want to re-prompt and re-collect input from the user if they make an unparsable input error. Let's break our example up a bit to simplify this new code:

```
Console.Write("And, what is your age: ");
string playerAgeString = Console.ReadLine();

int playerAge = 0;
while(!int.TryParse(playerAgeString, out playerAge))
{
    Console.Write("Please try again. What is your age: ");
    playerAgeString = Console.ReadLine();
}

Console.WriteLine("Awesome, you are " + playerAge + " years old.");
```

Take a close look at what has changed before reading on. First, we are now collecting the player age as a separate string. Second, we now pass this string to the TryParse() method that is in the while loop header. The TryParse method returns true or false depending on whether or not the parse operation is successful. If you look closely, we have a ! (not) in front of our int.TryParse() which tells our while loop to keep running as long as we are unsuccessful in our parsing. Third, we have a separate int variable for the player age that is set using the special "out" parameter in the TryParse() method. Maybe now it's more clear to all you brave adventurers why I waited for a bonus level to throw this useful, but somewhat-complex bit of code at you.

When you run the program for yourself and try a few bad int inputs, you should see something like this as output:

```
And, what is your age: 100.65
Please try again. What is your age: 57,312
Please try again. What is your age: applesauce
Please try again. What is your age: 47
Awesome, you are 47 years old.
```

For the curious, the code for parsing a float is similar:

```
Console.Write("How many hours of video games do you play per week: ");
string playerGameTimeString = Console.ReadLine();

float playerGameTime = 0;
while(!float.TryParse(playerGameTimeString, out
playerGameTime))

{
     Console.Write("Please try again. What is your age: ");
               playerGameTimeString = Console.ReadLine();
}

Console.WriteLine"Awesome, you play " + playerGameTime +
" hours of games per week.");
```

Code this for yourself and try some bad input. It should loop until you enter a parsable float. It's more code, it's more complicated, but it's also more robust – your program won't crash with bad number input.

TryParse() and Input Validation

If you've taken the time to read this bonus level and if you think that TryParse() is a great way to keep your program from crashing with unparsable input, you might be wondering if you can mix TryParse() with input validation (see Level 9) in the same loop? The answer is yes, but hold on because it gets pretty wild.

Let's start with our integer example from the previous section (though the same idea would apply to floats too). Let's assume that when we ask the player for the age, we want (a) a parsable integer and (b) a number that is greater than 18 – assume we are collecting data for adult players only. Here's how we can check for both in the same loop:

```
Console.Write("And, what is your age: ");
string playerAgeString = Console.ReadLine();

int playerAge = 0;
while(!int.TryParse(playerAgeString, out playerAge) || playerAge < 18)

{
```

```
    Console.Write("Please try again. What is your age: ");
    playerAgeString = Console.ReadLine();

}
Console.WriteLine("Awesome, you are " + playerAge +
" years old.");
```

In this update, our while loop checks for two conditions – bad input or a value less than 18. Trying it out would look something like this:

```
And, what is your age: 100.65
Please try again. What is your age: applesauce
Please try again. What is your age: 6
Please try again. What is your age: 14
Please try again. What is your age: 21
Awesome, you are 21 years old.
```

And, while I don't want to discriminate against older players, here is proof that an upper condition could also be added:

```
while(!int.TryParse(playerAgeString, out playerAge) || playerAge < 18 ||
playerAge > 150)
```

Code this example for yourself and try some bad input, low values, and high values to see how this works in the end.

ToLower() Makes String Input (A Bit) Less Sensitive

Since this bonus level is all about making our console programs a bit less sensitive to "bad" input, let's take a look at one more common issue that we have when users enter strings and characters. Here is some code to consider:

```
Console.Write("What is your name: ");
string playerName = Console.ReadLine();

if(playerName == "Aaron")
    Console.WriteLine("Cool, that's my name too!");

Console.WriteLine("Welcome " + playerName);
```

There isn't much to this little example – the player enters a string, presumably their name, and if it's the same name as mine, we output an extra message. If the player runs the program five times and they enter these as the input strings, how many times will "Cool, that's my name too!" pop up:

```
aaron
aarON
I'm the ultimate player!
Aaron
Aaron The Brave Adventurer
```

If you're not sure, code this example and try it out – don't forget to run it five times and enter the five strings above. When you're done, you should find that only the fourth input – "Aaron" – makes the if-statement true and triggers the "Cool" message. When we compare strings using ==, we are asking for an exact match, and unlike number input, with strings, we have to worry about uppercase and lowercase input too. To be clear, the only string that will make our if-statement true is "Aaron", and while "I'm the ultimate player!" and "Aaron The Brave Adventurer" are completely different, so too are aaron and aarON.

To make our program a bit less sensitive to strings with strange capitalization, we can use the ToLower() method like this:

```
Console.Write("What is your name: ");
string playerName = Console.ReadLine();

if(playerName.ToLower() == "aaron")
    Console.WriteLine("Cool, that's my name too!");

Console.WriteLine("Welcome " + playerName);
```

ToLower() does exactly what you might think it does – it turns all uppercase letters to lowercase. Notice that I also adjusted my string literal to be all lowercase as well. Now, whatever string the player enters, we'll compare a lowercase version to our literal "aaron". If we were to run it again with the same five input strings as before, the comparison would see:

```
aaron                         - becomes aaron
aarON                         - becomes aaron
I'm the ultimate player!      - becomes i'm the ultimate player!
Aaron                         - becomes aaron
Aaron The Brave Adventurer    - becomes aaron the brave adventurer
```

Now, three out of five of our strings will successfully make our if-statement true. This doesn't really help with wildly different strings like "I'm the ultimate player!" or "Aaron The Brave Adventurer", but it does help when our players make small capitalization mistakes in their input. If you're wondering, there is also a ToUpper() that converts all lowercase letters to uppercase if you prefer to go in that direction. And it's worth making a note that neither ToLower() nor ToUpper() affect any numbers, spacing, or punctuation in our strings. Finally, both ToLower() and ToUpper() work on the char (character) data type as well. I'll leave you with this updated example to try out:

```
char repeatProgram = 'Y';
while (char.ToUpper(repeatProgram) == 'Y')
{
     Console.Write("What is your name: ");
     string playerName = Console.ReadLine();
     if (playerName.ToLower() == "aaron")
        Console.WriteLine("Cool, that's my name too!");

     Console.WriteLine("Welcome " + playerName);
     Console.WriteLine("Do you want to run this awesome program again?: ");
     repeatProgram = char.Parse(Console.ReadLine());
}
```

31

Bonus Level 4: The Return of Decisions, Decisions

In this very short Bonus Level, we're going to take a closer look at how conditional logic (if-statements and loops) work and we'll introduce a new kind of decision structure called a switch statement. Let's get right to it, shall we?

The Bare Truth

In Level 7, we saw our first bit of conditional logic in an if-statement that looked like this:

```
if (1 < 2)
{
    Console.WriteLine("1 is less than 2");
}
```

If you've gone through Levels 7, 8, and maybe even 9, that statement might seem pretty simple now. But, we can actually write ifs that are even simpler in syntax like this:

```
if (true)
{
    Console.WriteLine("The truth shall set you free!");
}
```

Some people find this example helpful, and others find it confusing – that's why I didn't put it in Level 7. It's helpful because it makes the idea that if statements run when the condition is true very clear. It's confusing because it's code that we wouldn't normally write. It would be very unusual to use boolean literals in our conditions because they are hardcoded "true" or "false" values:

```
if (false)
{
    Console.WriteLine("The truth shall set you free!");
}
```

DOI: 10.1201/9781003348481-31

```
else
{
    Console.WriteLine("This appears to be a falsehood!");
}
```

When we hardcode our conditions, we are saying that they will always be true (or false), no matter what happens elsewhere in the program. This means that our conditional logic is more-or-less useless and that's why we wouldn't normally write code like this. However, I do find that it makes the use of boolean flags a bit clearer.

```
Random rng = new Random();
int randomNumber = 0;
int heroHealth = 75;
bool isPoisoned = true;

Console.WriteLine("Hero starting health: " + heroHealth);
while(isPoisoned)
{
    Console.WriteLine("Oh no! Your hero has been poisoned!");
    heroHealth -= 15;
    randomNumber = rng.Next(1,100);
    if(randomNumber < 50)
    {
        Console.WriteLine("Your hero is no longer poisoned.");
        isPoisoned = false;
    }
}
Console.WriteLine("Hero final health: " + heroHealth);
```

In this example from Level 9, we're using the boolean variable isPoisoned as a flag for our loop to say that we are going to reduce the hero's health by 15 until they are cured. This is very similar to the if(true) example above, but now we're using a variable that can change instead of a hardcoded, and not-so-useful, literal.

Intuitively, we eventually come to understand that conditional operators like >, <, <=, ==, and so on drive our if-statements and loops, but did you know that they actually produce true and false values? Try running the following code to see the output:

```
Console.WriteLine(2 < 1);
int playerScore = 100;
Console.WriteLine(playerScore >= 100);
bool applesToOranges = "apples" == "oranges"; //this one is tricky, but cool
Console.WriteLine(applesToOranges);
Console.WriteLine('Y' != 'y');
Console.WriteLine(3.14159 >= 3.1415);
```

If everything goes well, you should see some true and false output on the console. Conditional operators supply the boolean values that our decision and looping logic need. Maybe this was clear to you before, but if not, I hope it's clearer now.

Switching Things Up with Switch Statements

Switch statements are a bit controversial among coders. Some people find them very intuitive and easy to use, while others find them unintuitive and awkward. If I'm being honest, I'm firmly in that second group of people, but in this section, we'll look at some examples so that you can decide for yourself if switch statements are for you.

Switch statements, sometimes called case statements, are an alternative to if-else-if statements. Here's an example from Level 8:

```
Console.Write("What is your hero's current health: ");
int heroHealth = int.Parse(Console.ReadLine());

Random rng = new Random();
int randomValue = rng.Next(0, 101);

Console.WriteLine("Your hero enters a room and rummages around in the
darkness …");

if(randomValue <= 25)
{
    Console.WriteLine("Your hero finds a health potion and feels
    refreshed!");
    heroHealth += 10;
}
else if(randomValue >= 90)
{
    Console.WriteLine("Your hero steps on a rusty nail. It really, really
    hurts.");
    heroHealth -= 10;
}
else
{
    Console.Write("The room is empty. Utterly empty.");
}

Console.WriteLine("Your hero continues their journey with " + heroHealth +
" health.");
```

And here's the same example using a switch statement instead of the if-else-if:

```
Console.Write("What is your hero's current health: ");
int heroHealth = int.Parse(Console.ReadLine());

Random rng = new Random();
int randomValue = rng.Next(0, 101);

Console.WriteLine("Your hero enters a room and rummages around in the
darkness …");

switch(randomValue)
{
    case <= 25:
      Console.WriteLine("Your hero finds a health potion and feels
      refreshed!");
      heroHealth += 10;
      break;

    case >= 90:
      Console.WriteLine("Your hero steps on a rusty nail. It really,
      really hurts.");
      heroHealth -= 10;
      break;

    default:
      Console.Write("The room is empty. Utterly empty.");
      break;
}

Console.WriteLine("Your hero continues their journey with " + heroHealth +
" health.");
```

Take a few minutes to look at the structure and syntax of that switch statement before reading on. Be sure to look at what's different and what's similar to the if-else-if example.

Here are some reasons to consider switch statements in your code.

- *Cases:* Even when we use if and if-else-if statements, we often talk in terms of "cases". Perhaps you've even thought about your logic in terms of true cases and false cases, or multiple cases for multiple conditions. Switch statements make the cases very clear with the case keyword.

- *Default:* The default keyword is a very clear indicator of what will happen if our cases aren't met.

- *Structure and syntax:* Sometimes people are drawn to the distinct structure and syntax of switch statements – they feel very code-y.

- *The need for speed:* If you do a bit of digging, you'll find articles online that say switch statements can run faster than large, complex, if-else-if structures.

In the end, it's up to you if you want to use switch instead of if-else-if statements in your program. If you find the structure more intuitive and clear, or if you are writing complex logic that is slowing your program down, give them a try. If you find them confusing with the different keywords, punctuation, and syntax, or if you're writing fairly simple programs that aren't running slowly, feel free to stick with if-else-ifs for now. If you're uncertain and want more examples before deciding, I encourage you to do some more digging and carry on with a self-directed switch-focused side quest of your own.

32

Bonus Level 5: A Matter of Scope

Variable scope is a programming topic that you don't really notice until something goes wrong. In fact, if you code all of the examples in the book as they appear, scope isn't a topic that we really need to cover at all. But when you start writing your own programs and games, you'll eventually create a variable in one part of your code, and it won't be accessible in another part. Maybe this has already happened to you and you want to know how and why this happened. This bonus level is here to shed some light on variable scope.

Curly Braces { } Define Variable Scope

Variable scope is the term we use to describe where a variable can be accessed. Many of the examples we've seen and coded are quite short and the variables we declare are accessible throughout the entire program. This isn't always the case though and curly braces { } are to blame.

In Levels 7, 8, and 9, I introduced the idea that if-statements and loops have before, during, and after parts. Some of our code happens before these structures, some happens during, and the rest happens after. What I didn't mention was that these "parts" are, in some ways, a matter of scope. Consider a simple example:

```
Console.Write("What is your score: ");
int playerScore = int.Parse(Console.ReadLine());
if(playerScore > 100)
{
    int bonus = 10;
    playerScore += bonus;
}
Console.WriteLine("Your final score is: " + playerScore);
```

There's actually nothing wrong in this example. The player is prompted for their score and if it's higher than 100, they earn a 10-point bonus. Let's make a small, but problematic change:

DOI: 10.1201/9781003348481-32

```
Console.Write("What is your score: ");
int playerScore = int.Parse(Console.ReadLine());
if(playerScore > 100)
{
    int bonus = 10;
    playerScore += bonus;
}
```

```
Console.WriteLine("You earned a bonus of: " + bonus);
Console.WriteLine("Your final score is: " + playerScore);
```

If you code this example, Visual Studio will flag that new (bolded) statement with a syntax error related to scope. Since the variable bonus was declared inside the if-statement curly braces, it is "local" to the if-statement and doesn't actually exist outside of those braces – strange, but true. Just to make it clear that it's the curly braces and not the if-statement that cause this issue, try writing and running this weird example:

```
Console.Write("What is your score: ");
int playerScore = int.Parse(Console.ReadLine());

{
    int bonus = 10;
    playerScore += bonus;
}
```

```
Console.WriteLine("You earned a bonus of: " + bonus);
Console.WriteLine("Your final score is: " + playerScore);
```

Even though this code doesn't make a lot of sense, it should still run properly if we move the declaration of bonus outside of the curly braces like this:

```
Console.Write("What is your score: ");
int playerScore = int.Parse(Console.ReadLine());
int bonus = 0;
{
    bonus = 10;
    playerScore += bonus;
}
```

```
Console.WriteLine("You earned a bonus of: " + bonus);
Console.WriteLine("Your final score is: " + playerScore);
```

Hopefully, from these examples, it's clear that the curly braces are doing something, and what they're doing is defining different scope regions in our code. Variables that are declared before a set of curly braces can be accessed and modified before, during, and after the braces. Variables that are defined inside of a set of curly braces can only be accessed and modified within those braces. This is why, in the first examples, playerScore can be used before, during, and after the if-statement, while bonus can only be used during.

Scope also has a role to play in our object classes as well. Take a look at this simplified version of our familiar Die class (pay close attention to the bolded variable declarations):

```
internal class Die
{
    private int numberOfSides;
    private int sideUp;
    public Die()
    {
        numberOfSides = 6;
    }
    public Die(int sidesIn)
    {
        numberOfSides = sidesIn;
    }
    public int GetNumberOfSides()
    {
        return numberOfSides;
    }
    public int GetSideUp()
    {
        return sideUp;
    }
    public void Roll()
    {
        Random rng = new Random();
        sideUp = rng.Next(1, numberOfSides + 1);
    }
}
```

There are many sets of curly braces in this code – one set for the class, one set for the constructor and each of the methods, and a set for the namespace that I removed to save some space. Each of these sets of curly braces defines a particular score region in our code. By declaring our attributes – numberOfSides and sideUp – at the top, or more accurately, inside of our class curly braces, we have ensured that they can be accessed throughout the class. This is an important feature of attributes since we need to be able to access and modify them in the constructor, accessor, mutator, and helper methods. On the other hand, any parameter variables like sidesIn will only be available in the method where they are defined – in this case, our constructor. Similarly, rng is only available in the Roll method. Trying to access sidesIn or rng outside of their constructor or method will result in a syntax error because their scope is limited.

The takeaway from this short bonus level is this – if you've declared a variable and can't seem to access it, you might be trying to use it outside of its scope. Take a look at where it's declared and even how you're trying to use it, and adjust the scope if necessary. Scope is especially important for if-statements, loops, methods, classes, and anywhere else that curly braces are lurking in your code.

I'll leave you with this analogy that I've used many times – curly braces are like little fences. Anything "born" outside the fences can go inside the fences and leave again. Anything that's born inside the fences spends their whole lives inside and can't escape. Maybe that's helpful to you, and maybe it's just a glimpse inside my overactive imagination.

33

Bonus Level 6: Let's Take This Online

WelcomeBraveAdventurer.ca

To help you on your journey, a companion website has been set up at https://welcomebraveadventurer.ca. There, you'll find:

- extra content
- links to other helpful sites and resources
- updated (or corrected) examples
- alternate Code Quests

Example Code and Visual Studio Projects

To help you, even more, on your journey, a GitHub repository has been set up at https://github.com/WelcomeBraveAdventurer. There, you'll find:

- Code for all the level and bonus level examples.
- Visual Studio projects for each of the code rewards.
- Visual Studio projects for each of the code quests.

You can explore the GitHub site using a browser, but to download code to Visual Studio, use the "Clone a repository" feature at the top of the "Get started" panel (Figure 33.1).

Then, simply type or paste the link to any of the projects (called repositories) in the "Repository location" field (Figure 33.2).

Finally, click "Clone", and enjoy!!

DOI: 10.1201/9781003348481-33

FIGURE 33.1
"Cloning" is an easy way to get a copy of a project that's publicly available on code storage sites like GitHub.com.

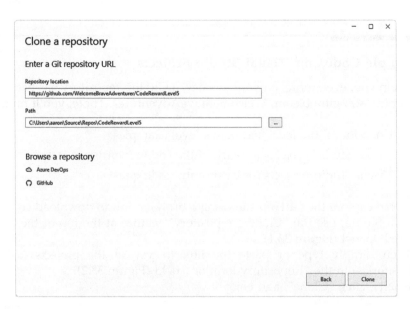

FIGURE 33.2
To clone a project, you'll need the URL (website address) from the GitHub (or similar) project.

Index

Note: Locators in *italics* represent figures and **bold** indicate tables in the text.